LANDSCAPES IN BETWEEN

Environmental Change in Modern Italian Literature and Film

MONICA SEGER

Landscapes in Between

Environmental Change in Modern Italian Literature and Film

UNIVERSITY OF TORONTO PRESS
Toronto Buffalo London

Toronto Buffalo London
www.utppublishing.com

ISBN 978-1-4426-4919-4

Toronto Italian Studies

Library and Archives Canada Cataloguing in Publication

Seger, Monica, 1980–, author
Landscapes in between : environmental change in modern Italian literature and film / Monica Seger.

(Toronto Italian studies)
Includes bibliographical references and index.
ISBN 978-1-4426-4919-4 (bound)

1. Italian literature – 20th century – History and criticism. 2. Italian literature – 21st century – History and criticism. 3. Motion pictures – Italy – History. 4. Landscapes in literature. 5. Landscapes in motion pictures. 6. Ecology in literature. 7. Ecology in motion pictures. I. Title. II. Series: Toronto Italian studies

PQ4088.S43 2015 850.9'36 C2014-905918-3

University of Toronto Press acknowledges the financial assistance of The University of Oklahoma and the College of William and Mary towards the publication of this book.

University of Toronto Press acknowledges the financial assistance to its publishing program of the Canada Council for the Arts and the Ontario Arts Council, an agency of the Government of Ontario.

University of Toronto Press acknowledges the financial support of the Government of Canada through the Canada Book Fund for its publishing activities.

Contents

Acknowledgments

This project begins and concludes with my appreciation for many wonderful colleagues and mentors scattered across landscapes near and far. I am grateful for early inspiration at the University of California, Santa Cruz, and the Università Ca' Foscari Venezia. Sincere thanks go to Shaul Bassi, Tonia De Chicchio, Paolo Venerando, and especially Margaret Brose. For strong grounding and encouragement in the continuation of my studies I thank a wonderful cohort and faculty in the Department of French and Italian at the University of Wisconsin-Madison. I was lucky to work with Stefania Buccini, Tom Cravens, Christopher Kleinhenz, Ernesto Livorni, and Kristin Philips-Court, all of whom significantly helped shape the dissertation that led to this book. I owe special thanks to Patrick Rumble, for careful guidance and an ongoing willingness to always pick up the phone, and to Rob Nixon, for continued support and an invaluable introduction to ecocriticism. Most of all I thank my dissertation advisor, longtime mentor, and critical interlocutor, Grazia Menechella. In addition, I owe deep thanks for the support of my University of Oklahoma colleagues Serafina Boggs, Stephanie Malia Hom, and Jason Houston.

I appreciate the feedback of all the friends who have contributed to this book as thoughtful readers, editors, and conversation partners, especially Hester Baer, Catherine Barrett, Lucas Bessire, Ryan Long, Stephanie Pilat, Jillian Porter, Matthias Rudolf, and Meghan Wieters. My thinking on this subject was further developed during a residency at the Asilo Bianco Cultural Institute in Ameno, Italy, as well as time spent in the archives of the RAI in Rome and at the Cineteca di Bologna. I am also thankful for inspirational and still-ongoing conversations with organizers and fellow participants of the 2012 Rome Seminar sponsored by Italian Studies at Notre Dame.

I was fortunate to have my work welcomed at the University of Toronto Press, thanks to the warm enthusiasm of the late Ron Schoeffel, along with Richard Ratzlaff and Anne Laughlin. The book benefited from the copyediting skills of Wendy Jacobs. The University of Oklahoma has provided me generous support for research and publication over the years. I am grateful to the anonymous readers of my manuscript, as well as the readers and editors at *The Italianist Film Issue*, who published an earlier version of Chapter 6 in article form.

Finally, my deepest thanks are reserved for my dear friends and family, whose belief in me and my work has never wavered. This book is dedicated to the memory of Dr. Charles E. Seger, the most tireless champion a person could have.

LANDSCAPES IN BETWEEN

Environmental Change in Modern Italian Literature and Film

Chapter One

Introduction: Exploring the Interstice

odore di erba che evapora
boschi cedui all'orizzonte
due turbine
le grondaie industriali
due torri di silos
i tralicci della luce
cavallette metalliche alte venti metri
con le zampe sottili
piccole tour eiffel campagnole
i fili elettrici scavalcano la campagna
hanno un itinerario tutto loro
devono andare
devono andare
non ha senso pensare che arrivi un gigante e ci stenda
il bucato[1]

– "Incontro con dio e con i miei morti a Biancade," Tiziano Scarpa

In Italy, as in much of the world, the physical nature in which many find delight, sustenance, or refuge is more often than not a modified nature – land repeatedly built upon and ecosystems forever altered. Such modified nature is rarely articulated in popular literary and cinematic representations of the Italian landscape, which instead offer images of gently rolling hills with poppies and poplars swaying in the breeze and nary an industrial drainpipe in sight. Images of idyll under the Tuscan sun may have much to offer an audience in terms of beauty and pleasure. We run a great risk, however, if they are the only representations of the Italian landscape to which we give heed. One of the crucial functions of imaginative texts is their ability to reflect the world – in all of its complications – to audiences, so that they may begin to make sense of it. Texts such as Scarpa's, cited above, or those of other authors and filmmakers discussed in this book, play a crucial role in contemporary processes of environmental reckoning. Depicting physical reminders of use and manipulation alongside those of persistent natural beauty, such texts explore possibilities for a modified idyll while challenging readers and viewers to confront difficult environmental realities.

To represent Italy's lived landscape today is indeed a thorny task. For the authors and filmmakers that take it on, such a task does not add up to a lament for what has been lost so much as the development of an ethics of coping. Such a task requires understanding how to make the most of a modified natural environment. Essential to this process is the realm of the *interstice.* The interstice is the gap between two objects of concrete meaning, the space between tissues in the body, the break in content of a printed text, the pause in time. When it comes to the physical environment, interstices arise in those oft-ignored spaces that bridge areas of defined use, such as built structures and cultivated plots, with undeveloped land. The abandoned factory site overgrown with shrubs is an interstitial landscape, as are the untended strips of land bordering the state highway, the oceanfront plot dotted with dwellings that will forever remain half-built, and the polluted watershed not yet rehabilitated. The interstice is the unaccounted-for in-between.

Italy's interstitial landscapes provide a model for thinking about the peninsula's natural environment in its entirety. While spaces of non-use and namelessness in the landscape are often considered to be without aesthetic value, their lack of definition also contains great potential for what may yet grow, or be grown, as well as great relief from prescriptive social order and predetermination. They give us space to breathe, teach us to observe closely before forming judgment, and remind us of the continued transition of the lived world as well as the beauty in the unadorned. They also offer an immediate experience of the natural environment through direct contact with earth, water, and air while still exhibiting traces of the built environment, of the culture from which nature simply cannot be divorced. These are the spaces explored in the chapters that follow, as represented in select literary and cinematic texts by Italo Calvino, Pier Paolo Pasolini, Gianni Celati, Simona Vinci, and the duo Daniele Ciprì and Franco Maresco. From the late 1950s to today, these authors and filmmakers address the challenge of coming to terms with the unique physical character of the contemporary Italian landscape.

Calvino and company shape a framework for appreciating the material at hand, however degraded it may be, and advocate in particular for an ecological sensibility of the interstice. They highlight its role as a physical manifestation of the complicated dialogue between nature and culture. In this, their texts suggest that Italy's interstitial landscapes *do* hold value, thanks to the very same attributes for which such landscapes are often ignored in popular representations, ranging from Tacitus's *Germania* (ca. 98 AD) to Bernardo Bertolucci's *Stealing Beauty* (1996), and beyond.

Attributes of the interstitial Italian landscape, such as Scarpa's silos, are overt markers of second nature. This is not a Jamesonian second nature, "when the modernization process is complete and nature is gone for good."[2] Rather, second nature is understood on the following pages as a less absolute realm, as the natural environment that is no longer (if it ever was) primary, that is, untouched by the human but instead profoundly engaged with it. As in the work of scholars such as Frederick and Lawrence Buell, William Cronon, and Ursula Heise, this need not mean that nature is "gone for good," simply that it is inevitably in relationship with culture.

The nature/culture debate is a long-standing one, dating to Aristotle and beyond. It is deeply anchored in the fields of philosophy and anthropology, where questions of divide, dichotomy, and binary have been explored at great length.[3] In these fields nature is often approached as a problematic theoretical construct, one that can easily encompass various notions of human nature and the non-social environment at large. The approach to nature/culture in this book's analysis of literature and film differs quite notably, and quite simply. While *culture* is indeed understood here as the social forms and material trappings of the human, *nature* is understood primarily in light of its physical expressions: the water of the Po River, the trees along the Appian Way, the arid hillside on the outskirts of Palermo.

Interstitial landscapes are fertile ground in which to explore the intricacies of such spaces, for they are tied to realms both human and non. In their proximity to and, often, participation in the built environment, interstitial landscapes disallow the sort of "back to the wild" narrative favoured by early North American naturalists and philosophers such as Thoreau and Emerson. At the same time, such landscapes still facilitate a direct experience of the natural environment and maintain the ability to inspire an awareness of the nonhuman. As in Scarpa's poem, the smell of grass and the sight of woods can still be experienced in the presence of electric cables stretching across the countryside and industrial drainpipes below.

On page and screen, the voices considered in this book engage with one another in dialogue about a changing country. From Calvino to Ciprì and Maresco, they trace Italy's post-war economic resurgence or *boom economico*, subsequent developments in industrial growth and housing construction, and a widespread culture of consumption. Each of the authors and filmmakers discussed acknowledges both the benefits and the harms of the technological advancements, financial growth, and upward movement in class structure to which the boom led so many Italians. These authors and filmmakers also express great unease. They are troubled by subsequent shifts in affiliation and communication between individuals and with what they depict as a waning contact with the rapidly changing natural environment.

Underscoring all of the above is a shared interest in environmental health. The categories of nature and culture, urban and rural, history and pre-history are not detached from symbolism in the texts considered here. Equally important, however, is a clear plane of ecological concern. Critical attention to the environmental impact of factory run-off, reckless development, and large-scale pollution permeates the texts analysed in this book. Such attention to the physical impact of human action serves as strong social criticism in an unabashedly environmentalist light. By choosing to represent on page and screen the degradation underway, by framing a landscape that is far from serene, Calvino and company direct their audiences' gaze to a complicated natural environment. They encourage us to find the life that it still contains, just as they warn of the potential for further damage. Their texts beg the following questions: What is the role of the natural environment in today's Italy? How much, or how little, is it valued? How is this complicated by the realities of environmental modification, pollution, and even nuclear disaster? Perhaps most importantly, how do contemporary Italian protagonists adapt over time in their relationship to a degraded natural environment? How do they continue to dwell in such a space, and what are the larger implications of such adaptation?[4]

Informing these next chapters are the traditions of ecocriticism and landscape studies. While the first opens a discourse on the ways in which the realms of nature and culture shape one another, the second focuses its attention on the idea of landscape as a historical and aesthetic construct. As Cheryll Glotfelty, editor of *The Ecocriticism Reader*, explains: "Ecocriticism takes as its subject the interconnections between nature and culture, specifically the cultural artifacts of language and literature. As a critical stance, it has one foot in literature and the other on land; as a theoretical discourse, it negotiates between the human and the nonhuman."[5] Glotfelty's *Reader* (1996) is one of the earliest theoretical texts in this ever-developing field, yet her definition still rings true, as cited above, especially for the sort of reading this book displays in the name of eco- or environmental criticism. Ecocriticism is a natural fit for the authors and filmmakers discussed here, given its focus on the nonhuman world and acknowledgment of the ongoing exchange and overlap in discourses about nature and culture.

While ecocriticism has historically been rooted in North American traditions of nature writing, scholars have widened their reach beyond national borders in the past decade, and the field has benefited immeasurably. Only in very recent years, however, and very sporadically at that, has ecocriticism overtly labelled as such reached Italian shores. This is so despite a long presence of environmentally attuned literary analysis in Italian studies. Of late, a select group of scholars has turned a sharper critical gaze to representations of the nonhuman in Italian texts, often privileging physical nature over its symbolic iterations. In underlining the formal and thematic importance of the natural environment to a work, these scholars contribute to a reassessment of plot- and person-driven narrative while also directing the gaze of readers and viewers to yet another manifestation of a complicated modern Italy. Investigating the shapes and functions of the natural terrain in Italian literary and cinematic works are Patrick Barron, Giorgio Bertone, Serenella Iovino, Abele Longo, Tullio Pagano, Elena Past, Massimo Quaini, Anna Re, Silvia Ross, and others. These scholars perform important critical work: examining the roles of the human and nonhuman in crafting landscape, exploring the ethics of ecological engagement, turning an environmentally critical eye to the city and landscapes of the urban, and, finally, advocating for landscape's primacy of place in texts canonical and otherwise.[6]

More present among critical works coming from both Italy and Italian studies is an approach rooted in landscape studies, a field that boasts a rich inter- and trans-national history.[7] By focusing on landscape as a terrain that is observed and framed by brush, camera, or language, scholars such as John Brinckerhoff Jackson and Susan Herrington, as well as Rosario Assunto, Bertone, and Quaini present a critical approach less concerned with the state of physical nature than with what this says about the state of humankind. In so doing, they also acknowledge the role of myth in our conceptualization of nature and the interconnectedness of nature and culture as theoretical categories. Quaini writes: "Sono infatti convinto che il paesaggio non è interessante come categoria analitica per leggere l'ambiente o il territorio in termini scientifici, ma lo è in quanto contenitore di miti, sogni ed emozioni, in quanto accumulatore di metafore per capire le contraddizioni e i problemi del nostro tempo."[8] While I oppose the first half of Quaini's statement, I am in full accord with the second. Through consideration of landscape, of how writers and artists present the natural environment as well as how societies choose to interact physically with it, we have the opportunity to analyse the values, fears, and aesthetic ideals of a given age.

A landscape scholar reflects on the human-made history inherent in any particular natural vista. He or she looks at a valley and think about how the river flowing through it has been used by humans over time and how such use may have shifted the river's flow or contents, just as it may have shifted the banks along its side. He or she also considers how such history affects modern observers and the ways in which such observers relate to both river and valley – how they physically traverse the setting, how the fruit, fish, or shelter there might be used, and, what is most important, some might say, how observers think about that river and valley. In short, a landscape-focused approach is concerned with the histories of use and technology, as well as with aesthetics, tradition, and myth, and how they shape our conception of a particular stretch of land or span of sea. In *Landscape and Memory*, Simon Schama asserts that "before it can ever be a repose for the senses, landscape is the work of the mind. Its scenery is built up as much from strata of memory as from layers of rock." He notes further: "It is our shaping perception that makes the difference between raw matter and landscape."[9] The message behind Schama's work, along with that of Italian scholars like Bertone and Quaini, is that any particular landscape is culture before it is nature.[10]

I do not, of course, deny the imprint of history, psyche, and so on in landscape. Nor do I agree, however, that the mind is at work in landscape before the senses are. One of the unique qualities of landscape is precisely that it engages the senses just as immediately as it engages the mind, if not even sooner. More significantly, such an anthropocentric tack as that inherent in the above citation ignores the role of nature in the shaping of land throughout time, as well as the status of the nonhuman in that land's current state. This is where ecocriticism plays a crucial role. Like landscape studies, ecocritical approaches give great consideration to the presence of culture in spaces of nature. They tend, however, to direct their focus at least as much on the physical reality of a space as on the institutions that shape our response to it. Michael P. Cohen cites the editors of a *New Literary History* special issue on ecocriticism as noting that the field "claims as its hermeneutic environment nothing short of the literal horizon itself, the finite environment that a reader or writer occupies thanks not just to culturally coded determinants but also to natural determinants that antedate these, and will outlast them."[11] Cohen's argument bears repeating because of the agency it so definitively attributes to the nonhuman. It is precisely this sort of agency that can be lacking in landscape studies, leading to a subsequent and potentially dangerous overlooking of nature.[12] In studying represented landscapes with an eye for the active role of nature, we remember just how much in the physical world is beyond human control, just as we note the long-term effects that human modifications inflict on the natural.

The relationship between human and nonhuman nature is indeed complex. In this book I approach this relationship with the belief that nature and culture are and have always been engaged in conversation, at times raucous and at times polite. I hold that the natural spaces to which protagonists turn in the texts analysed here are crafted vistas, shaped through relationships to the human and its ideals. In no way, however, does this fact diminish such spaces' status as physical nature, or their ability to foster concrete ecological engagement. In this light, my critical approach is enriched by other disciplines and other thinkers involved with the negotiation of meaning, forms of identity, cultural production, and the effects of history. Giorgio Agamben's work on the figure of the sacred man is particularly useful, as it provides a human parallel to the interstitial landscape, both entities simultaneously included and excluded from socio-political consideration. Also critical in the following chapters are notions of dwelling and temporal horizon, as discussed by Heidegger, Husserl, and Gadamer, as well as key feminist critiques by scholars such as Julia Kristeva.

Italian lands have long been inhabited and cultivated. In the past century, however, both the Italian landscape and its inhabitants' relationship to it have undergone exceedingly rapid change as the result of industrial, agricultural, and technological innovation. This is particularly the case subsequent to Italy's economic boom of the mid-1950s to early 1960s, which "forced Italians into a modern, industrial world," and away from rural tradition.[13] What follows is a survey of boom-era effects that have had the greatest impact on the texts examined in Chapters 2 through 6.

Despite its lengthy history of civilization, Italy became a democratic republic through popular referendum only in 1946, three years after armistice with the Allied powers. Upon foundation, this new Italian government faced a serious task: resurrecting a country that had suffered years of bombardment, widespread structural damage, and internal political and social upheaval during World War II. As a result, government officials launched a multi-year plan of economic and social reconstruction almost immediately. Italian efforts were greatly buoyed by the US-funded European Recovery Program (ERP), or Marshall Plan, established in 1947. Lasting until 1951, the ERP sought to promote international trade and general war recovery while also rebuilding means of production. The Italian industrial sector was assumed to have suffered heavy structural damage during the war due to bombing, and the ERP dedicated a great deal of money to its being rebuilt. As it turned out, however, the country's industrial zones, primarily located in the north, were not nearly as damaged as first suspected. Attention and funds directed from Italy and the United States towards the world of industry thus had very quick and widespread positive effects, eventually leading to Italy's major industrial growth in the mid-1950s. The primary items produced in this expanding factory culture included textiles, methane gas, hydrocarbons, steel, and petrochemicals.

While an increase in production of domestic goods is to be expected after wartime, the numbers in the Italian case are staggering. From 1945 to 1946 the amount of raw silk produced in the country more than doubled from 855 to 1,990 tons, while the amount of cotton-based clothing items jumped from 16,436 to 102,305 tons. Lead production saw a similarly vast increase, from 21,140 tons during the period 1941–50, up to 40,390 tons in 1951–60.[14] Conversely, the production of cultivated grain showed smaller gains, accompanied by standard dips: 3,563 tons of rice were produced in 1945, compared to 4,885 in 1946 and 6,355 in 1947, while 41,766 tons of wheat were produced in 1945, then 61,256 in 1946, and 47,021 the following year.[15]

Such lopsided growth in output brought with it a shift in employment structure, with workers once involved in agriculture moving into the world of industry across all economic levels. Percy Allum draws attention to the "substantial growth of the salaried urban middle class (white collars) at the expense of the self-employed rural middle class (peasant farmers)," as well as "similar growth of the industrial and service working class and the decline of farm laborers."[16] Italians who had once worked in the fields moved into factories and urban-centred businesses at great rates. Geographic shifts, logically, followed. Southern Italy had always been poor compared to the northern half of the country, and the financial assistance granted to the industrially rich North only furthered this divide.[17] Residents of the South thus moved north with hopes of attaining higher incomes, just as rural dwellers moved towards city centres throughout the country. In veering away from an existence that was largely agricultural towards one that was more industrial, many Italians were also distanced from lifeways based on fundamental contact with the natural environment. Thus, just as watersheds and air quality were becoming increasingly polluted by factory production, residents found themselves suddenly less well positioned to note indicators of environmental change. Many also had greater concerns, such as securing employment after years of economic hardship. The lakeside community of Gozzano, in the region of Novara, north of Milan, offers a prime example. From 1926 to 2009 Gozzano was an active production site for Bemberg, a German-based multinational corporation known for its particular brand of rayon. Bemberg produced the fabric right along the southern shore of the subalpine Lake Orta, consequently releasing high levels of copper and ammonium sulfate directly into the lake on a daily basis. Lake Orta was heavily and repeatedly polluted from Bemberg's production process until 1980, when the Italian parliament passed protective legislation to limit the release of industrial waste into freshwaters.[18]

Although pollution of the lake was immediate and intense, decades passed before many residents of Gozzano and surrounding areas took note. They had greater concerns than the slow death of the fish they had once eaten, or the clouding over of Lake Orta's formerly clear waters. Antonietta C. began working at the Bemberg factory in 1960, the lean times of World War II still thick in the air for much of Italy, despite the country's rapidly growing economy. In 2012 I had the opportunity to speak with Antonietta about industrial legacies and environmental change in Gozzano. She stated that in the 1960s no one in the area thought about the negative ramifications of factory runoff, so great was the community's need for employment opportunities. As she explained, Bemberg "ha dato da lavorare tanto a tutta la zona," thus addressing a much more immediate concern than the continually evolving process of environmental degradation.[19]

Italians slowly began to settle into a resuscitated economy at about the same time that Antonietta went to work at the Bemberg factory. As the 1960s progressed, increased earning potential led to greater spending power, and industry became a stimulus for social change with a wide-reaching impact. Alongside greater production of material goods and the resulting rise in individual income came a culture of consumption never before experienced in the Italian peninsula. Domestic electronics, such as refrigerators and televisions, began entering private homes in the North and social centres in the South on a large scale. As Christopher Duggan notes, the percentage of Italian families owning a refrigerator rose from 13 to 55 per cent between 1958 and 1965.[20] The introduction of television into the Italian mainstream in 1954 had a particularly broad impact on consumerism.[21] This was especially apparent beginning in 1957, via the television program *Carosello*, which aired from 8:50 p.m. to 9:00 p.m. every night, just before children went to bed. The program contained a series of vignettes, generally comic sketches lasting approximately one minute and forty-five seconds, and ending with the promotion of a product. Everything from hair pomade to kitchen appliances was advertised in this format. The program was revolutionary: Every evening across a country long divided by regional and lexical diversity, all Italians could sit down, whether at home or at a neighbourhood gathering space, to watch the very same content ultimately promoting the very same products.[22] The impact of a television-fuelled consumer culture is still felt today and has become a trope much explored in the literature of the past two decades. That impact, and in particular a refusal of it, is arguably one of the strongest incentives for a return to the external landscape, as discussed in the work of Simona Vinci and explored here in Chapter 5.

All of the geographical transitions of the mid- to late 1950s necessitated a significant increase in structural development, and quickly. New homes were required to accommodate new workers, and people of all social strata were quick to take up opportunities for new construction, buying and building on any plot of land available. Calvino's *La speculazione edilizia*, considered in Chapter 2, overtly addresses the ramifications of this trend. The rapid increase in urban and semi-urban housing often took place without any forethought to the subsequent need for increased social services and community structures. As a result, many Italians found themselves confronted with a lack of public transportation, schools, and other necessary services. Families with the means to do so responded by seeking "salvation in private spending and consumption: on using a car to go to work, on private medicine and on private nursery schools in the absence of state ones."[23] The turn towards private resources prompted a growing trend of individual family isolation. Paul Ginsborg observes that "each nuclear family unit tended to be more closed in upon itself, and less open to community life or to forms of inter-family solidarity."[24] This heightened focus on the private nuclear family marks a sizable shift in both attitude and community structure for an Italian populace long attuned to extended kinship structures and social networks.

As the literature and film from both this period and those that follow suggests, a retreat from community life was to provoke both a sense of alienation and a lack of concern for common spaces. In 1975, the pioneering Italian environmentalist and cultural critic Antonio Cederna remarked on this change: "Negli ultimi trent'anni abbiamo assistito al rifiuto costante o al costante fallimento di ogni tentativo di pianificazione urbanistica, al culto esclusivo del lotto edificabile e della mappa catastale, all'indiscriminata depredazione di un bene (il territorio appunto) considerato, anziché patrimonio collettivo e risorsa per definizione limitata e non reintegrabile, terra di nessuno."[25] With a focus turned inward, towards the prosperity and well-being of the individual and the isolated family unit, most people extended little concern to the landscape that lay beyond their own fence.

As a consequence of diminished general interest in public space, the Italian landscape was allowed to suffer. It did so at the hands of unregulated construction, industrial pollution, the cutting of more than one hundred thousand trees to allow for road widening, and the refinement of three times the amount of oil necessary for internal consumption.[26] Growth of the industrial sector was most prominent not in the largest of urban centres but in smaller cities and their surrounding semi-rural areas, which offered more space for new construction. The world of the factory was thus brought into direct contact – physically, not just ideologically – with the countryside and the natural landscape it hosted. In this atmosphere, the terms *industrializzazione difusa*, "diffused industrialization," and *campagna urbanizzata*, "urbanized countryside," entered the lexicon.[27]

Limited state controls existed to govern the building boom and speculation of the 1950s and 1960s in many parts of the country. An important government-regulated building program did exist in the guise of INA-casa, a project of the Istituto Nazionale delle Assicurazioni. A public-housing project dedicated to constructing homes for the working class, INA-casa was active in two phases, 1949–56 and 1956–63. INA-casa projects were generally located on the periphery of urban areas, where land was cheap. This urban exodus led to a marginalization of the lower classes of cities such as Rome, while shifting the peripheral edge and blurring its boundary with the land beyond.[28] Chapter 3 looks explicitly at these issues in the work of Pier Paolo Pasolini.

There were few building codes in place to regulate private construction, however, and no well-organized bodies to govern in which areas and to what density contractors and private citizens were allowed to build. Fiorentino Sullo, a founder of Italy's Christian Democrat Party, did try to introduce urban planning legislation in 1963 but it died before ever reaching the parliament floor.[29] As such, Simonetta Tunesi notes, "By the seventies no Italian city could boast more than three square meters of green areas per inhabitant."[30] As recently as 1991, in fact, Italy – just a bit larger than the state of Arizona – still laid claim to two to three times the amount of cement found in all of North America.[31] This freedom of expansion was not simply the inevitable result of shifts in population and economy but the result of clear political decisions, as the Italian governments of the 1950s and 1960s "decided to allow the maximum degree of freedom to private initiative and speculation in the building sector."[32] After years of wartime poverty and destruction, government officials were more than willing to give free rein to the prosperous building industry and the landscape sector. Not only would such an action further stimulate the economy, but the visual symbol of strength and growth the new construction provided was also sure to aid public morale.

Just as the freedom provided to speculators was deliberate, the attitudes behind this decision were not unprecedented. As Tunesi points out, "The divide between civil society and the natural environment is deep-rooted. Following the unification of Italy, national efforts concentrated on creating administrative structures and on providing support to the manufacturing industry of the North."[33] In terms of social current, these national efforts "marked the detachment of Italian intellectuals from their natural environment." This phenomenon was then further "accentuated as a result of the idealist approach characteristic of Italian culture in the twentieth century and the eclipse of scientific culture."[34] It is important to recognize that attention had been directed towards industry as a unifying, revenue-building entity in Italy well before the mid-twentieth century. The disregard shown for the landscape during the 1950s and 1960s was not new. The frenzy with which it was borne out in the advent of a newly potent industrial age, however, was.

A caveat must be addressed in light of Tunesi's statement, as her reminder, while fundamental, easily supports a nature/culture binary if not unpacked. Widely inhabited and cultivated for millennia, the landscape of the Italian peninsula has forever been modified and conceptualized in one way or another by the framework of human culture. This book is not intended to investigate representations of a natural landscape invaded for the first time by the trappings of culture. Italy had long been crossed by thoroughfares, its fields and streams parceled out as discrete properties, by the time the texts studied herein were composed. My concern lies, rather, with the rampant environmental transition that occurred in the wake of the country's post-war industrial expansion and the ways in which individual voices responded to a subsequent upset in relations with the landscape. As the primary texts considered in the following chapters demonstrate, a potential means of coping with this transition is to turn away from a notion of divide between "civil society and natural environment" and focus instead on the merger of the two.

One of the pockets of culture to most sharply acknowledge a post-war shift away from an experience of primarily rural livelihood was Italy's literary scene, just as in flux as the social and environmental landscapes of the time. The journal *Il Menabò* initiated a debate surrounding literature and industry that was to have a lasting impact. Founded by Elio Vittorini and Italo Calvino in 1959, *Il Menabò* was dedicated to printing a balance of literary writing and critical inquiries linked by a particular theme. In 1961 it elected to respond to cultural shifts of the previous decade. The editorial board dedicated the journal's fourth issue to the question of how literary fiction might adapt to the new reality, and requisite new linguistic code, of the modern factory experience. While the entirety of the issue is dedicated to the theme, it was Vittorini's opening essay that prompted the most dialogue.

In the preface to the articles that follow, Vittorini declares that contemporary Italy has transitioned from a natural society to an industrial one and that narrative literature must catch up:

> I significati di una realtà dipendono dagli effetti infiniti che si producono in essa a partire da una certa causa. La realtà contadina ha preso via via i suoi significati dal mondo grandioso e mutevole degli effetti che

la coltivazione del suolo ha messo in moto. E la realtà industriale è dal mondo degli effetti messo in moto a mezzo delle fabbriche che può prendere i significati suoi.[35]

Vittorini holds that experience leads over time to the formation of the symbols that make up language. The realm of rural existence, he states, had formed its codes throughout the ages based on daily practices rooted in relationship to the land. As this was the majority experience in Italy until the 1950s, narrative traditions had historically relied on just these codes. With the advent of a newly reinvigorated industrial culture, however, the majority experience was moving away from the countryside and so, argues Vittorini, must the codes used by a reinvigorated literary tradition. Italy had entered a new world, he explains, one with a new set of symbols, and literature ought to abandon the old natural codes and adopt those of the factory. Like the futurists at the advent of Italy's first industrial revolution, Vittorini proclaimed that one could not effectively describe a new reality with an old language.

Regardless of whether it had much effect on the literature produced in its wake, Vittorini's article set the tone for what was to be a decade of debate over the public role of the intellectual, the responsibilities of literature, and the use of language.[36] It is of most importance to this book in that it demonstrates the truly broad impact of industrial culture during the economic boom. Furthermore, it establishes the intellectual climate in which Calvino and Pasolini approached their texts of industry and nature, and the intellectual inheritance of Celati, Vinci, and Ciprì and Maresco. Calvino and Pasolini were both directly involved in the debate, and their responses to the questions of new literature and new language diverge greatly. As those familiar with modern Italian literature well know, Calvino and Pasolini's views are often opposed in terms of both style and professed ideology, and some readers may be surprised to find them grouped together here. This is particularly true as they were engaged in a very public polemic over the accommodation of multiple linguistic codes in a literary text.[37]

Of greater concern than divergent attitudes and poetics is the fact that both men felt that the writer, and to this we may safely add the filmmaker, holds a responsibility to represent the world in which he or she lives. Calvino frames his argument explicitly in terms of history. In "Il midollo del leone" (1955), he writes: "Il romanzo vive nella dimensione della storia. […] Il vero tema d'un romanzo dovrà essere una definizione del nostro tempo […] dovrà essere un'immagine che ci spieghi il nostro inserimento nel mondo."[38] As an author, Calvino is wrapped up in representation of the current age. This does not necessarily mean a *realistic* depiction of the age – Calvino began his fantastic trilogy shortly after penning the above statement – but an exploration of trends, ideologies, and anxieties of the times.[39] Pasolini echoes Calvino to an extent, while also framing the discourse more directly in terms of language, specifically a national language. In his widely reprinted 1964 essay "Nuove questioni linguistiche," Pasolini states: "Se la nuova realtà italiana produce una nuova lingua, l'italiano nazionale, l'unico modo per impossessarsene e farlo proprio, è conoscere con assoluta chiarezza e coraggio qual è e cos'è quella realtà nazionale che lo produce." He concludes that "mai come oggi la letteratura ha richiesto un modo di conoscenza scientifico e razionale."[40] Like Vittorini and Calvino, Pasolini calls for literature to confront head-on the reality that it represents. Such confrontation occurs in all of the texts considered in the present study. From Calvino's early realist novellas to Ciprì and Maresco's recent films of apparent non-place and alternate reality, all of the texts discussed here are in fact deeply engaged with, inspired by, and anxious about the realities of contemporary Italy.

The geographic and social shifts of the 1950s and 1960s laid the groundwork for the decades to follow in terms of both environment and cultural production. As for more recent years, Italy continues to hold a greater percentage of cultivated land, compared to other countries: 47 per cent national land cultivation as of 2012, with 38 per cent worldwide. With the exception of grain production, which has remained largely steady, overall cultivation has in fact gone down in the past three decades, while the use of natural resources has gone up. From 1990 to 2009, domestic electricity use increased by 23 per cent nationwide. Urban air quality continues to be a grave concern, especially regarding nitrogen dioxide: in 2010, 64 per cent of the major cities in Italy reported levels beyond the accepted standards. The authors of Legambiente's 2012 report note that critical situations are to be found in much of the Po Valley.[41] Pollution in this area is reflected in the water quality of the Po River, which has received a rating of 3 (polluted) from the Legambiente since 2003. It ought to be noted that this does mark improvement since the 1989–2003 rating period, in which the water quality was at a 4 (very polluted). Recycling efforts also continue to improve: annual tonnage of materials recycled from *raccolta differenziata*, separated waste collection, increased from 3.7 million in 1999 to nearly 10.8 million in 2009.[42]

An emphasis on private spaces and private means has remained a dominant part of Italian culture. Between 1958 and 2010 the number of passengers using private transport, such as cars or scooters, increased nine-fold, from just over 100 million per kilometre to about 918 million per kilometre. The cultural stronghold of television has only grown stronger and, according to many, significantly more damaging. While the 1970s saw the introduction of private television networks, the past three decades have ushered in a long-standing era of talk-show hosts, reality stars, and *veline*, highly sexualized showgirls, as cultural models. As for literary culture, much has changed as a handful of mainstream publishing houses have grown ever larger and the life of the literary magazine has died out. The possibility of debates such as those that played out on the pages of *Il Menabò* has grown ever slimmer. By no means, however, does this suggest that Italian authors, artists, and filmmakers are no longer engaged in representing the contemporary world. It simply means that the rules of engagement continue to shift, just like the physical landscape.

It is an understatement to write that much has already been said about Italo Calvino's work, yet where else could this study begin? Through repeated commingling of industry and nature, in works set within the city as well as those set outside of it, Calvino fully introduces a portrait of a second, or modified, nature to post-war Italian literature. He opens investigations of the darker side of an ever-developing Italy by exploring industrialization's environmental and ideological consequences. His work displays a growing understanding that there is no going back in terms of industrial growth, urban development, and the social attitudes they foster. At the same time, his work launches the debate carried on by voices to follow: how to adapt in relationship to modern nature. Rather than propose a cut-and-dried division between the realms of nature and culture, Calvino repeatedly considers one in relation to the other, recognizing the necessity of each to post–World War II Italian existence.

In light of both environmental degradation and interstitial landscapes, Calvino's early works are particularly interesting. Texts such as *La nuvola di smog* (Smog, 1958) are narrated from within urban centres and look outward towards signs of a natural space that is either polluted or beyond the urban protagonist's reach. Others, like *La speculazione edilizia* (A Plunge into Real Estate, 1957), take place outside of the city, featuring landscapes in development and suffering from factory runoff. The emotional response to environmental change contained within these works also embodies a state of transition. At times Calvino's protagonists express a sense of defeat at the waning of the natural. The narrator of *La nuvola di smog*, for example, notes: "Questo parco, questo fiume, – io pensavo, – possono stare solo in margine, consolarci del resto, una bellezza antica non può nulla contro una bruttezza nuova."[43] At other times, though, Calvino's protagonists suggest a certain acceptance, moving forward to foster modified relationships with a modified landscape, as in the conclusion of *La formica argentina* (The Argentine Ant, 1965):

> Eravamo dinanzi a casa: il bambino succhiava il suo giocattolo, mia moglie s'era messa su una sedia, io guardavo il campo infestato, le siepi, e di là una nuvola di polvere insettifuga salire dal giardino del capitano, col continuo stillicidio delle vittime. Questo era il mio nuovo paese. Presi bambino e moglie e dissi: – Andiamo a fare un giro, andiamo fino al mare.[44]

The mixed attitudes expressed within these texts, something between bitter acceptance of the "new ugliness" of the urban and a fragile hope for contact with an adapted nature, show Calvino to be engaged in a still-unfolding intellectual process, setting the stage for those to come.

An attention to representations of a shifting physical reality would be incomplete without a consideration of the visual. Pier Paolo Pasolini's films of the 1960s provide a prime example. They explore transitions from agrarian to cosmopolitan ways of life and utilize degraded landscapes to engage with questions of ideological as well as environmental destruction. Pasolini's message is clear: Entry into the market economy, the urban realm of commerce and exchange – what the director speaks of in Marxian terms as an entry into history – is inevitably an assault on the basic spirit of human character. It is a transition that turns individuals into the nonsensical professors of *Uccellacci e uccellini* (The Hawks and the Sparrows, 1966), so wrapped up in abstract analysis, or drives them to despair, like the alienated family members of *Teorema* (Theorem, 1968), no longer able to speak to one another.

The natural environment serves in these films and others as a physical marker of such transition and its detrimental effects, mirroring a modern degradation of human character in landscapes scarred by erosion, trash, and half-completed construction. In this operation Pasolini often employs landscape to reflect the state of a protagonist caught in the interstice between urban and rural social structures. Such protagonists are depicted as *omines sacri*: figures on the edge of a society, still connected to an older way of life and not able to thrive in the same way as their cosmopolitan peers. They are visually tied to a physical object that marks the shift from one way of living to another: a bridge or road leading out of the city, or ancient ruins bordering Rome. Some protagonists are able to make the leap from overgrown fields to smoothly paved highways, while others, like the homonymous Accattone, are killed in the process.

While Pasolini makes effective symbolic use of landscape, he also calls upon viewers to consider the true physical state of the natural environments that he films. Pasolini has rarely been discussed in terms of environmentalism, less even than Antonioni, for whom landscape is a fundamental emblem of alienation. Yet Pasolini's films of the 1960s ask to be read ecocritically. For example, *Teorema* and the short *Che cosa sono le nuvole?* (What Are Clouds? 1967) are overt in their marriage of environmentalism and social commentary. Laura Betti's character in the first film buries herself in dirt as an act of protest against bourgeois modernity, confirming her connection to an agrarian culture while simultaneously revealing how little uncultivated earth remains in the rest of the film. The protagonists of *Che cosa sono le nuvole?* also find themselves buried at film's end, this time in a heap of trash. Only when fully immersed in human-made and human-discarded objects do they remember to look up and note the blue sky above – so beautiful precisely due to the contrast between it and their immediate surroundings.

Of the three authors considered here it is Gianni Celati who writes most overtly about the processes of observing and narrating the natural world. Whether watching and recounting in the first person in *Verso la foce* (Toward the River's Mouth, 1989), recording what others have observed and relayed in *Narratori delle pianure* (Voices from the Plains, 1985), or flexing his muscle as a storyteller in *Quattro novelle sulle apparenze* (Appearances, 1987), Celati's agenda is explicit: By serving as witness to the world as it unfolds, we use language to ground ourselves in reality. More often than not he finds the unfolding of the world to be reflected in the changing landscape, a realm forever damaged by industrial waste but still very much habitable – if we can just remember how to see the land before our eyes.

Towards the end of *Verso la foce*, of his works the most directly focused on an interstitial environment, Celati grows increasingly sceptical of his powers of description. He is urgent, however, in his need to observe and record:

> D'un tratto risuonano richiami di gabbiani, uno chiama e altri rispondono. Anche le parole sono richiami, non definiscono niente, chiamano qualcosa perché resti con noi. E quello che possiamo fare è chiamare le cose, invocarle perché non diventino tanto estranee da partire ognuna per conto suo in una diversa direzione del cosmo, lasciandoci qui incapaci di riconoscere una traccia per orientarci.[45]

This need for a "trace by which to orient one's self" is the driving force in his works, one which recalls Calvino's lost modern souls and looks forward to Simona Vinci's unsettled millennial protagonists. By honestly recording the landscape in language, Celati works to retain a relationship to it, modified or degraded as it may be.

His is a nature decidedly intertwined with culture, and he is interested not so much in seeking a contrast between untouched country and city – that for which Pasolini longs – as in physical signs of give and take between the two. This may come in the guise of abandoned factories overgrown by wild plant life, or in the rambling, vine-like framework of country roads. In his acceptance of a nature/culture mutuality in today's post-industrial Italian landscape, Celati writes from a point past that in which we find Calvino and Pasolini. Firmly acknowledging an overlap, he moves beyond the grief and uncertainty in the other men's texts without discounting the landscape that remains, urging readers to work with the material at hand in hopes of remaining grounded in reality.

Simona Vinci takes up where Celati leaves off, increasingly so as her body of work expands. Over the past fifteen years she has moved more overtly into discussion of the landscape, starting with a symbolic treatment of the earth as womb in the novel *Dei bambini non si sa niente* (What We Don't Know about Children, 1997) and heading outward towards the politics and environmental impact of development in the novella *Rovina* (Ruin, 2007), published ten years later. Vinci (b. 1970) is the ideal final author for this study. She carries forth a tradition of landscape-oriented literature, demonstrating lessons learned from her predecessors while deftly engaging with the Italian culture of today.

Entirely her own is the connection she draws between nature, the human body, and expression, from *Dei bambini non si sa niente* on. From an exploration of collective bodily control and contact with the earth in this early text, Vinci has moved ever more towards issues of individual self-control, often connecting a character's relationship to her physical being with her ability to express herself through language. Interstitial landscapes enter the equation as the realm in which her protagonists begin to address their tied tongues and deprived bodies. As in the works of the authors above, Vinci's protagonists search for a compass by which to orient themselves, yet for them a distancing from the land is often tied to a distancing from the self. Again like the authors above, Vinci is as committed to tracing the landscape's actual environmental reality as she is to noting its symbolic potential.

While Vinci's texts are full of running waters and female bodies, the films of Daniele Ciprì and Franco Maresco are short on water and devoid of women. In those considered here, *Lo zio di Brooklyn* (The Uncle from Brooklyn, 1995), *Totò che visse due volte* (Totò Who Lived Twice, 1998), and the shorter *A memoria* (By Memory, 1996), the directors portray an arid outer Palermo inhabited only by men and prohibitive of any nature/culture distinction that may yet remain. As Abele Longo writes, "The 'urbanized countryside' or 'sprawling city' is a defining characteristic of their films and signals the breaking down of boundaries which were at one time distinct and inviolable, necessary in order for the urban and the rural to exist in relation to one another."[46] In their total contamination of these two realms Ciprì and Maresco challenge viewers to reflect on the function served by boundaries both physical and ideological, depicting a scenario in which we can no longer gaze out at the countryside from within city limits. The interstitial is thus simultaneously everywhere and nowhere in the directors' work.

Ciprì and Maresco enter into dialogue with Celati and Vinci for their exploration of life lived in a degraded environment, as well as for their attention to the body and communication in relationship to nature. Where Ciprì and Maresco transcend the two authors is in their vision of an Italian society so beyond issues of factory run-off and housing development as to have entered into a phase of regressive social relations and obsessive focus on physical need. In a windswept zone of decomposing buildings and freely roaming pigs, Ciprì and Maresco's overtly corporeal characters spend their days attentive only to their immediate physical desires. They live out a temporally narrow existence, marked by an absence of history or future, and the presence of a horizon that cannot be clearly perceived. In this light, the directors represent nature not as something in need of protection or celebration but rather an entity, scarred and resilient, that might just outlive humankind.

Lawrence Buell writes that physical nature serves as "humanity's codependent and coconspirator in coping with the fact/awareness that the nature one engages must now inescapably be – if indeed has not always in some sense been – not pristine but the effect of 'second' (i.e., modified) nature."[47] He sets up an intriguing relationship. If, as Buell posits, physical nature helps us cope with the ways we have changed nature, this assumes also that it first prompts an awareness of the sentimental attachment we hold to nature: "coping" implies coming to terms with a sad or difficult situation, here identified as the modification of the natural environment. In the above formulation, an awareness of emotional attachment to nature is linked to an awareness of our own actions, for who modified nature if not humanity? Both such types of awareness are palpable in the literary and cinematic representations of Italian landscape examined in the following chapters. The authors and filmmakers considered in this book confront the ways in which modern existence has modified the natural environment, while demonstrating just how much we need that environment if we are to cope with modern life. In so doing they shed light on a fundamental capacity of contemporary Italian literature and film that has been, as of yet, studied far too little.

Chapter Two

Economic Expansion, Environmental Awareness in the Early Works of Italo Calvino

In 1958, Italo Calvino writes: "An instinctive inclination has always pushed me toward the authors of yesterday and today in which the terms nature and history (one could also say society) appear together."[1] He then lists great authors of past eras who have drawn the relationship between nature and history, or society, to the forefront of their texts. He lauds in particular Balzac, for his discovery of the natural "organic" vitality of the city. While this essay, "Natura e storia nel romanzo," sheds light on Calvino's tastes as a reader, it also speaks to his general attitude regarding nature and culture, suggesting that he believes them to share a relationship of exchange.[2] Nature is certainly "co-present" with history and society in the author's work. Raised by botanists and himself a former student of agronomy, Calvino (1923–1985) displays a careful engagement with the environment throughout his vast oeuvre. He moves from partisan-inhabited woods in his World War II-era first novel, *Il sentiero dei nidi di ragno* (The Path to the Spiders' Nest, 1947), through the adventures of the bumbling proletarian in *Marcovaldo* (1963), a man trapped between city realities and country desires, all the way to the myriad environments observed by his final novelistic protagonist, Palomar (*Mr. Palomar*, 1983). So many of his texts – whether realistic or fantastic, set in the present moment or otherwise – consider human relationships to the nonhuman world. What's more, they portray an Italian landscape in the throes of modification and an Italian subject undergoing the murky process of achieving environmental awareness.[3]

From among Calvino's many works, my interest lies with a pair of the author's novellas originally published in the 1950s: *La speculazione edilizia* (A Plunge into Real Estate, 1957) and *La nuvola di smog* (Smog, 1958). The first focuses on land speculation in a town along the Ligurian

Riviera, while the second considers the urban-industrial at large and the ways in which atmospheric pollution may connect communities and their bioregions across geographic and cultural boundaries. Together they work towards the development of a newly fluid understanding of landscape, one that acknowledges and accepts a modified, degraded, or second nature. At the same time, they point to the dangers of saddling the natural environment with development and pollution. They suggest that Calvino's underlying issue of narrative concern in the 1950s, even more than changing class structure or the role of the post-war intellectual (two themes well documented in his work), is one of ecological awareness. Rather than launch a platform of direct environmentalist action, the author explores the ideological difficulties posed by the very act of acknowledging a changing environmental reality. In this he proposes a model of indirect action, the first important step towards the development of an ethics of coping in Italy's ecologically geared literature and film of the later twentieth century.

In 1958, the two novellas were published together in the *Racconti*, or "Stories," a collection of fifty-three of Calvino's shorter works written between 1945 and 1958. The *Racconti* are divided into four sections: "Difficult Idylls," "Difficult Memories," "Difficult Loves," and, finally, a "Difficult Life." In this last section *La speculazione edilizia* and *Smog* appear. Like many of Calvino's shorter works from the period, both feature disaffected, intellectual, middle-aged men. These men hover on the brink between a desire to abstain from involvement in the world and a rather festering sense of *impegno*, political or social commitment. They are unhappy with their lives and feel at odds with the direction of mainstream society yet are unwilling to live outside of it or to protest its confines. It is easy to see them as removed or alienated in their daily lives. In a 1970 essay on the *Racconti*, J.R. Woodhouse writes that Calvino employs a "Rousseauistic scale of personages" in these works. That scale, according to Woodhouse, ranges from man as an animal at peace in the woods to man completely detached from nature and thus completely alienated.[4] While Woodhouse places the protagonists of *A Difficult Life* at the furthest end of this scale, I am not convinced that they are as alienated or detached as they have often been read.

Indeed, these individuals struggle to find meaning in the lives they lead and connection to the societies within which they dwell.[5] But they do find meaning and connection, setting their desire not to care about their surrounding conditions, to remain aloof, in contrast with a reality of caring quite deeply. Pitting this tension against descriptions of chemically altered landscapes and reckless construction, Calvino explicitly makes *caring* an ecologically geared undertaking. He positions readers for what Serenella Iovino calls an "ethical-environmental reading," which explores the ways a text might be "uno strumento che aiuti il lettore immaginare un universo di valori più esteso, un momento di consapevolezza."[6] By depicting scenarios, rather than simply espousing unilateral beliefs, Calvino puts the reader in the powerful position of imagining, of contemplating different social and environmental realities.

Although *La speculazione edilizia* and *La nuvola di smog* share many similarities, one important distinction arises between the two when it comes to awareness of the natural environment. The first text is consumed with landscape, one particular landscape as well as the very notion; the second text focuses on the issue of air quality, raising environmental concerns of a less individually framed and thus more universal scale. This does not put the texts in opposition to one another but rather leads to an enriched environmental discourse. Studied in tandem, *La speculazione edilizia* and *La nuvola di smog* reflect an ecocritical approach engaged with both bioregionalism and transnational environmentalism, what Ursula Heise and others refer to as *eco-cosmopolitanism.* The two texts show Calvino to be engaged with questions about the particularities of unique landscapes, as well as those environmental elements that connect residents of areas far-flung. The author's novellas of the 1950s are thus particularly intriguing from an ecocritical perspective – and are particularly representative of an early economic-boom era critical inquiry – for two reasons. Together, they model a process of acknowledging environmental change. At the same time, they attempt to balance considerations that are both bioregionalist and eco-cosmopolitan, both local and global.

First proposed by Peter Berg in the 1970s, bioregionalism emphasizes local community and relationship to place. It privileges social networks based in a sense of geographic specificity over those associated with concepts like *state* and *nation.* As Berg writes in 1978, "The term refers both to geographical terrain and a terrain of consciousness – to a place and the ideas that have developed about how to live in that place."[7] A bioregionalist approach locates community through a shared sense of place grounded in physical rather than ideological realities. An eco-cosmopolitan or transnationally environmentalist approach shares some of bioregionalism's concerns but applies them on a much broader scale. As proposed by Heise, eco-cosmopolitanism also interprets community as based in shared relationships to place and environment that negate the national. At the same time, it stretches far beyond the bioregion to consider similarities in how the "cultural means by which ties to the natural world are produced and perpetuated, and how the perception of such ties fosters or impedes regional, national, and transnational forms of identification."[8] By engaging with both approaches in his work, Calvino anticipates a very twenty-first-century debate on local versus global environmental realities. On the other hand, his work is firmly rooted in the Italy of his day, a country experiencing industrial growth just as it grapples with notions of national identity and transnational allegiance a decade into the Cold War.

La speculazione edilizia was first published in 1957, when Calvino left the Italian Communist Party, the *Partito comunista italiano* (PCI), of which he had been a member since 1944. A vocal and active presence in the party for more than a decade, Calvino, along with many others, had grown dissatisfied with its direction throughout the 1950s. After party leaders made the decision to pull the PCI away from Soviet communism in 1956, Calvino withdrew from the PCI entirely. He cites the difficulty of balancing his roles as writer and political activist in the 7 August 1957 edition of the daily paper *L'Unità*: "Credo che nel momento presente quel particolare tipo di partecipazione alla vita democratica che può dare uno scrittore e un uomo d'opinione non direttamente impegnato nell'attività politica sia più efficace fuori dal Partito che dentro."[9] This statement informs much of Calvino's literary work from the mid-1950s onward, when he depicts protagonists who choose to enact just such a remove, men who are neither "directly engaged" nor fully cut off from social concerns. Notably, many of these same protagonists are never truly comfortable with their ambiguous stance, unsure of how to comport themselves without the grounding of party politics or established social role. They are unable to identify that "particular type of participation" that Calvino suggests a "man of opinion" adopt. Calvino himself, however, *is* successful in such a venture. He participates in contemporary democratic life through his fictional texts, reflecting society to itself in a new form, one that provides the distance often needed to perceive more clearly and, subsequently, more critically.

In the case of *La speculazione edilizia*, that reflection centres on the culture of land speculation and development during Italy's economic boom. The editorial history of *La speculazione edilizia* is, unlike the straightforward story it contains, rather complicated. The work was initially composed between April 1956 and July 1957, a particularly intense period in Calvino's trajectory. During this time Calvino was expanding his writerly voice through both critical essay and fictional prose, moving between sharply penned essays, such as "Il midollo del leone" (The Lion's Marrow, 1955), and the fantastic narrative of *Il barone rampante* (The Baron in the Trees, 1957) and *Il visconte dimezzato* (The Cloven Viscount, 1959). *La speculazione edilizia* first appeared in its entirety in September 1957, just one month after the *Unità* article cited above, as part of the twentieth issue of the literary journal *Botteghe Oscure*. The novella was featured again the following year in the aforementioned *Racconti*. This second publication gave the author an opportunity to edit the work further and, in the process, further edit his public image.

As Claudia Nocentini and others note, when compiling materials for the *Racconti* Calvino made careful decisions about which texts to edit heavily and which to omit entirely. One of the former was *La speculazione edilizia*. Fearing that some sections of the novella too closely described his real-life friends and family in his home town of San Remo – that is, reflected actual life too directly – the author removed a significant amount of text. He also pulled an entire chapter, which he later described as "una specie di storia della Riviera ligure e di Sanremo in particolare."[10] In the Mondadori-published collection of Calvino's *Romanzi e racconti*, Bruno Falcetto notes that the removal of these portions reflects the author's general desire at the time to restrain both autobiographical references and overt political commentary. Falcetto writes that the decision to cut particular passages and stories reflects a "sicura definizione del proprio stile, che prevede una scelta sempre più decisa della strategia della 'visione indiretta' […] anche per dire dei problemi di oggi."[11] With the term *visione indiretta*, Falcetto cites from "Lightness," the first of Calvino's *American Lessons* (1985). In this essay Calvino heralds "indirect vision," captured in a mirror, as representative of the relationship the poet ought to have with the world. He argues that the poet, or writer, should offer a distanced image of the world, one that reflects lived reality but takes it out of the harsh light of immediacy. It follows, then, that the original description of San Remo in *La speculazione edilizia* would have been too close to historical reality for Calvino, too strictly documentarian, and at the same time too politically involved and critical.

Asked by Mondadori to prepare an "Oscar," or paperback, edition of *La speculazione edilizia* in 1963, six years after its initial publication, Calvino once more changed his position. He decided to reinsert almost all of the edited descriptions, as well as the missing chapter, in order to present the work in its original incarnation, and because he felt they were, among other things, "utili alla completezza del quadro."[12] The missing chapter is an important aid to understanding the social current that grounds the work. It conveys a sense of cautious rebirth, depicting a late-1950s Liguria shaken from lazy slumber by the economic possibility of post-war industrial growth and a newly revived tourist economy.[13] In this chapter, number XIV, the author writes that "la colonia stabile di *** era costituita da quel ceto medio-borghese che s'è detto, abitatore d'agiati appartamenti nelle proprie città e che qui tale e quale riproduceva (un po' più in piccolo; si sa, si è al mare) gli stessi appartamenti negli stessi enormi isolati residenziali e la stessa vita automobilistico-urbana."[14] Never named, the city of *** emerges in this chapter as a tourist destination for a developing middle class, a designation largely embraced by its inhabitants. It also emerges rather clearly as a predominant Ligurian coastal locale, which is to say San Remo. Calvino's decision in 1963 to reinsert the identifying chapter and thus to present a complete portrait of an actual time and place, underscores the author's inability to distance himself fully from contemporary reality. It also suggests a conflictual engagement with bioregionalism, as Calvino draws a clear parallel between local landscape and the society that it houses, while refusing to identify the region in question through the specificity of naming. By avoiding overt identification in this way, he leaves readers to imagine the city of *** as any community experiencing the cultural and environmental shifts of Italy's economic boom.

Thus a portrait of transition, *La speculazione edilizia* hinges on the brink between acceptance and rejection of change in terms both social and environmental. Environmentally, this manifests as a tension between desire for the unbuilt landscape to be left in peace and tentative recognition that change is inevitable and may, in fact, reinvigorate that landscape. Mired in the tension are three characters representing three distinct paths in the face of such change: the novella's protagonist, Quinto; his mother, Signora Anfossi; and the developer Caisotti. The book begins shortly after Quinto has decided to sell Caisotti part of the family property on which his mother still lives. Along with his brother, a rather minor character in the work, Quinto has decided, specifically, to sell a section of his mother's garden. Distraught by the construction-induced metamorphosis in which he finds his home town upon every return, he hopes to sever once and for all his painful attachment to the land by jumping right in to the local building craze.

This craze, against which the novella is set, is indeed historically accurate: During the 1950s Liguria boasted one of the highest rates of Italian housing development, along with Lombardy and Emilia-Romagna. In 1959, for example, more than 50 dwellings were built in the region for every 1,000 residents. As a measure of comparison, Tuscany gained 30 to 40 new dwellings for every 1,000 residents. All of northwest Italy, in fact, underwent rapid growth. From 1951 to 1961, the number of dwellings in the area grew from 3.35 million to 4.23 million, an increase of almost 1 million, or nearly 37 per cent. This is the highest percentage of growth for all regions surveyed by the Italian National Institute of Statistics (ISTAT). While a good portion of these dwellings surely went to house new workers employed by the growing industrial sector, many were also the coastal vacation homes described in Calvino's once-omitted chapter XIV.

Linear and short on dynamic plot shifts, *La speculazione edilizia* is primarily concerned with conveying Quinto's immobility in the face of a quickly shifting Italian society and landscape. A former partisan, like Calvino himself, very involved in the PCI, Quinto is described as now disenfranchised and searching for a sense of identity.[15] Unbound from any clear ideology or sense of self, he attempts to define his personality with every step in the text, often acting in direct opposition to his instinct so as to be bold, daring, the picture of the man that he thinks he ought to be. Always suspecting that he does not fit in, he mistrusts his inclinations and acts against them in hopes of falling in line with popular standards and stances. He is the image of the apathetic intellectual described by Calvino in the aforementioned "Il midollo del leone."

For Calvino, "La ribellione contro la propria natura, caratteristica dell'intellettuale che non riesce a integrarsi, è il marchio di condanna di tanti che pure si credono, si vorrebbero, uomini nuovi, rinnovatori della storia."[16] Following this logic, Quinto's decision to act against his nature is the self-condemnation of a man who does not fit in to mainstream society. Calvino's use of the conditional *si vorrebbero* in the citation above is notable in regards to such men. While the apathetic intellectual "would like" both to be new and to renew, his desire remains unfulfilled. Like Quinto, he would like to welcome change in his life but is unable to do so, this inability to embrace new codes blocking him from an active role in the historical renovations occurring all around.

In his marginal position, Quinto embodies the interstitial. Though not shunned by society, he struggles to function successfully within it. Readers may simply understand him to be alienated by capitalism and modernity – an easy dupe – and he is.[17] There is more to it than that, however, when we note his negative response to change. Quinto finds himself caught between a fading, culturally stratified existence and an emerging post-war sensibility that allows for greater social mobility. Pondering the state of contemporary Italian culture one day, he muses, "Prima viveva sul privilegio, però aveva radici solide. Ora gli intelletuali non sono borghesi e non sono proletari."[18] For Quinto, the lack of social stratification and clear party identification in late 1950s Italy is drawing intellectual culture towards collapse; the lack of clear boundaries is only negative.

He feels just the same when it comes to his native landscape. Like individual inclination, his relationship to the natural environment of the Riviera is deeply felt and something that he has always known. And again, like his most spontaneous inclinations, this primary landscape is something from which he tries to distance himself in daily practice but to which he is undeniably still deeply connected. We read that Quinto, "Nei suoi ritorni a xxx sceglieva sempre itinerari mezzo in campagna o lungo la marina, dove c'erano da riscoprire sensazioni d'una memoria più sedimentata, marginale o minore. In città no, tutto era brutto."[19] Before beloved vistas of country and seaside, Quinto gives licence to his feelings, taking pleasure in reconnecting with memories tucked deeply away.

This habit becomes troubling when he witnesses the once-familiar landscape change. It is not simply the Ligurian landscape but the image of that landscape precisely as he has always known it that awakens Quinto's sentiment. We read at the story's outset that, arriving each time in town by train, Quinto moves to "alzare gli occhi dal libro (leggeva sempre, in treno) e ritrovare pezzo per pezzo il paesaggio – il muro, il fico, la noria, le canne, la scogliera – le cose viste da sempre di cui soltanto ora, per esserne stato lontano, s'accorgeva: questo era il modo in cui tutte le volte che vi tornava, Quinto riprendeva contatto col suo paese, la Riviera."[20]

He reconnects by visually repossessing, surveying the landscape as he has always seen it on approach. When the land becomes disfigured by "un sovrapporsi geometrico di parallelepipedi e poliedri, spigoli e lati di case," he likens it to a part of himself that has been amputated.[21] *Il suo paese*, as he has known it, has been changed by others, and its new state of being throws Quinto off balance. His love of the land is complicated specifically by the fact that, like the rapidly evolving political ideologies of his friends, his object of affection is quickly passing him by. Possessing a real and deep attachment to the land, he is also deeply distressed and, in fact, alienated by its changing image.

The full reference to a sense of amputation, noted above, reads: "Ecco, ora, lì, quel suo paese, quella parte amputata di sè, aveva una nuova vita, sia pure abnorme, antiestetica, e proprio per ciò – per i contrasti che dominano le menti educate alla letteratura – più vita che mai. E lui non ne partecipava."[22] Rather than participating in the new life, Quinto finds himself "legato ai luoghi ormai appena da un filo d'eccitazione nostalgica, e dalla svalutazione d'un'area semi-urbana non più panoramica."[23] Again, he has been left behind in the wake of a changing society. As Quinto watches familiar vistas shift form, he finds that his sensibilities, in this case preferring country or seaside to urban views, are once more not in sync with the mainstream. From his train window it seems that people are only too eager to fill the landscape with cluttered construction. Instead of suffering defeat in silence, he strikes out to join the masses, attempting to fit in with the majority through denial of his true inclination. Imitating the environmentally damaging behaviour of his peers, he enters into the world of hasty land speculation by selling and building on his family plot. Behind what reads as a rather nonchalant decision to sell lies great unrest. Calvino writes of Quinto at the novella's beginning: "La vista d'un paese ch'era il suo, che se ne andava così sotto il cemento [...] pungeva Quinto," but "bisogna dire che egli era uomo storicista, rifiutante maliconie, uomo cha ha viaggiato, eccetera, insomma, non glie ne importava niente di niente."[24] The text is written in the third person but this passage, like many, clearly reflects Quinto's voice. While the first half of the above citation speaks to a love of nature, the second speaks to just how compartmentalized his views of nature are. For although Quinto allows himself momentarily to experience sadness at the sight of vanishing land, he quickly reassures himself with the understanding that it is becoming something else. Explaining that he need not care for nature because he believes in history, Quinto implies that belief in or identification with one realm must automatically negate similar feelings toward the other. He tells himself that nature and history – interchangeable for Calvino, as we recall, with society, what we may indeed call *culture* – simply cannot coexist. History, for Quinto, trumps nature. Not so, for Calvino.

In the essay "Natura e storia nel romanzo," cited at the outset of this chapter, the author argues that to represent truly the current age we must "trasportarci violentemente dalla parte di ogni fenomeno, ogni modo di pensare che giudichiamo negativo, entrare nella sua logica interna portandola alle ultime conseguenze, vivere insomma la negatività 'al grado eroico.'"[25] To understand an era's zeitgeist, he argues, one must try to enter its logic from all angles, even and especially those found to be most troubling. Calvino refers to this act of engaging the negative as a *mimesi della negatività*. If Quinto represents the author's successful attempt at a mimesis of negativity in *La speculazione edilizia*, Calvino thus argues through his fictional character that nature and history do, and must, coexist.[26] Through his foray into speculation, Quinto lives out a desire for separation to its fullest extent by replacing the land dearest to his family with new construction. Rather than see the landscape of *** partially changed by construction – and thus exist as a hybrid of nature and "history" – he attempts to turn it all from one category to the other.

In Quinto, Calvino proposes the first and most thoroughly explored of three paths for living out a shifting nature/culture dynamic. Quinto's path is guided by the sense that nature is irrevocably desecrated once changed at all, a view still common today. As William Cronon observes, "As soon as we label something as 'natural,' we attach to it the powerful implication that any change from its current state would degrade and damage the way it is 'supposed' to be."[27] The notion of untouched nature certainly has its appeal, but we set ourselves up for continual disappointment if that is what we seek. As Quinto himself struggles to recognize, a binary attitude simply cannot be sustained in a post-industrial world, especially for those who want to maintain a positive relationship with the natural environment. The challenge for the ecologically minded individual, then, lies in sifting out dynamic change from that which is degrading and damaging.

Paired against Quinto is the builder Caisotti, a stumbling agent of uncritical and indeed potentially damaging change. Caisotti is an unusual complement to Quinto, not so much a double as an opposite, a missing half representing all that Quinto feels he lacks, along with all that he fears. Caisotti is a recent arrival to the Anfossis' Ligurian community, having come from the mountains to seek his fortune. He is rough-edged and often described as frazzled and unkempt, as though he has spent the night in his modest office. Socially, he embodies both the positive potential and the painful struggle for the upwardly mobile individual in Italy of the late 1950s. He is someone from the rural working class who has come to the city, a space of relatively greater structure and law, to make a name for himself.

Both Caisotti's manner and his social station unnerve Quinto. Yet his status as a perennial loser, an outsider to be looked down on and mistrusted, pulls at Quinto's heartstrings. On hearing his town acquaintances heartily dismiss Caisotti's business practices and general character, Quinto, we read, "Addesso si sentiva solidale con Caisotti come con un vittima: tutta la città voleva schiacciarlo, tutti i benpensanti s'erano coalizzati contro di lui, e quel muratore montanaro, armato solo della sua natura rozza e sfuggente, resisteva."[28] In his outsider status, Caisotti inhabits the other half of Quinto's interstitial realm. Like Quinto, he is neither fully of nor apart from his social milieu.[29] He has surpassed Quinto, however, by resisting the community's opposition and existing within its framework on a prominent formal level, via his socially recognized professional identity as builder.

Understanding Caisotti's persistence early in the story, Quinto once again regrets his past intellectual and political engagement, which he now finds pointless: "Ora ce l'aveva coi suoi amici delle grandi città del Nord in cui era vissuto per tutti quegli anni, anni passati a far progetti sulla società futura, sugli operai e gli intellettuali." While Quinto and his friends were busy talking, "Ha vinto Caisotti."[30] The game has been won by those too ambitious or perhaps too driven by base need and desire to waste time philosophizing. It is not an easy route that Caisotti has chosen, and we see him struggle at every step. In fact, although repeatedly cited as a cement-hungry brute with no concern for aesthetics – an issue with which Quinto is frightfully obsessed – Caisotti is rarely depicted in the act of construction, and his building projects are repeatedly stalled. He is instead always waiting for more cement to arrive, in feverish anticipation of the chance to cover the earth with new buildings. As such, he represents a constant threat, a looming reality of increased speculation founded on the desire to create ever more manmade structures and move further up the social ladder through financial gain.

Caisotti's involvement in the covering up of landscape and his role as new modern man are complicated by his associations with nonhuman nature. The uncouth builder is repeatedly likened to an animal, cited for his brute affect, and associated with the imagined sexual prowess and fertility of a beast. He is also, like an element of the natural world, coming into an increasingly complicated relationship with city life and social code. When first introduced into the narrative he is described as "squalo, squalo e toro che sbuffa dalle narici," possessing "una specie di fragilità infantile," but also an aspect "dello squalo, o dell'enorme crostaceo, del granchio."[31] Later in the text he is downgraded from the specificity of individual animals to the generality of the beast at large, described as acting "come di bestia che si vede in gabbia," "un irresponsabile, un selvaggio [...] una bestia," and a "bestia smarrita," ready to unleash his rage at any moment.[32] His base passion is only underlined by recurrent suggestions that "dal paese è scappato perchè ha riempito di figli naturali tutta la vallata," as well as innuendos of intimate relationship to his employees: illegitimate children, lovers, or simply fellow refugees from rural existence.[33]

Such descriptions recall Agambian categories, specifically the philosopher's discussion of the bandit or werewolf figure, "a monstrous hybrid of human and animal, divided between the forest and the city."[34] Caisotti fits the bill, a shark-bull-crustacean of a man ideologically stuck between the Anfossis' relatively urban town and his original mountain home. In his discussion of the bandit, Agamben specifies that "the life of the bandit, like that of the sacred man, is not a piece of animal nature without any relation to law and the city. It is, rather, a threshold of indistinction and of passage between animal and man, physis and nomos, exclusion and inclusion."[35] Once more the description is applicable to Caisotti. Legally, he enters into relationship with the unnamed town through his business relationships. Socially, however, he is not given the respect offered to any other member of the community and is continually referred to as an outsider.

While Caisotti is portrayed as a simple, straightforward, and uncouth character, his contribution to the narrative is anything but. To begin, his bumbling nature and lack of acceptance by the community negate Quinto's vision of the speculating class as a club of omnipotent new leaders. If Caisotti is any example, the speculators and developers are in fact struggling. What's more, Caisotti's social status, operating within the society while not of it, distinctly mirrors the threshold status of the landscape, which is transitioning from a relatively bare state to one of urban (dis)order. Because of such mirroring, our initial impression of Caisotti, master of cement, as somehow contrary to nature becomes complicated. Caisotti and the landscape share a fundamental trait, that of interstitiality. He thus destabilizes any remaining trace of a nature/culture binary, as the zeitgeist of Calvino's speculator class is one fuelled by Caisotti's raw, "beastly" nature.

The final path proposed in *La speculazione edilizia* is that of Signora Anfossi, a somewhat marginal but meaningful figure who is most often referred to simply as *la madre*. Signora Anfossi is generally found quietly toiling away in her garden amid Caisotti's slow-moving construction, working with the hope that she might at least "salvare il salvabile," save what might still be saved.[36] Unlike Quinto, who thinks one thing and voices another, Signora Anfossi is quite direct in her spoken regret about the changing Ligurian landscape. As a result she is a much less tormented individual than either her son or Caisotti. By acknowledging her grief and communicating it to others she is able to come to terms with the physical reality of her environment and culture, serving as a model for contemplation and recognition of change.

Parallels have been drawn between Signora Anfossi and Calvino's own botanist mother. Claudia Nocentini writes, in fact, "Just as the first-person narrator is a representation of the author distorted in a negative sense, so the portrait of the mother is totally positive and seems to be a tribute to Eva Mameli Calvino."[37] While it is difficult to verify just how much Signora Anfossi is meant to evoke Eva Calvino, it is easy to note her representation of the maternal in general, as underlined by her common designation as "the mother." Lexically tying Signora Anfossi to her maternal function does run the risk of reducing woman to the monodimensional role of caretaker, as Signora Anfossi is, notably, the only female character of significance in the text. Furthermore, her connection to the landscape of her unnamed town – a space under construction at the desire and service of others – echoes the sort of woman/nature parallel critiqued by contemporary ecofeminists like Val Plumwood and Stacy Alaimo.[38] As they and others rightly note, women and nature have long been linked in such a way that assigns them less agency and worth than the pairing of men and culture. Calvino does veer into such essentializing territory, but he also complicates it. Explicitly linked to the environment, Signora Anfossi is shown to be more forward thinking in her relationship to change and acceptance of nature/culture overlap, rather than binary, than the male characters in the text such as her son.

The first thing Signora Anfossi does each time Quinto returns to their family home is show him the *novità* from their terrace, indicating the physical transition underway and, in the process, articulating a new vision of hybrid or modified landscape. She tells her son, "Là i Sampieri soprelevano, quello è un palazzo nuovo di certi di Novara [...] ora guarda che scavo," continuing on, "vieni da questa parte, ora; qui a levante, vista da toglierci non ne avevano più, ma guarda quel nuovo tetto che è spuntato: Ebbene, adesso il sole alla mattina arriva qui mezz'ora dopo."[39] Just one page after Quinto has described his preferred static landscape his mother verbally ruptures that vision. She details what vistas are shifting form and how that affects her relationship to the environment, encapsulated in the passage above in the form of sunlight. Due to new construction, the sun reaches her home a half-hour later than it used to, thus changing her daily contact with the nonhuman environment and, we might assume, shades of her habitual routine. Recalling certain principles of bioregionalism, she notes how ways of living are shaped by the particularities of place.

Quinto responds to his mother's sentiment by finding her old and out of touch. He is repulsed by her "serene sadness," considering it the foolishness of an older generation unable to face the workings of history. Yet he is the one to bristle at the physical signs of history's passing, here in the guise of rubble and cement. And while Quinto may view his mother as part of a dying breed, Calvino's underlying narrative suggests just the opposite. Not exactly languishing behind closed doors, Signora Anfossi is most directly connected to the land through the practice of gardening, a cultivation of new life and continued growth that welcomes the cooperation of nature and culture.

Like Quinto, Signora Anfossi feels connected to her environment, but she succeeds where her son cannot: she is able to maintain a sense of place by recognizing and even participating in the dynamic life of her surroundings. By immersing herself in the garden space, she is forced to recognize and work within the ebbs and flows of natural growth cycles, while serving as daily witness to the construction also taking place upon the land. The differences between Signora Anfossi and her son are most clearly outlined by his choice of land to sell, an area called *della vaseria*. This is the piece of family property to which Quinto feels the least attached, an area whose name means essentially "for the pots," and which was used at one time or another as a kitchen garden, a hen hoop, and a storage area for items such as vases and tools. Not surprisingly, the space for which Quinto holds the least sentiment is an interstitial one often in visible flux. For his mother, however, this area has become through the years a favoured spot. As the narrative goes, "Quest'orto, la madre, via via sminuito il fabbisogno familiare di verdure […] la madre era andata invadendolo delle sue piante da giardino, facendone una specie di luogo di smistamento, di vivaio."[40] We read that as her parents and husband died and her sons moved out of the family home, Signora Anfossi dedicated more and more time to the plot, working the earth such that "così il terreno aveva rivelato doti d'umidità e d'esposizione specialmente raccomandabili per certe piante rare, che accolte là provvisoriamente vi s'erano poi stabilite [...] aveva ora un suo disarmonico aspetto, tra agricolo, scientifico e prezioso."[41] Thus, as it turns out, the land of least importance to Quinto is humid, fertile earth well suited to the growth of new plants, plants that might enrich the natural landscape if given the opportunity.

After first introducing the land *della vaseria,* Calvino subsequently writes of it as a *vivaio,* a term that emphasizes its life-giving, vibrant character. Not only has the land itself undergone transition, it now serves as a transitional breeding ground, allowing plants to blossom before being moved elsewhere. This word *vivaio* is consistently translated in dual-language dictionaries as *nursery,* meaning a place in which something is "bred, nourished or fostered."[42] In both Italian and English the term can be used for plants, people, even ideas. Where the Italian is particularly pertinent on its own is in its obvious root, *vivere,* to live. A true testament to Signora Anfossi's resilience and acceptance of transition, she has created a *vivaio,* transitional sanctuary of new life, out of the deaths and absences in her family.

The ripe nature of the *vivaio* is not meant to encourage a reading of nature/culture binary in the text. As a place structured and tended by human hands the garden cannot exactly be considered separate from the realm of culture. We might instead view the garden in general, and Signora Anfossi's *vivaio* in particular, as evidence that collaboration between nature and culture does not equate a remove from the natural world. Tended by human hands, the garden provides space for the nonhuman to flourish and allows for direct contact with the earth. In demonstration of such flourishing, Signora Anfossi's garden is a place of unrestrained, free-willed growth, as emphasized by the above description of its "disharmonious aspect." With the *vivaio* our environmental focus shifts from Quinto's attachment to the natural landscape, which quickly proves itself to be of a static romanticist ilk, to his mother's acceptance of plurality, a precursor to trends of our own current era beyond the postmodern.

In considering the function of the garden it is helpful to turn to the early work of Michael Pollan. In his book *Second Nature,* Pollan identifies the garden as a "midspace," a "place that admits of both nature and human habitation."[43] As midspace, the garden bridges nonhuman physical nature with the human capacity for reason and an aesthetic sensibility. Within this space, according to Pollan, the gardener "doesn't feel that by virtue of the fact that he changes nature he is somehow outside of it. He looks around and sees that human hopes and desires are by now part and parcel of the landscape."[44] A gardener, Signora Anfossi is one step ahead of Quinto in that she can negotiate two realms as they overlap and blend into one another. Pollan holds that the "second nature" of the garden is still very much *nature* and that "the 'environment' is not, and has never been, a neutral, fixed backdrop; it is in fact alive, changing all the time in response to innumerable contingencies, one of these being the presence within it of the gardener."[45] In this light, the garden and its keeper serve as ideal guides for conceptualizing a modern relationship to the land, leading us towards an understanding of the role played by the human hand in the landscape all around, while still celebrating the vibrancy of nature.

And yet Calvino does not let his work conclude with the happy sort of ending that might simply celebrate the potential in Signora Anfossi's garden; that would be too easy. The signora does indeed embody a positive alternative to the Quintos and Caisottis of the world, but her path surfaces as the least dominant of the three represented in the text. As *La speculazione edilizia* comes to an end, Calvino leaves his characters as unresolved as he found them and only further entrenched in the implications of their changing terrain. On the novella's final pages we read that Signora Anfossi "era in giardino. I caprifogli odoravano. I nasturzi erano una macchia di colore fin troppo vivo. Se non alzava gli occhi in su, dove da tutte le parti s'affacciavano le finestre dei casamenti, il giardino era sempre il giardino."[46] In this same moment her sons' environment and actions are quite different. While she obstinately maintains her role as gardener, Quinto and his brother negotiate the power of property ownership in a space ever more removed from nature. We read:

> La stanza, con le persiane chiuse, era in penombra. Loro, seduti con fasci di carte sulle ginocchia, rifacevano il conto di quando si sarebbe ammortizzato il capitale. Il sole spariva presto dietro l'edificio di Caisotti e di tra le stecche delle persiane la luce che batteva sull'argenteria del buffet era sempre meno, era adesso solo quella che passava tra le stecche più alte e si spegneva a poco a poco, sulle curve lustre dei vasoi, delle teiere.[47]

After this morose description the tale ends, with ellipsis points pairing two images, two potential environments and attitudes, side by side. It confirms neither the ecologically minded option, the garden remaining a place of new life, nor the option more likely to endure, the construction under way. Both scenarios exist conditionally and both require a measure of sacrifice. The mother's garden, full of flowers bursting with almost too much life, retains its grounding function. This is only so, however, if she does not raise her head to face the reality immediately in front of her. Her garden and thus her direct contact with the natural world persist on the condition that Caisotti's building, or another one like it, does not continue to occupy even more land. Quinto's situation is then conditioned in the opposite direction. He can live out the glory of the proprietor, already tenuous based on the temporary nature of his economic stability, but his relationship to nature, once dear, has been duly compromised: The sun's light barely reaches past Caisotti's building to Quinto's place at the table, surrounded as he is by the trappings of modern society as he understands it. It is the outsider Caisotti, noticeably absent in these concluding passages, who has come the closest to succeeding at something: His building, in the end, is complete.

As Franco Ricci reminds us, in the work of Calvino, "Nature is never simply innocent, nor is industry always lethal."[48] There are no easy choices, no clear distinctions when it comes to finding a balance between nature and culture in the author's work. They are already too entwined. With *La speculazione edilizia,* Calvino does not answer but rather offers a new question. He asks how humanity might go forward in a culture of mass production, construction and consumption without losing sight of the natural world. His work suggests that we have no choice but to move beyond any notion of static nature/culture binary, just as it confirms that modern Italy's attraction to progress and growth ushers in an era of significant rupture to the landscape. Readers are left pondering how to strike a proper balance, so as to embrace progress and innovation without damaging both the nonhuman world and the untamed human spirit that it attracts.

La nuvola di smog poses similar questions from a distinctly new angle, situated within the urban industrial at large. This novella is, in certain ways, a smaller work than *La speculazione edilizia.* It is briefer in terms of both page number and narrative time span, and it features a less-developed cast of characters. Most strikingly, it works at times to undermine its own status as a serious text or realistic narrative through a heavy-handed use of gag and hyperbole. Rather like in his *Marcovaldo* tales of the same period, Calvino's narrative can linger in this work just on the edge of fable. It blurs the lines of specific temporal identification and encourages readers to seek a punchline or moral that, not surprisingly, never quite comes. Much as in those tales, the environmentalist tack is so overt in *La nuvola di smog* that we run the risk of brushing it aside so as to focus solely on its symbolic function, taking the smog of the work's title to represent the ideological haze of the modern alienated worker. To do so, however, would be to deny a real engagement with tough, historically prescient questions. Amid colourless descriptions of place and humour-filled caricatures of people, Calvino employs *La nuvola di smog* to confront the role of pollution not only in post-war Italy but in the industrialized world at large. Along the way, he probes the ethical responsibility of both industry and the private individual.

The second novella of Calvino's "Vita difficile," *La nuvola di smog*, like its predecessor, has a rather complicated editorial history. The work first appeared in 1958, in the journal *Nuovi Argomenti*, then again that same year in the collected *Racconti*, only to be paired with the novella *La formica argentina* (The Argentine Ant, 1965) seven years later by Einaudi's Coralli imprint. In 1964 the two novellas were then published in another Coralli edition with a third novella, *La giornata di uno scrutatore* (The Watcher, 1963). On the occasion of this final publication Calvino writes, in the third person, "*La nuvola di smog* è un racconto continuamente tentato di diventare qualcos'altro: saggio sociologico o diario intimo; ma a queste tentazioni Italo Calvino riesce sempre a opporre la sua tattica difensiva a base di gags comiche e di scrollate di spalle."[49] As its author admits, *La nuvola di smog* dances along the edges of social criticism, gingerly confronting a difficult reality head on while echoing Calvino's own struggles with personal accountability and the real effects of social action. That it actually achieves these ends is often shaded from our sight by the author's strategic use of tone, and it is up to the pragmatic reader to navigate around his protective roadblocks in search of the work's denser core.

La nuvola di smog is the story of an unnamed man who has recently moved to a new city, again also unnamed, to take a job writing copy for a factory newspaper under the direction of a corporate head. He rents a squalid room in a dusty apartment, has a girlfriend he sees on occasion and with whom he has difficulty communicating, and generally feels passionless about his current existence. He does reserve a certain measure of passion, directed towards his obsession with the city's dirt, from which he never manages to feel clean. He is a rather sad character leading a rather mundane life, one more in a series of Calvino's socially maladjusted leading men. Only ever identified through the auto-referential *Io*, the protagonist acts largely in adherence to his perceived social role – he does what he thinks others expect him to do – even when this generally opposes his instincts, much like Quinto in *La speculazione edilizia*. He goes to parties when he would rather stay in, claims to support common political beliefs when he in fact does not, and so on.

The novella begins just as he arrives in his new city and takes stock of his situation. He states: "Lavoro nuovo, città diversa, fossi stato più giovane o mi fossi aspettato di più dalla vita, m'avrebbero dato slancio e contentezza; adesso no, non sapevo vedere che il grigio."[50] Were he someone else, if he had greater faith in the workings of the world, he would feel greater enthusiasm for his situation. As it is, he is resigned to considering life as something that occurs around him regardless of his input, something that has become covered in dirt and shrouded in smog. Throughout the text, Calvino's protagonist struggles with both the symbol and the reality of smog; it mirrors the lack of grounding and the alienation of modern urban man, but it is also an actual, physical reality, an atmospheric byproduct of nearby factories. The book's primary plot and climax centre simply on his growing clarity regarding both the source and potential impact of this smog. Although he states a desire for anonymity in his immediate environment –and both protagonist and place remain unnamed in the text – he ultimately cannot deny a growing sense of responsibility to confront the larger environmental impact of industrial culture. As the novella progresses, the protagonist becomes increasingly engaged with the effects of industrial pollution on the immediate urban landscape, this pollution's eventual global legacy, and the social response to both.

Titled "La Purificazione," the paper for which he writes is an internal publication of the Organization for the Purification of the Urban Atmosphere of Industrial Centres. While all of this sounds very eco-positive, it is complicated by the fact that the EPAUCI, as the organization is known, runs the largest chemical plant in the region. The paper is a biweekly publication expressly dedicated to addressing the atmospheric effects of the EPAUCI's productive existence. The great irony in this text, what Calvino would have called the "comic gag," is twofold. The protagonist is a staunch city dweller who fancies himself to be quite cosmopolitan. Again, like Quinto in *La speculazione edilizia*, he sees himself as a modern citizen of the world and states early in the text that he prefers to avoid feelings of place attachment altogether. Yet he has moved to his new city to focus explicitly on place and environmental specificity, through his work as writer and editor of "La Purificazione."

Here we find the first part of *La nuvola di smog*'s comic gag: a disenfranchised character possessing neither attachment to nor awareness of place has been commissioned to act not only as an environmental advocate but also as an environmental advocate for a very specific region. About starting this job and meeting his new supervisor, he states: "Di motivi ideali non ne avevo nè volevo averne; volevo solo fargli un articolo come piaceva a lui, per conservare quel posto, nè migliore nè peggiore di un altro, e continuare quella vita, nè migliore nè peggiore di tutte le altre vite possibili."[51] He has simply found himself in the position of working for "La Purificazione," through no true interest of his own, as all things hold the same objective value in his eyes.

The EPAUCI is run by a certain Cordà, a self-proclaimed "devout environmentalist" and, as it happens, a captain of industry. EPAUCI and its publication are side projects initiated, funded, and overseen by Cordà's industrial conglomerate, Wafd. Herein lies the work's second gag, simultaneously comic and tragic: the entity behind "La Purificazione" is itself the largest source of pollution in the city. Readers must then wonder how truly devout Cordà's environmentalism can be. Midway through the text the protagonist asks himself just this. Late on a deadline, he meets with Cordà to read over a new issue of "La Purificazione" at the Wafd headquarters. As he stands in the director's office while Cordà approvingly reads his pledges of atmospheric heroism, the protagonist has ample time to gaze out at the flaming smokestacks past Cordà's glass walls. In slow shock he reveals:

> Io, che tante volte di fronte a lui, negli uffici dell'Ente, sfogavo il mio naturale antagonismo di dipendente dichiarandomi mentalmente dalla parte dello smog, agente segreto dello smog penetrato nello stato maggiore nemico, ora capivo quanto era l'ingegner Cordà il padrone dello smog, era lui che lo soffiava ininterrottamente sulla città, e l'EPAUCI era una creatura dello smog, nata dal bisogno di dare a chi lavora per lo smog la speranza di una vita che non fosse solo di smog, ma nello stesso tempo per celebrarne la Potenza.[52]

The scope of the EPAUCI and its publication is to promote a positive environmentalist image of the corporation, thus soothing any doubts held by employees about the nature of their polluting work. The EPAUCI also seeks with the paper to keep its working population in a sort of limbo, as they simultaneously produce and decry the smog. Digesting confident text such as "Lo risolveremo? Lo stiamo risolvendo," readers of "La Purificazione" are motivated by the thought of moving towards a positive common goal, a state brighter than the present because of the cleaner air the paper loosely promises.[53] Happy with this projected future, they then continue their process of atmospheric pollution. Neither the gravity of the situation nor the proper actions one might take to eradicate it are ever fully addressed in the paper. Cordà manages to keep his newspaper readers at arm's length from their environmental reality by emphasizing the magnitude of their still-nebulous situation. As he exclaims to the protagonist, "Siamo una delle città in cui la situazione atmosferica è più grave, ma nello stesso tempo la città in cui si fa di più per essere all'altezza della situazione!"[54] Cordà is deftly able to keep reader concern high while simultaneously maintaining a position of power over his audience. This is achieved through a manipulation of fear – readers of "La Purificazione" certainly do not want things to get worse – complemented by the pretence that hope is enough to sustain and thus pacify them.

That his city is one among many affected by smog might open the door for Cordà, who dictates the paper's contents, to a printed discussion of shared environmental realities, a more national, global, or even eco-cosmopolitan perspective. It could, then, pave the way for a sharing of knowledge among other captains of industry, which might eventually lead to stronger problem solving and environmental standards. The Great Smog that occurred in England just six years before the publication of *La nuvola di smog* provides a notable example from another centre of Western industry and surely served as inspiration for Calvino's work. This real-life incident of severe pollution lasted from 5–9 December 1952, when a combination of still skies, cold weather, and massive coal residue created a blanket of smog over the city of London, the likes of which had never before been seen. In the following months upwards of eight thousand Londoners died from lethal fumes produced during the five days. The positive result of this environmental disaster was the Clean Air Act passed by the British Parliament in 1956. This legislation controlled both industrial and domestic smoke sources, and marked in England "the dividing line between the general acceptance of air pollution as a natural consequence of industrial development, and the understanding that progress without pollution control is no progress at all."[55] Calvino's Cordà is distinctly not interested in actively pursuing such an understanding. Instead, he manipulates an interpretation of risk in order to shape a discrete community within his city, distanced from and elevated above, as he says, "altre città rivali del nostro stesso paese," thanks to "La Purificazione" and its vague promises of localized environmental repair.[56]

Perhaps the most stunning attribute of the inherent contradiction in Cordà's stance, and the most comic, is that he appears truly blind to it. Thinking that it will please his supervisor, the protagonist writes an article portraying his new city as less polluted than others in Europe. Rather than compliment him on the article, however, Cordà is quick to retract it and present a counter-argument based in statistics on the levels of fossil fuels burnt in the men's midst every day. He says, in all earnestness, "La situazione è seria, sì, più seria di quel che il suo articolo non lasci prevedere. Parliamoci da uomini: il pericolo d'inquinamento dell'aria delle grandi città è forte, abbiamo le analisi, la situazione è grave."[57] Cordà is only too ready to instil yet more fear regarding localized pollution. In order to understand the import of the EPAUCI's promised salvation, his readership must know that the environmental threat they face is just as great, if not greater, than that in other communities. Once his employee is appropriately impressed with the gravity of the situation Cordà then drops in his punchline: "Appunto perchè grave, ci siamo noi per risolverla."[58] Cordà and company declare themselves ready to resolve the situation precisely because it is so serious, and yet it is so serious precisely because of them.

Our interpretive task as readers is to determine both the veracity of Cordà's ideological claims and the scope of Calvino's authorial intent. Is Cordà truly a believer in both his smog-spewing factory and the need to save the environment? Is Calvino, then, using him to poke fun at big business and industry, perhaps at Italy's boom-era bourgeoisie? I would argue that readers are indeed to understand Cordà as truly ignorant to the contradiction that he represents. This does not, however, negate how he purposefully manipulates others' understanding of environmental concern in order to protect his privileged status, nor that he does so without taking any real action to resolve the worsening pollution. As far as we are able to glean from the text, Cordà's only environmentalist turn is to oversee a journal promising an action that is always only forthcoming. Whether or not they feel real to him, his intentions boil down to words on a page, ultimately not even authored by him but by a paid employee.

On realizing the conflict behind Cordà's claims to environmentalism, the protagonist is motivated to consider the smog in a new light. It is this realization that serves as the novella's climax, as its protagonist finally comes into a state of awareness and, as a consequence, his own true environmentalism. Smog is no longer a figurative concept out to harm the vitality of the city but a physical reality produced by the city's greatest barons. Fully cemented in the scene inside the Wafd offices, cited above, the groundwork for this eco-awakening is laid in chapter 2 of *La nuvola di smog*, in which the protagonist takes an extra-urban jaunt with his girlfriend, Claudia. She is all that the protagonist is not: full of exuberance and social grace, aware only of beauty, and often associated with colour and animals, two elements starkly absent from the rest of the grey text.

Desperate one day to shield her from the city's grime, and to be far from the social arenas in which their differences are greatest, the protagonist takes Claudia to a hillside beyond the urban centre. Once they arrive, she is struck by an instance of natural beauty, while he is spellbound by the urban view that distance reveals. He explains: "Lei, senza ascoltarmi, era presa da qualcosa che aveva visto volare, uno stormo di uccelli, e io restavo lì affacciato a guardare per la prima volta dal di fuori la nuvola che mi circondava in ogni ora, la nuvola che abitavo e che m'abitava, e sapevo che di tutto il mondo variegato che m'era intorno solo quella m'importava."[59] While Claudia is enchanted by the beauty of the nonhuman world, he is transfixed by the darker realities of an ongoing merger between worlds human and non. It is in this realization that he finally commits to commitment: He acknowledges truly caring about something – smog.

Notably, the protagonist's first true awareness of the smog as a unique atmospheric entity is only possible through removed observance and the chance it provides to gaze upon his city as a contextualized landscape. He marvels: "Un senso di vasto m'aveva preso [...] guardando i molteplici aspetti del paesaggio [...]. Fu allora che vidi quella cosa," referring in the final sentence to the cloud of smog.[60] These unassuming lines contribute to a growing ecocritical platform in that they succinctly alert readers once more to Calvino's nature-*with*-culture approach. By viewing the city as just one part of the *paesaggio*, the landscape, the protagonist inserts his gaze into a larger discussion of what defines nature, and of how to approach landscape and environment in a heavily industrial age. He recognizes as a piece of the landscape not only the city but also "quella cosa," the smog, byproduct of urban industry. And by declaring smog part and parcel of the landscape, as much as the birds that attract Claudia's gaze, he signals ahead to the decidedly second-nature landscapes explored by Gianni Celati in the 1980s, as I discuss in Chapter 4.

The category of landscape is relatively new. Giorgio Bertone writes that "paesaggio è parola solo moderna, borghese, colta, scaturita come getto di fonte a lungo compressa nelle buie viscere della terra."[61] Bertone's suggestion that humankind suddenly leapt from a raw, uncritical relationship with the land to a place of bourgeois remove is, on its own, rather troubling. His insistence, however, on the correlation between modernity and a need to frame and temper that upon which we gaze, or within which we move, is quite useful. As he underlines, the very notion of landscape resolutely confirms a relationship of exchange between the natural and the cultural. When we approach the terrain before us our responses – emotional, aesthetic, and intellectual – expose our cultural positioning through dependence upon reason, ideology, and scales of value. As Calvino's unnamed protagonist says, "La bellezza va inventata continuamente."[62] Our gaze cannot help but be shaped by the world in which we live.

Scholars such as Bertone and Massimo Quaini focus heavily on the culture inherent in any given landscape. Quaini even goes so far as to write, "Il paesaggio non è interessante come categoria analitica per leggere l'ambiente o il territorio in termini scientifici, ma lo è in quanto contenitore di miti, sogni ed emozioni, in quanto accumulatore di metafore per capire le contraddizioni e i problemi del nostro tempo."[63] While I agree wholeheartedly that a society's approach to landscape reflects the myths and the problems of its age, these categories need not exclude the physical, scientific reality of the environment, as Calvino's narratives show. If this means that in order to feel environmental concern or act in stewardship for a place we must view it within a particular frame, so be it.

By having his protagonist direct a landscape-oriented gaze onto the city, Calvino challenges readers to reconsider the values we place on diverse types of space and reminds us that the natural environment exists within cities, as well as beyond them. By then focusing his text on air, an element that resists confinement to any particular space, he suggests that all spaces warrant environmental concern. In this Calvino once again anticipates more recent environmentalist trends, such as the environmental justice movement, for air is available to and used by all people. He also promotes the sort of eco-cosmopolitanism that the character Cordà negates in *La nuvola di smog*, as air certainly does not recognize national borders, and concerns regarding air quality may be felt in any site of industrial or chemical activity.

Gazing first upon the city from afar, then upon a site of chemical production from the offices of upper management, Calvino's protagonist is able to finally move beyond his own obsession with localized smog and understand contaminated air as a wide-reaching environmental threat. His first step reflecting an increasingly global awareness is to reprint news from a foreign paper, which cites air pollution in its area due not to smog but to atomic radiation. Cordà chides him for this action, exclaiming incredulously: "Ma, senta, dottore, lei a questo pericolo della radiotività ci crede?"[64] The protagonist does believe in such danger, and from that point on he continues to insert articles concerning nuclear radiation into the pages of "La Purificazione." Turning to hazardous situations and sources of pollution located elsewhere provides the protagonist a certain measure of journalistic protection, as it distances him from Cordà's complicated directives regarding the EPAUCI's environmental image. Quite simply, the protagonist is no longer drawing attention to the organization's own role as mass polluter. More significantly, this shift in focus indicates his awareness not only of place at large but also of other bioregions and communities, and the ways in which they might differ from and resemble his own. The trend of transnational awareness continues in his writing as, amid data on coal, combustible oil, and their physiological consequences, he adds further data regarding atomized zones. Dropping the glib promises of the early days of "La Purificazione," he uses the paper as a format for drawing his local environmental risk scenario into a broader early Cold War context. By employing the notion of atmospheric threat to reach toward the global, the protagonist destabilizes his corporate supervisor's manipulation of atmospheric pollution as, instead, something regionally specific. Where Cordà uses air quality to limit his readers to the particular – we have it the worst so we must fight the hardest – the protagonist treats it as a platform through which to encourage a longer-range, thus ecologically deeper, engagement.

La nuvola di smog, small work that it may be, spans wide in geographic scope in its final chapters due to such explorations of common environmental risk. They are greatly enhanced by a very simple but significant narrative element: anonymity. As in *La speculazione edilizia*, the setting of *La nuvola di smog* remains unnamed; the tale unfolds simply in "the city." In truth, the omission of a place name in the first novella does quite little to mask its location and character. The narrative is so full of specific references – Liguria, a semi-urban seaside town, a vacation destination for northern city dwellers, full of florists, and so on – as to root the story in a specific place. This is ultimately one of its greatest strengths, as Calvino uses the text to explore both the benefits and the limitations of a regionally specific approach to environmental concerns. By contrast, the city enveloped by and in *La nuvola di smog* is truly anonymous. As an industrial centre we may assume that it is located in north-central Italy, but we may assume little more than this. It could be any city of the industrially rich West. That fact only underlines further the commonality of, well, smog. In this, Calvino's economic boom-era text anticipates a very postmillenial trend towards eco-cosmopolitanism, as theorized by Heise and others – a critical understanding of environmental realities that cross geopolitical boundaries.

In the essay "Il mare dell'oggettività" of 1960, Calvino writes:

> Rivoluzionario è chi non accetta il dato naturale e storico e vuole cambiarlo. La resa all'oggettività, fenomeno storico di questo dopoguerra, nasce in un periodo in cui all'uomo viene meno la fiducia nell'indirizzare il corso delle cose, non perchè sia reduce da una bruciante sconfitta, ma al contrario perchè vede che le cose (la grande politica dei due contrapposti sistemi di forze, lo sviluppo della tecnica e del dominio delle forze naturali) vanno avanti da sole, fanno parte d'un insieme così complesso che lo sforzo più eroico può essere applicato solo al cercar di avere un'idea di come è fatto, al comprenderlo, all'accettarlo.[65]

We might hesitate to call Calvino's protagonist in *La nuvola di smog* a revolutionary. In the end it is unclear whether he will in fact take any action to address the environmental reality at hand beyond slipping musings on nuclear threat into a factory newspaper. And yet, our unnamed antihero does not, in the words of Calvino, accept the "dato naturale e storico." While he may not yet know how to effect change, he has developed the desire to do so, a crucial beginning. As he observes towards the end of the work, "Uno vede tante cose e non ci bada; magari queste cose che vede hanno un effetto su di lui ma lui non se ne accorge; poi comincia una volta a collegare una cosa con l'altra e allora improvvisamente tutto acquista significato."[66] Increased awareness eventually lends a deeper meaning to the world around, a new significance. The challenge, then, is what to do with this new significance. With his ecologically geared novellas of the 1950s, Calvino proposes a first step, depicting protagonists who expose their own struggles in the movement from *oggettività* to *coscienza,* so that readers may, perhaps, follow suit.

Chapter Three

Pier Paolo Pasolini: Boundaries and Mergers in (Ex)Urban Film

From his earliest poetry of the 1950s to his final films of the 1970s, Pier Paolo Pasolini (1922–1975) investigates the physical space in which subjects negotiate social reality. So very much of his work addresses landscape, one that is often Italian and always portrayed in relation to city structure and urban development. Yet landscape, and certainly the Italian *paesaggio*, might not be what first come to mind for most readers when they encounter his name. Ideology, critique, class; poetics, allegory, style; scandal, heresy, sexuality – all of these terms are likely to precede landscape. And not without reason: whether on page or screen, Pasolini's texts are wrapped up in the above categories, fiercely so.

All of that engagement does not, however, negate his attention to the relationship between humans and the earth. In fact, one can hardly address the above categories in Pasolini's work without stumbling across his equally strong engagement with the physical environment and the modern Italian landscape. But Pasolini's environmental focus has not yet received its due attention, especially when it comes to film.[1] While much of his writing, both poetry and prose, addresses the natural environment, it is through film that he most directly engages the contemporary interstitial terrain between urban and rural, and between built and unbuilt environments. It is here that he continues the conversation about adaptation and coping raised by Calvino's novellas of the 1950s, bringing us one step further in consideration of a manipulated and multiaxial Italian landscape. Focusing on a transition to ever more urban life in his films, whether in the guise of character or land, the director asks viewers to question the lived realities in which we participate, realities that host changes to land as well as lifestyle. At the same time, he struggles against his outdated investment in binary categories, particularly when it comes to the very relationship between nature and culture. While Pasolini overtly embraces a nature/culture binary in first-person texts cited below, his cinematic work suggests an understanding that such a binary is ultimately impossible. The tension between these two modes of thought marks a decisive turning point in the recognition of a second-nature state in modern Italian literature and film. It posits Pasolini's work as a bridge between a form of tentative acceptance and the development of active strategies for coping with the modified environment.

In writing about Pasolini's cinema here I use the terms nature and landscape rather interchangeably, with the full knowledge that they have long been considered discrete and even, at times, oppositional entities.[2] As addressed previously in this work, landscape is very much a cultural construct. To cite Martin Lefebvre, "nature is that which we usually conceive of as existing independently from us, whereas it is our (real and imaginary) interaction with nature and environment that produces the landscape."[3] Such human interaction leads some to oppose the category of landscape to that of nature, whether interpreted as "metaphysical concept" (the nonhuman in general), "realist concept" (physical nature, as in land and sea) or "lay concept" (the space that is commonly opposed to the urban environment).[4] Film, however, moulds these notions of nature into landscape by default. In framing a section of sea or sky, using manmade machinery to capture its image, and then packaging this image for the viewer's gaze, it envelops the natural in a human-made framework. And yet what it represents still pertains to the natural world; film is still able to capture the metaphysical notion of nature, as well as, more concretely, its physical or lay realities. For this reason it is particularly difficult and unfruitful to separate the categories of nature and landscape when it comes to film; rather, it is difficult to even consider a nature that is not somehow also landscape. All of this makes both the medium of film and the notion of landscape apt vehicles for a contemporary manifestation of nature, one that is distinctly secondary in its engagement with culture. Pasolini spent his career actively exploring just such sorts of relationship in the tension between being and representation. While he ostensibly advocates for a clear distinction between nature and culture, his work reveals a visual fixation with the very realm in which they overlap. This is, of course, just one of many productive contradictions to be found in Pasolini's theory and practice.

An emphasis is thus placed in this chapter on films that attempt to address a separation of nature and culture while also displaying an intermingling or, as Pasolini would more readily state, a "contamination" between the two in the contemporary landscape of 1960s Italy.[5] This chapter also considers the ways in which the director's attention to interstitial landscapes (those spaces where city meets country, no matter the era in question) is mirrored in his preferred human protagonists, Agambian *homines sacri,* who rest in the edgelands of social acceptance. Such a correspondence is unique; a similar one can rarely be found in the films of other landscape-oriented directors of the 1960s, such as Michelangelo Antonioni, and even then it is faint.[6]

Pasolini's attention to interstitial space and the merger of scapes urban and rural serves as the point of transition in this book between studies of landscape in the written texts of Italo Calvino (Chapter 2) and Gianni Celati (Chapter 4). Like Calvino's *La speculazione edilizia* and *La nuvola di smog,* Pasolini's films address exurban construction while expressing an evolving environmentalist sentiment: painfully aware of change to the landscape yet not quite sure what to do about it. While Calvino's protagonists work to come to terms intellectually with a transitioning environment, Pasolini's protagonists physically inhabit it, dwelling in the zone where the physical manifestations of nature and culture collide. And like the Celati of *Verso la foce,* to be considered in Chapter 4, Pasolini obsessively, albeit often oneirically, reflects the lived world and the trod-upon land back to viewers, "observing and recounting," as Celati will argue one must. The texts that result invariably touch upon the themes of industry, construction, and waste, which dominate landscape-oriented Italian texts in the later twentieth century. At the same time, they are marked by a particularly sharp attention to the potential *discomfort* caused by the meeting of diverse ways of life and defined types of space.

On the porous quality of defined realms, Giorgio Agamben explains: "Together with the process by which the exception everywhere becomes the rule, the realm of bare life – which is originally situated at the margins of the political order – gradually begins to coincide with the political realm, and exclusion and inclusion, outside and inside, *bios* and *zoe,* right and fact, enter into a zone of irreducible indistinction."[7] Agamben speaks of metaphorical or ideological space here, but his conceptualization may easily be applied to and further explicated by considerations of actual physical space. Just as the elements of life generally classified as personal – how and what we eat, with whom we share a bed – are inevitably brought into the realm of politics, so are physical spaces ostensibly separate from one another caused to intermingle as subjects transition from one realm to another. We can best understand the crucial role played by landscape in Pasolini's films if we perceive Agamben's "zone of irreducible indistinction" as a boundary in the process of being crossed.

A clear separation between bare life and political life is not possible, yet there is still a particular, even physical, realm in which their merger takes place: the realm of interstice, edgeland, or borderland. In the words of Gloria Anzaldúa, "Borderlands are physically present wherever two or more cultures edge each other, where people of different races occupy the same territory, where under, lower, middle, and upper classes touch, where the space between two individuals shrinks with intimacy."[8] The definition is easily extended to Pasolini's treatment of space; his landscapes do, after all, host the meeting of two different cultures, the open land and rudimentary structures pertaining to subproletarian, agrarian, or "prehistoric" life and the developed zone pertaining to the bourgeois existence of the modern polis. Such newfound intimacy does not come empty handed, but instead carries with it a whole slew of uncertain identities and frictions that are both productive and irreconcilable.[9]

A brief survey: A teenager walks free-form through the fields abutting his peripheral Roman housing complex, slowly circling the ruins of Etruscan aqueducts, crumbling stones jutting organically from the earth. He is home here. Later he brings a girl to this same space and cements his relationship to it through his ability to identify birdcalls, a skill that his urban paramour might only dream of. Next, an infant held by his mother in a bright green field looks up to the shocking blue sky above, safe and secure in a setting of hopeful new life and nurture. After this, two men – in truth, marionettes cut free from their handles – are tossed from the back of a garbage truck into a dumping ground beyond the city's edge in what is, apparently, their first experience of the outside world. Lying immersed in refuse they look up to see clouds and open sky for the very first time, marveling at the beauty of the nonhuman. Those same two actors, now playing father and son, stroll jauntily along a highway still under construction amid otherwise untouched land. Moving towards their rubble-filled ex-urban village they chat casually of trash-filled waters, false teeth, and DDT in one smooth breath, and viewers cannot help but connect the three. Finally, an anguished industrialist runs through barren desert, his body as naked as the land he traverses, while far away a woman buries herself in the trash-riddled dirt of a construction site, her tears nurturing the life that may yet grow from this ground. *Mamma Roma* (1962), *Edipo Re* (Oedipus Rex, 1967), *Che cosa sono le nuvole*? (What Are Clouds? 1968), *Uccellacci e uccellini* (The Hawks and the Sparrows, 1966), and *Teorema* (Theorem, 1968) – films spanning the predominant decade of Pasolini's career – grimly acknowledge pollution and pesticide use, and celebrate what they posit as a "pure" spirit of nature, while lamenting a distancing from it in modern society. The above titles ascribe agency to the landscape by focusing on it as much as on human characters, often drawing a parallel between the two.

Plaintive odes to the earth or calls for its protection, Pasolini's lingering landscape shots are also expressions of desire for a way of life he fears lost. The teenager mentioned in the list above, for example, Ettore of *Mamma Roma*, eventually dies due to his distancing from the ruins and the grass surrounding them. This transition and its definitive conclusion condemn Ettore's entry into urban modernity, his physical and psychological distancing from the land. They also underscore Pasolini's sumptuous, panning shots in the film with remorse for a collective decision to shun the peace of a simple life in nature. This is so much the case as to prompt one to ask whether the symbolic value of nature does not trump its physical reality in the director's oeuvre, whether the natural landscape does not in fact serve *only* as emblem of a simpler way of life lost. As Pasolini readily attests, however, both levels of signification, symbol and reality, exist comfortably in his cinematic work.

Pasolini had already established himself as a writer when he began making films. By the release of his first feature-length film, *Accattone* (1961), he had two full-length novels, four volumes of poetry, and the first of many important collections of essays under his belt. Although he continued to write prolifically after this first film, Pasolini felt that the moving picture opened new possibilities of expression, and he explored these possibilities in approximately one film a year from then on until his death. In articles on film and semiotics included in the volume *Empirismo Eretico* (Heretical Empiricism, 1972), particularly in the widely noted "Cinema di poesia," the director attributes his preference for film to what he sees as the medium's close relationship to reality.[10] Ever a lover of juxtaposition, Pasolini finds cinematic representation – a thoroughly modern form – to hold a closer relationship to myth, prehistory and dream, and, at the same time, nature and basic reality, than verbal language.[11] Just as cinema and myth mesh for the director, so too do dream and lived reality, as he views the realm of dream to simply be a most immediate and unmediated representation of daily life. Written and spoken languages, on the other hand, are much more filtered modes of communication in his view, and thus a limited means of representation. As Pasolini explains, there are certain images, such as visual gestures, that we associate with language, while there are "quelli legati a ricordi e sogni," which "prefigurano e offrono se stessi come il premesso 'strumentale' della communicazione cinematografica."[12]

Such a stance would suggest that the language of cinema is at least in part pre-linguistic, very much akin to the semiotic as later elaborated by Julia Kristeva: a means of communication related to the pulses and rhythms of the body, not yet maintained by the symbolic realm.[13] Already here we note a connection between cinema and the natural in the broadest sense, a close relationship between the moving image and the world of drive and seasonal cycle. Such a relationship is only confirmed by Pasolini's assertion that, unlike the relative elegance of the spoken, "La communicazione visiva che serve da base del linguagio filmico è, al contrario, estremamente grezzo, quasi animalesco," and so, "concreta, mai astratta."[14] Pasolini's theories of cinematic representation thus support his treatment of nature as a physical, and not solely symbolic, realm on two counts. Adamant that the material he chose to film was indeed raw reality, he shot on location rather than in studio, often in the Roman periphery under construction. Furthermore, in choosing a medium he found closer to the realm of the natural than other means of representation, in presenting "reality reproduced with reality," the director underlines a fascination with what he considered to be less mediated or culturally crafted experiences of the world, while still allowing for multiple levels of signification in his work. Filmic representation is of course still a mediation of reality, as much as literature albeit through different means. What is important to note here is that Pasolini operated on a different belief: According to his cinematic poetics, film is less manipulated than literature and thus more immediately connected to the lived world.

All of the above means that in the film *Uccellacci e uccellini* the unfinished highway upon which stroll protagonists Totò and Ninetto (portrayed by actors Totò and Ninetto Davoli) is indeed a highway. It appears, in fact, to be the A1, the Autostrada Uno or Autostrada del Sole that now stretches from Naples to Milan. Begun in 1956, in the full throes of Italy's recovery efforts and just shy of the subsequent economic boom, the A1 stands as an emblem of post–World War II civic progress ripping right through formerly open lands, soon to bring quick travel and exchange of goods to the Italian people, and automobile exhaust and industrial waste into the Italian countryside. This unfinished highway can also be read as a road of life, a symbol for the unknown course of human existence mulled over by the film's protagonists in their often-surreal encounters with the denizens of surrounding lands. Such an interpretation is strongly encouraged by the film's opening printed citation: "Dove va l'umanità? Boh!" (Where's humanity going? Dunno!). Without clear indications (the road is at one point flanked by street signs pointing to both Cuba and Istanbul) or a finished path, the highway offers no information as to where it may take its passengers. Following this lead, Giuliana Bruno views the film on a wholly allegorical level, arguing that with *Uccellacci e uccellini* Pasolini depicts a non-place. Citing the aforementioned signs, along with others bearing invented street names and odes to the unemployed, day labourers, and runaways, she proposes that in opposition to a very place-centred film such as *Mamma Roma, Uccellacci e uccellini* holds no relationship to particular place. Rather, she views the film as "a moving allegory of the joint itinerary of history and social space."[15]

This final assessment rings true on many levels. References to other times and cultures are repeatedly made in the film, and allegories of class conflict run rampant, no more so than in the titular episode featuring the hawks and the sparrows. At the same time, however, the particular history and social – as well as geographical – space foregrounding the film ought to be given more credit. The aforementioned opening reference to DDT, only used as an agricultural insecticide after World War II, sets the film in the post-war West, while also pointing to the sort of burgeoning environmental awareness launched by measures such as the British Clean Air Act, cited in Chapter 2. A later reference to Ninetto's upcoming job with Fiat also serves as an indication of post-war socioeconomic growth, while further refining the location to Italy. References to birth control and feminist struggle, while introduced in an absurdist episode featuring a travelling circus of humanity, are incredibly prescient. And not even mentioned yet are the film's final minutes, dedicated to documentary footage of the 1964 funeral of Palmiro Togliatti, who had helped lead the aforementioned PCI since 1927.

Finally, frequent shots of a large metropolis in the distant background of many scenes locate the film explicitly in the Roman outskirts. The easily recognizable Palazzo della Civiltà Italiana and Basilica of Saints Pietro and Paolo, both built as part of Rome's EUR (Esposizione

Universale di Roma) neighbourhood, often jut out in deep centre frame. For viewers familiar with Pasolini's extant oeuvre, scenes filmed against this now iconic backdrop – such as when Totò and Ninetto stroll on and under the highway construction site or when Ninetto, joyful after a bout of innocent flirtation, runs through grass and grain, leaping off mounds of dirt – recall the director's earlier Roman films. The particularly striking later scene reads very much as an ode to *Mamma Roma*'s Ettore, as in both films an adolescent boy expresses his romantic joy and energy in the outdoors, emblems of organized city life hovering in the far background.

Taken as a whole, such scenes and references clearly tie *Uccellacci e uccellini* to a particular time and place. The film captures the same postwar Roman outskirts featured in *Accattone* and *Mamma Roma*, but a few years richer and a few years more developed. And as in those films, the city centre looms as dominant active agent, instigator of the changes taking place in the foreground, such as economic disparity and widespread but unfinished and unguided construction.[16] For the reasons considered above, a designation of non-place for the setting of *Uccellacci e uccellini* runs a bit shy of the mark. Like Pasolini's other works, the film comfortably bridges the gap between universality and specificity of place, landscape included.

The landscape that it represents is one undergoing significant change as the Roman population rapidly expands. More perhaps than any other city, Rome quickly felt the effects of Italy's late 1950s industrial expansion, economic resurgence and internal migration, as more and more workers and their families flooded the capital in search of a steady job and better life. Population growth and, subsequently, environmental change, were most notable in the frenzy of Roman construction that occurred from the end of World War II to the mid-1960s. As Stephanie Pilat writes, the city more than doubled in area between 1940 and 1966.[17] Much of this expansion was guided by the government led INA-casa (Istituto Nazionale delle Assicurazioni) housing program, which sought to provide housing for the working poor. Like the Fascist-designed *borgate*, or slums, built for workers in previous decades, INA-casa neighbourhoods, such as the Tiburtino, were generally built on the city's edge. Pilat notes that unlike Fascist planning strategies, which imposed spatial order, INA-casa designs instructed planners to "take the natural landscape into account."[18] She also notes, however, that the INA-casa neighbourhoods ultimately had the same effect as the Fascist designs, which isolated Rome's working poor on the outskirts of town. What's more, by doubling the footprint of an already large city, all of the construction that occurred in the 1950s and 1960s, whether government sanctioned or not, covered up vast quantities of formerly open land and changed the face of Rome to include an ever-present bulldozer.

Pasolini assigns this transitioning Roman landscape great weight not only in *Uccellacci e Uccellini* but in the majority of his films. In so doing, he underlines landscape's abilities as storyteller and powerful narrative agent. At the same time, he explores the ways in which landscape can also be a temporary escape from authoritative narrative. Writing of the "autonomous landscape" in film, Martin Lefebvre investigates the filmed earth's capacity to serve as spectacle unto itself, distracting the viewer from its other functions as setting or narrative agent. He notes, "When I *contemplate* a piece of film, I stop following the story for a moment, even if the narrative does not completely disappear from my consciousness [...]. The interruption of the narrative by contemplation has the effect of *isolating* the object of the gaze, of momentarily freeing it from its narrative function."[19] In this way, the filmed land can simultaneously be a narrative setting and an autonomous isolated space, both storyteller and story breaker; it allows viewers to take part in a sensory experience beyond the structure of language. Once again we might consider the parallel images of the characters Ettore and Ninetto as they leap from the remnants of ancient structures now mounded into the waving dry grass of the Roman hillside, a shifting cloudscape and the hint of mid-construction public housing in the background. Such scenes speak to the transition of society, space and adolescent subject. At the same time, they provide a break in the narrative progression of each film, allowing viewers to, as Lefebvre writes, *contemplate*, focusing on the physical elements captured within the frame.

Pasolini thus values landscape both for its narrative and non-narrative functions, of that we can be sure. One may still ask, though, whether the director can be considered to have worked with an environmentalist sentiment. Again the response is yes, and again one sensibility is couched among others, a distinct environmentalism wrapped up in a broad social critique. I cite here two examples, moving from page to screen. In 1975, Pasolini published an opinion piece in the national daily paper *Corriere della Sera.* Titled "L'articolo delle lucciole" (The Firefly Article), the article is often referred to as "La scomparsa delle lucciole" (The Disappearance of the Fireflies). It lambasts an increasingly base consumer culture and the Democratic-Christian leadership that

Pasolini felt created it, and likens consumerist 1970s Italy to Nazi-fascist 1930s Germany. At the same time, it warns of a deceptively innocuous marker of environmental degradation: the reduction of Italy's firefly population over the course of the previous decade.

Pasolini explains: "Nei primi anni sessanta, a causa dell'inquinamento dell'aria, e, soprattutto, in campagna, a causa dell'inquinamento dell'acqua (gli azzurri fiumi e le rogge trasparenti) sono cominciate a scomparire le lucciole. Il fenomeno è stato fulmineo e folgorante."[20] His use of fireflies as a focal species here is significant. On a symbolic level, the firefly suggests unexpected brightness, open movement, unstructured and free-form expression – all of the qualities that Pasolini fears humans lose with full immersion in the worlds of history and capital. On a physical level, fireflies serve as an important measure of environmental health, a sort of canary in a coal mine, were anyone to notice. Of the delicate creatures, Kazama et al. note that "their population density is correlated to the availability of healthy habitats."[21] As the general environmental health of a particular area declines, so does the health of its fireflies. Urban development and pollution from chemicals commonly put to domestic use, such as those found in pesticides, are at particular fault for the population decrease.[22] As Gianni Celati observes in the 1980s, these same factors contribute to the poor health of the Po River watershed, affecting not just the river but the valley at large. The Italian firefly is a small being in a world of much bigger concerns, but Pasolini's attention to its condition indicates a sharp critique (note his use of the adjectives *fulmineo* and *folgorante*: "instant" and "striking") of the health of the greater Italian ecosystem.

Pasolini goes on in this article to relate impaired environmental health to an overgrown consumer culture, arguing that both stem from increased industrial production. He writes of the leveling of diverse cultural strata into one mass, owing to what he describes as the violent approval of industrialization. Citing the oppressively homogenous industrial culture of pre-war Germany, he explains, "In Italia sta succedendo qualcosa di simile: E con ancora maggiore violenza, poiché l'industrializzazione degli anni Settanta costituisce una 'mutazione' decisiva anche rispetto a quella tedesca di cinquant'anni fa."[23] The Italian public of the 1970s is not faced with "new times," he writes, as was Germany, but with a fear of the *end* of times, situated as Italy is in "una nuova epoca della storia umana, di quella storia umana le cui scadenze sono millenaristiche."[24] Millenarian deadlines, apocalyptic deadlines – while this is no doubt dramatic language, it is at least in part warranted by the grounding of Pasolini's critique in a clear indicator of environmental pollution and what might now be understood as climate change. The director concludes his argument by returning once more to the image of the firefly: "Ad ogni modo, quanto a me (se ciò ha qualche interesse per il lettore) sia chiaro: io, ancorché multinazionale, darei l'intera Montedison per una lucciola."[25] His stance is environmentalist just as it is broadly anti-industrial. In nominating the firm Montedison, at that time and still today a massive industrial holding company, he dismisses the worlds of industry and agribusiness. With this article Pasolini reveals himself to be informed and concerned about the state of the natural environment as well as that of society, an environmental activist just as he is a social one.

A similar approach, situating environmentalist investigation in a more universal social critique, is to be found in his film work. *Teorema* (1968) presents a prime example in its tale of a bourgeois industrialist's household unraveled by the arrival of a mysterious guest, a spirit representative of the natural world. The film's primary focus is on the relationships that emerge between each family member and their guest, who is only ever refered to as "the visitor." His presence causes all those with whom he interacts to enter into ideological crisis, to yearn for organic experience, and to question the capitalist power structure in which they participate. This is signalled most overtly by the pairing of the film's opening and closing scenes. The first is marked by documentary-style footage of the excitement surrounding a factory just turned over to its workers. The latter then depicts the industrialist father character – who may well be the man who handed over that factory – stumbling naked through the desert, bare against earth marked only by the shadows of quickly passing clouds, time moving ever forward.

The visitor himself, played by Terence Stamp, is a character far from crisis. He is full of silent grace and fluid sexuality, not outwardly attached to any era or social class, and most often framed in bright sunlight that flows from behind, fixing him as a messenger from another realm. Each member of the industrialist's household, including the maid Emilia, has a unique and private relationship to the visitor, always based in sexual encounter. Silvestra Mariniello comments, "L'ospite, bello e silenzioso, lettore di Rimbaud, si inserisce con estrema naturalezza nella famiglia e il suo rapporto con i vari personaggi che la compongono non è fatto tanto di parole, ma di gesti, di sguardi, di una complicità e di un'intesa quasi muta."[26] It is his *naturalezza* that is both so intriguing and so disarming; in contrast, each of his interlocutors becomes frightfully aware of his or her remove from organic life and feeling. Following Mariniello's lead, we might say that he is nature come to dismantle history, just as he dismantles the hetero-normative family structure.

The visitor's relationship to Silvana Mangano's character, the housewife, is particularly emblematic of a connection to the nonhuman world. She is first able to observe him closely when he runs one morning, minimally clothed, through woods behind the family home. In a point-of-view shot moving between Mangano's face and the visitor in the distance, the camera tracks Stamp's lean frame while he runs with abandon. He passes first through trees and then across an open swathe of green earth, sunlight glinting from his skin. From woods and field the camera returns to Mangano, now on a deck of the home and removing her clothes to lie down and, it seems, masturbate. Stamp soon arrives at the house and runs up stairs to the deck, where she apologizes in embarrassment. The camera first lingers in close-up on the mixed emotion on Mangano's upturned face, then shifts to the visitor hovering over her, his full body filmed in a medium shot. He is framed against trees, blue sky and sun, the latter shining so brightly behind him as to gradually wash his image into the solar halo behind it, dissolving him into the natural landscape to which he so clearly belongs. As he moves slowly towards Mangano, a combination of bare skin, bright sky, and gentle smile, his offered embrace reads as a gift, one act of the healing mission that he has come to fulfil. The visitor has similar encounters with each member of the household, all at first joyful yet ultimately troubling, as the characters subsequently question their staid conceptions of identity and social structure.

His effect on the maid Emilia, played by a fantastically somber Laura Betti, is especially relevant to this discussion, for it carries the weight of environmental awareness most overtly.[27] The encounter between the visitor and Emilia occurs inside the family home, yet it too is prompted by her excitement and discomfort at seeing him at ease in the outdoors, reading poetry while he relaxes in a lounge charge. Although the bourgeois family members come undone after their encounters with the visitor – the son questioning his art, the daughter becoming ill in his absence – the subproletarian Emilia gains a deeper focus in life. After their encounter, Emilia leaves her employers' home to return to her village. Here she eventually undergoes a transformation to sainthood. She passes her days on a bench in the sparse communal courtyard, an environment that, not surprisingly, evokes an earlier time through the presence of chickens running about, well but cheaply dressed old men on bicycles, and children playing with sticks and leaves. Remaining still, she eats only nettles and gains the abilities to levitate and to cure illness through her gaze.

The film's final scene of Emilia is the most impressive and, from an ecocritical perspective, the most meaningful. Rising up from her seated perch, she walks through the main entrance of the courtyard, accompanied by an older woman, played by Pasolini's mother, Susanna. Viewers are immediately struck by the contrast of worlds as the camera follows the women's brief pilgrimage. Although Emilia's community and its courtyard dwellings seem Pasolinianly prehistoric – surfaces plain and bare, clothing unattached to era – the area just beyond her village community is decidedly modern. The road is in fact a highway, flanked by streetlights and guardrails. Urban housing complexes, billboards, graffiti, and factory smoke abound. Momentarily still, Emilia stares out directly in front of her. As the camera pans to reveal her point of view, we see that she is fixated on a new construction site, which at this point is no more than a gaping hole in the earth, with apartment complexes visible behind it, indicating the city beyond. She has arrived with the help of her compatriot, whose peasant-black clothing is an anomaly amid the modern rubble, to bury herself in the earth, in front of a resting bulldozer.

The image of the construction site as an open wound conjures Pasolini's long poem of 1956, "Il pianto della scavatrice" (The Tears of the Excavator). The poem describes the cultural and spatial hybridity of peripheral Rome: the last fields on the edge of town, the boys of the *borgate* taking the tram home from work, the poet trapped "lontano dalla città e dalla campagna." It also describes the 1950s construction boom, in a language of sentient suffering:

> Ma tra gli scoppi testardi della
> benna, che cieca sembra, cieca
> sgretola, cieca afferra,
> quasi non avesse meta,
> un urlo improvviso, umano,
> nasce, e a tratti si ripete,
> così pazzo di dolore, che, umano,
> subito non sembra più, e ridiventa
> morto stridore. Poi, piano,

rinasce, nella luce violenta,
tra i palazzi accecati, nuovo, uguale,
urlo che solo chi è morente,
nell'ultimo istante, può gettare
in questo sole che crudele ancora splende
già addolcito da un po' d'aria di mare.
A gridare è, straziata
da mesi e anni di mattutini
sudori – accompagnata
dal muto stuolo dei suoi scalpellini,
la vecchia scavatrice: ma, insieme, il
fresco
sterro sconvolto, o nel breve confine
dell'orizzonte novecentesco,
tutto il quartiere ... È la città,
sprofondata in un chiarore di festa,
– è il mondo. Piange ciò che ha
fine e ricomincia. Ciò che era
area erbosa, aperto spiazzo, e si fa
cortile, bianco come cera,
chiuso in un decoro ch'è rancore;
ciò che era quasi una vecchia fiera[28]

In the poem the world cries for that which was once "grassy area, open clearing" and is now ruled by a bulldozer. It is not the world that cries in the film, however, not the earth, but Emilia, its representative. As the two women reach the torn earth at the bulldozer's edge, Emilia lies down and helps her companion to cover her body with dirt, even sprinkling it across her own face. Her muted, peasant-black clothing blends into the land as a train passes in the background and a melancholy contemporary jazz score plays. Before the older woman leaves, Emilia begins to cry a steady stream of tears, only her eyes visible amid the dark earth. In voiceover she says: "Non aver paura. Non sono venuta qui per morire ma per piangere ... e le mie non sono lacrime di dolore. Sono una sorgente che non sarà una sorgente di dolore."[29] Stopping mid-sentence, she leaves viewers to complete the line. Emilia's calm tone implies that her tears will be productive rather than a source of pain. We can only assume that, like the water required for a plant to grow, her tears will feed new life in that offended dirt.

By focusing on the potential for growth in a terrain torn asunder, well on its way to being covered in cement and deeply enmeshed in the processes of urban development, Emilia indicates her acceptance of a second-nature state. Like the gardening Signora Anfossi in Calvino's *La speculazione edilizia*, she works with the material at hand, defiantly so. In this light, the scene recognizes the possibility of merger between the categories of nature and history Emilia is connected to an earlier time (and is suggestive, in fact, of Pasolini's earlier, simpler life in Emilia-Romagna with his mother, who is present as an actress in the scene). Yet she shows her willingness to engage in the life of the urban contemporary, as well as her hope for its fertility despite obvious denigration. Hers is an act of coping with and adapting to contemporary realities by acknowledging the land as "ciò che ha fine e ricomincia," just as in the poem cited above.[30] At the same time, one can argue that by laying in the dirt, Emilia engages in a physical act of defiance, marking the land with her life-giving body (represented by tears) as a space not for construction or merger but only for natural cultivation and growth. It is the second reading that Pasolini supports elsewhere, through his professed belief in the overt aesthetic separation of nature from culture.

In 1974, Radiotelevisione Italiana (RAI) broadcast a twenty-minute documentary entitled *Pasolini e … la forma della città* (Pasolini … and the Form of the City). Directed by Paolo Brunatto, the piece was part of a series, "Io e …" (Me and …), which aired from 1972 to 1974 and was produced by Anna Zanoli.[31] Like other projects Zanoli produced for RAI, "Io e …" seeks to shed light on otherwise neglected monuments or works of art identified as national treasures by a selected cultural authority. In the case of "Io e …," that role goes to Luigi Malerba, Giorgio Bassani, Giulio Einaudi, and other literary and artistic icons of the time. For his episode, Pasolini selected the town of Orte, a hilltop community in the Lazio region northwest of Rome. The episode alternates between close shots of the director standing in a low field, looking up at Orte, and point-of-view shots toward the town. It is narrated entirely by Pasolini, who is frequently shown behind a camera, to emphasize his role as film director and the authority of his aesthetic judgment. He chose the town of Orte, as he explains, in order to speak about the form of the city in general, an antique "work of art" that he finds threatened by the architectural addition of something modern or "somehow foreign."

In the program's final minutes, Pasolini delivers a concluding message while standing among sand dunes down by the sea, waves crashing behind him. As he narrates, Pasolini explains that Orte is endangered by new construction, and he expounds his opinions about the countryside and nature in general. As the camera pans over the recently built public-housing developments at Orte's farthest edge, Pasolini expresses great indignation. What offends him most is the buildings' modernity: "Il fatto che appartengano a un altro mondo, hanno caratteri stilistici completamente diversi da quelli dell'antica città di Orte e la mescolanza delle due cose infastidisce, è un'incrinatura, un turbamento della forma, dello stile."[32] He is made uncomfortable at the site of this contamination, modern structures clashing with Romanesque ones, in spite of his noted predilection for mixing cultural forms in his own cinematic work.

What particularly disturbs him about the architectural mash-up is its effect on what Pasolini considers a once-clear division between city and country, nature and culture. He specifies: "Avendo io scelto come tema del mio argomento la forma della città, vorrei precisare che la forma della città si manifesta, appare, si rivela a sua confrontata con una fondale naturale."[33] The city's physical identity takes shape through contrast with the surrounding natural landscape. In Pasolini's view, the city needs the natural environment; it depends on it in very close relationship, yet it is strictly a relationship of distinction or difference, which must be respected. As he explains: "Ma sempre si pone il problema di rispettare il confronto tra il confine naturale tra la forma della città e la natura circostante."[34] Those offensive apartment buildings cause such problems for the director precisely because they do not demonstrate the appropriate level of respect: "Vengono a turbare soprattutto il rapporto fra la città e la natura."[35] In their position on the interstice, built on the very edge of a long-developed hilltop just before it slopes to open land below, the buildings blur a formerly clear boundary between the ancient city of Orte and the landscape beyond. Pasolini notes at the outset, "La forma della città di Orte appare in quanto tale perchè sulla cima di questo colle bruno divorato dall'autunno, con questa bruma davanti e contro un cielo grigio."[36] Jutting out from the edge of the hill in all their modern architecture of state-apparatus necessity, the housing projects insert themselves into a once-pleasing portrait of distinction between open nature and composed city. They blur the lines not only between spaces but also between ways of living. These buildings house the new working class, those just barely surviving in the world of modern commerce, somewhere between the urban environment in which they are required to operate and the natural spaces that offer, according to Pasolini, a gentler life.

Distinctly unlike Calvino in this regard, Pasolini is all too ready to embrace a nature/culture binary, at least overtly. By focusing on ex-urban border zones in which differences between spaces cultivated and otherwise are so visually evident, and by contrasting country with city, and pre-history with the modern, Pasolini's stance reflects a binary ideal not unlike that of Calvino's Quinto Anfossi in *La speculazione edilizia*. On the surface, his is a nature "opposed to culture, to history, to convention, to what is artificially worked or produced, in short to everything which is defining the order of humanity."[37] Pasolini's films explore just this sort of binary between the world untouched by man and the world he has overrun. As Matthew Gandy has commented on the director's work, "We are presented with an uncompromisingly essentialist reading of nature as a physical embrace around the everyday world of bourgeois reality."[38] To prove Gandy's point, we need only turn to the documentary cited above or the examples listed at the outset of this chapter. In the opening scenes of *Edipo Re*, for example, the visual connection between a mother's soothing breast and the surrounding open field and sky is explicit and indeed essentializing, as are later connections drawn between the worlds of the father, war, and social order. In this film and others, nature and culture appear to be strictly opposed, just as they are classically gendered.

And yet, there is an obsessive quality to Pasolini's focus on the merger of uncultivated land with cityscape that goes beyond the annoyance he claims so staunchly in reference to the town of Orte. Much of the director's work in fact displays a steady fixation with the visual overlap of nature and culture, featuring open land in dialogue with urban structure and the development underway. Emilia's act of self-burial in *Teorema* is just one example of the director's insistence on the very spaces that trouble him so. The whole of *Uccellacci e uccellini* is another, literally bridging the city and the country, as is the short film *La terra vista dalla luna* (The Earth as Seen from the Moon, 1966).[39] Pasolini's portrayal of a shantytown on the outskirts of Rome in this last title exemplifies what Keala Jewell, Gianni Biondillo, and J.D. Rhodes consider the director's eye for the "ugly," so sharp is his insistence on the transitional spaces bordering the thriving metropolis. That insistence leads me to believe that Pasolini felt more than mere *fastidio;* rather, his work displays a fascination with the interstitial spaces between city and country. In this light, I read Emilia's self-burial as an instance of progress in Pasolini's unfolding ecological sensibility, a moment in which we see him consider the actual possibility of a productive relationship to modified nature.

About the edgeland spaces "where urban and rural negotiate and renegotiate their borders," Paul Farley and Michael Symmons Roberts write:

> So much might depend on being able to see the edgelands. Giving them a name might help, because up until now they have been without any signifier, an incomprehensible swathe we pass through without regarding: untranslated landscape. And edgelands, by and large, are not meant to be seen, except perhaps as a blur from a car window, or as a backdrop to our most routine and mundane activities. Edgelands are part of the gravitational field of all our larger urban areas, a texture we build up speed to escape as we hurry towards the countryside, the distant wilderness. The trouble is, if we can't see the edgelands, we can't imagine them, or allow them any kind of imaginative life. And so they don't really exist. The smaller identities of things in the edgelands have remained largely invisible to most of us.[40]

By directing his attention to Italy's edgelands, what I refer to here as interstitial landscapes, Pasolini contributes to the study and nurture of an imaginative life for those spaces and subjects somehow left behind. At the same time, he hones in on the largely unspoken physical effects of a particular cultural moment in a particular geographic space. In this he raises concrete environmental concerns while furthering a post-war investigation of the modern Italian landscape and how society might cope with this landscape's distinctly second nature, albeit in spite of himself. Finally, he contributes to the deeper study of interstitiality at large permeating his work, from an interest in peripheral neighbourhoods to an interest in socially marginal individuals and socially oppressed classes.[41]

As noted at this chapter's start, Pasolini's career-long engagement with interstitial landscapes is directly tied to and underscored by his parallel engagement with interstitial people. Focusing on protagonists who are caught between bare life and that which is modern and, for him, necessarily urban, he consistently directs viewers to the often indiscernible middle realm in human as well as environmental form. Through figures such as the aforementioned Ettore of *Mamma Roma* and Ninetto of *Uccellacci e uccellini*, as well as the homonymous *Accattone* and even the mythical *Medea* (1969), the director explores the appeal as well as the lack of social acceptance granted to human protagonists who straddle the divide between old and new, rural and urban.[42]

Agambian *homines sacri,* such figures are both sacred and damned: Medea is shunned by her husband, and neighbours cross themselves when Accattone walks by, as though he were a ghost.[43] Notably, the discomfort that these protagonists prompt in others echoes the discomfort that Pasolini expresses regarding undefined spaces in the land. Like the modern apartment houses on the edge of Orte that so disturb his vision, figures such as the impoverished pimp Accattone blur the distinction between historical, bourgeois consciousness and an earlier way of being. And just like the landscape of Orte fascinates Pasolini, his protagonists inspire a particular fascination in those around them as well as great sympathy from the director himself.

Much of that sympathy derives from these protagonists' inability to survive in modern society. When audiences first meet Pasolini's prototypical protagonist Accattone, for example, we are inundated with references to his predestined death. As the film opens, on a dare from friends, Accattone has just jumped into Rome's Tiber River, on a full stomach. It is a banal discourse, indicative of just how much free time his cohort of pimps and hustlers has, but the conversation allows Accattone's companions to joke about his status among the living. They all hold that the proposed act will kill him, yet one of the group asks what is he living for anyhow? Accattone himself comments that he will jump in with his jewellery on, out of a desire to "die like the pharaohs." And just prior to diving full-bellied into the water, he mutters, "Diamo la sodisfazione al popolo" (Let's satisfy the people), a rueful acknowledgment that the *popolo* in fact desires his death.[44] From the film's opening scene, it is clear that Accattone is not long for this world.

Similarly, the landscapes upon which Pasolini hones his lens from this first film to his last are destined to certain defeat – or at least certain destabilization. More precisely, they cannot continue on in their current state without adapting to modernization. Like the character Accattone, such spaces are surrounded by the signs of impending change: The Autostrada del sole that dominates the open landscape in *Uccellacci e uccellini* is in the process of expansion, and the bulldozer in *Teorema* will most likely start back up the next morning, despite Emilia's desired truce. Where such spaces differ from Accattone, however, and where land surpasses man in this formula of parallel interstitiality, is in the natural environment's ability to tolerate a certain level of modification. Although Accattone is simply unable to survive either physically or ideologically in organized urban society, finally dying by film's end, his interstitial landscape equivalents are not as easily eradicated.[45] Pasolini does not feature landscapes that are fully cemented over and built upon or those that are fully polluted; instead, he explores spaces that are mid-process, host to emblems of city as well as country, culture as well as nature.

Thus probing the tension of the interstice, he invites viewers to rest awhile in the discomfort of uncertainty regarding just how *much* change the Italian landscape can take. In the process, he conveys an urgent need to recognize all of the changes underway just as he reveals that the natural environment can still be accessed, even if the life that it hosts has become a bit less bare. Pasolini's is not a positive affect by any means, but neither is it entirely negative. Pushing up against the very thing that he finds troubling – the mergers of nature and culture; history and pre-history; open space and urban structure – he demonstrates a deep engagement with contemporary realities, exposing both the limitations of a binary ideology and the challenges of moving beyond it.

Chapter Four

Observation and Acknowledgment in Gianni Celati's *Verso la foce*

Gianni Celati (b. 1937) has created texts for public consumption since the late 1960s. Throughout this time he has worn many hats – as a writer of fiction, composer of critical essays, professor, translator, and more recently, film-maker.[1] In all of these roles, he has focused on interpretation and representation of the contemporary. He has directed a steady gaze towards the scene before him, be it the immediate plane of individual experience or that of the expansive external world, the physical vista or the social. His texts suggest that Celati himself tends not to make such distinctions. The physical and social landscapes are one and the same for him; individual experience and the external world are intimately connected. The message behind his work is that if we do not observe the world at hand closely we are likely not only to destroy it but also to lose our connection to self. This view is no truer than in the reflective, first-person *Verso la foce* (Toward the River's Mouth, 1989).

Celati's work stands as the middle and strongest statement of an attention to environment-in-crisis that runs throughout the works considered in this book. Italo Calvino, the first author discussed here, broaches the topic as a new and rather nebulous phenomenon. On the other end of the spectrum is Simona Vinci, discussed in Chapter 5, who depicts an Italy in which the ideas of environmental threat and crisis have been incorporated into the culture of the everyday. It is in Celati's *Verso la foce* that these ideas are most pressingly fleshed out, having fully entered into social consciousness, yet having done so recently enough as to still be startling. With this text the author places two different categories of danger to the environment – industrial pollution and nuclear disaster – side by side to examine the response of communities as well as that of the land itself.

Celati began his writing career as an essayist, commenting on twentieth-century intellectuals such as James Joyce and Mikhail Bakhtin for neo avant-garde journals like *Quindici* and *Il Verri*. He then evolved as a writer of fiction with his first published novel, *Comiche* (Slapstick Silent Films, 1971), followed by subsequent experiments with the novel and the short-story form. During these years Celati primarily wrote about the abstract and the absurd in the lives of outsider characters, such as the awkward young Danci in *Avventure di Guizzardi* (The Adventures of Guizzardi, 1973). This novel was the first work in what is often referred to as a comic trilogy, or trilogy of *racconti comuni*, everyday sorts of tales. Next in the series came *La banda dei sospiri* (The Group of Spirits, 1976), then *Lunario del paradiso* (Heaven's Almanac, 1978), after which Celati published nothing for seven years. He returned to the public realm with *Narratori delle pianure* (Voices from the Plains, 1985), a collection of thirty short stories primarily set in north-central Italy's Po Valley. This work features a more meditative, less overtly comic voice than that in his previous texts. It also marks the beginning of the author's sharp focus on the importance of place and on the Po Valley in particular. His attention to this region is personal. Although he was born in Sondrio, Lombardy, near the Swiss border, Gianni Celati grew up primarily in Ferrara, not far from the banks of the Po.[2]

Celati is often noted for his attention to the act of storytelling, yet critics have also studied the role of landscape in his more recent work.[3] It is in this vein that I contribute to extant Celati scholarship, considering not *Narratori delle pianure* but the less-studied and yet more environmentally focused *Verso la foce*. Published in 1989, this series of the author's first-person musings on the small towns, rolling hills, and river embankments of the Po Valley presents the author in an inherently environmentalist light. Deeply concerned with faithfully representing the landscape of the *valle padana*, and deeply concerned by the degraded state in which he often finds it, Celati cannot help but draw his readers into an honest assessment of contemporary Italian nature with this work. For much like Calvino's *La nuvola di smog, Verso la foce* portrays the levels of pollution in north-central Italy with such candor as to forbid readers from turning away from the issue. At the same time, the notable tone of dismay present in the work is counterbalanced by a sheer delight in nature, a delight potent enough to remind us of the simple beauty of being, with awareness, in the outdoors. Celati calls society out for what we have done and are still doing to the environment, just as he simultaneously heralds nature's persistent energy. For this alone he ought to be considered not just a foremost contemporary Italian author but also a foremost contemporary environmental author, Italian or otherwise.

Relatively little has been written on *Verso la foce*. Narrative style is a subject of study in most of the articles that do address the work, and in each of these the role of observation features as a key, if not primary, element of analysis. How could it not? Celati himself so frequently ponders the act within his writing. In the extant criticism on *Verso la foce* there exists a divide between those who read Celati's narrative as emotionally distanced from his subject of observation and those who instead locate a strong sentimental current. In his work on the book, Mario Moroni writes of Celati as a "receptive entity" rather than an authoritative narrator.[4] He credits Celati's ability to keep his personality and point of view out of the spotlight with narrative descriptions that serve to open rather than close the landscape as a recipient of Celati's sentiment. Moroni argues, in fact, that the author is so successful in this venture that he shows no emotion at all towards the landscape. Niva Lorenzini also writes of Celati's sentimental remove from his subject and finds his landscape descriptions heavily influenced by what she considers to be the "impersonality" of the photograph, a medium with which the author has worked extensively.[5] Massimo Schilirò sees *Verso la foce* as a text of perceptive, imaginative experience in observation but also one of *svanimento*, disappearance and death of the villages and landscapes addressed in the work.[6] He notes, further, that the author prefers to remain on the outskirts of any landscape observed or town visited, and he seems to attribute this tendency to the sense that such spaces have reached their end. Each of these critics offers a unique reading, but they are all united in the distance they place between Celati and the landscape.

Marina Spunta and Patrick Barron read more life into Celati's landscape descriptions, just as they find his narrative voice to carry more overt sentiment. Spunta notes the contrast in spaces described in the work – some are Dantesque wastelands, others the very image of premodern idylls – and their ability to inspire Celati's "rinnovato sentimento di meraviglia per le cose semplici."[7] Barron, in turn, writes of communication and affection for space, the affection Celati expresses as well as that which the author hopes to inspire in others. While the analyses by Moroni, Lorenzini, and Schilirò provide important contributions – namely, those points touched on above – I align my work with that of Spunta and Barron. I do not deny a strong melancholia in

Verso la foce, nor do I deny that Celati's focus on pure observation and recounting often produces such a measured tone as to effect sentimental remove. At the same time, I hold that melancholy is a sentimentally derived response, one that negates the possibility of true detachment.

Ultimately, I wonder if *melancholy* and *remove* would not be better replaced with *contemplation* and *acceptance.* Celati tells readers: "Non si è mai estranei a niente di ciò che accade intorno, e quando si è soli ancora meno. Il corpo è un organo per affondare nell'esterno, come pietra, lichene, foglia."[8] By likening the body to a stone, a leaf, lichen calmly nestled in among the landscape, he sets up the human subject as just another natural element, ideally as at home in field or riverbank as any non-human subject there. This relationship of belonging negates the possibility of distance between the external world and the body, which is both the vessel that carries us through the environment and the tool we use to voice its description. Much of Celati's commentary in *Verso la foce* suggests that a great part of society denies such a relationship – remaining behind closed doors, ignoring the effects of industrial runoff, speeding across terrain in enclosed vehicles, and so on. Celati, however, actively works to remind himself and others of a human connection to the landscape through direct immersion in and observation of the natural environment. In this light, never "estranged from that which happens around him," he is in a position to approach landscape description calmly, with ease, yet still sentimentally invested in the process. Where my analysis extends beyond previous studies of *Verso la foce* is precisely in its emphasis on this attention to and representation of the physical environment. Like other scholars, I consider Celati's aforementioned focus on the act of observation, not so much for its part in a solitary narrative process, however, as for the interchange of landscape, communication, and community to which it speaks.

By the time that Celati is writing *Verso la foce,* in the mid-1980s, the effects of pollution caused by the industrial culture of north-central Italy are to a great extent already known. The reality of nuclear threat, however, still feels relatively new and uncertain, yet incredibly present. As different from one another as they are, pollution and nuclear radiation both effect changes to the landscape and atmosphere that raise once more the question of just how "natural" today's nature is. More pointedly, they both trouble just what we might conceive of as natural anymore, for each process has the ability to transform the environment silently, changing the composition of flora, fauna, air, and water in ways not always visible. In their wake they leave a physical environment forever marked by the workings of culture – cultural waste, to be specific. With *Verso la foce* Celati poses two questions regarding environment in transition, both of which link an environmentalist investigation to his career-long engagement with what Rebecca West calls "the ceremony of linguistic exchange."[9] He asks first, how do we use language to put the shape-shifting world around us into a frame, to make an unknown threat more benign? And second, how can we, as humans, continue narrating the world around us when that necessitates acknowledging damage we have caused?

Celati expresses his environmentalism in *Verso la foce* by way of a gentle path, a route paved by his indefatigable inclination towards observance and exchange. The dedication to landscape and environment that he demonstrates in the work runs deep, motivated by his belief that observation is the key to forging communication and, subsequently, community. Towards the end of the text, while contemplating different styles of speaking about the world, he explains, "Sì è disposti all'osservazione quando si ha voglia di mostrare ad altri quello che si vede. È il legame con gli altri che dà colori alle cose, le quali altrimenti appaiono smorte."[10] Celati is inspired to communicate to others the vision of something already concrete, yet that act of communication is necessary to provide further meaning to the scene observed. His desire to communicate with those around him and his desire to see his surroundings vividly, with clarity, are so intertwined as to be one unique motivational force. The result is a steady gaze that never turns away from the relationship between human and land and thereby serves as a faithful witness to environmental change in the Po Valley.

Published as the third and final leg of a Paduan trilogy that includes *Narratori delle pianure* and *Quattro novelle sulle apparenze* (Appearances, 1987), much of *Verso la foce* was composed at the same time as the stories grouped in the first and second collections. All three works contain prose pieces scripted in a clean, simple Italian, short on dialogue but careful to recount the world as it has been lived. This includes both the world as lived by others and recounted to Celati and that experienced by the author himself. Compiled in the form of a travel diary separated into four parts, *Verso la foce* details Celati's meanderings through the valley of the river Po, at times accompanied by a travelling companion and at other times alone. While his entries trace the journey from one town to the next, they are consumed not so much with a long-term narrative arc as with conveying the experience of each particular place and time.

The text reads as a narrative ramble even more directly engaged with landscape, that which Celati sees before him and that in which his experiences take place, than either *Narratori delle pianure* or *Quattro novelle sulle apparenze*. The author begins a typical entry mid-way through the work: "Contro il cielo su un argine papaveri mossi dal vento, e un cielo così cupo, così pesante. Campagne vuote. Tutto questo mi dà voglia di scrivere, come se le parole seguissero qualcosa che è fuori di me."[11] In attributing so explicitly to the outside environment his desire to write, Celati establishes a direct relationship between land and language in his text. At the same time, just as it is more landscape-oriented than his other works, *Verso la foce* is also more overtly bogged down by the difficulties of shaping experience in language.

The author often struggles in his attempts to capture fleeting moments and immediate impressions. Striving for clear communication, he favours brief sentence structure, occasionally inverted syntax, frequent use of the superlative suffix *–issimo,* and the present and imperfect tenses. About the three Paduan texts, Marina Spunta comments that *Verso la foce* "testimonia il tentativo più acuto di liberarsi da una struttura narrativa concepita a tavolino e di far coincidere i momenti della percezione, osservazione e riflessione con quello della scrittura."[12] Her use of the word *tentativo* in this passage is precise and correct. Defined in the Italian as an "experiment to try to succeed at something," the notion of *tentativo,* attempt, captures perfectly the spirit behind Celati's relationship with language in *Verso la foce.*[13] He does all that he can to imbue his writing with the not-yet-filtered sensation of initial comprehension – the observations of the body as leaf, as it were – yet it is very much an experiment, one at which he is unsure of succeeding. For how can a written account ever truly capture the unfiltered rawness of immediate impression? This is a monumental challenge, but rather than be paralysed by its weight, Celati is motivated to only try harder.

The text is divided into four sections. The first and longest, "Un paesaggio con centrale nucleare" (A Landscape with Nuclear Reactor), details a walking tour in the Cremonese countryside in the days immediately following the 1986 explosion at the Chernobyl nuclear power plant in Ukraine, then part of the Soviet Union. The second section takes Celati wandering along the banks of the Po; the third focuses in particular on Ferrara and its surrounding areas, home over the years to *bonifiche,* land-reclamation projects. The final section (A Voyage Full of Uncertainties) follows the author and a friend as they ostensibly search for a group of German ethologists along the Po delta.[14] In truth, though, Celati is more concerned here with locating the rawness of energy that he hopes to find as the land gives way to water, an energy he has been seeking all along.

While they do not overtly build towards a traditional narrative structure (introduction, building action, climax, and resolution), the four sections ultimately serve as three distinct movements in a larger whole. As though in a musical composition, each builds off the others to describe the often interstitial Po Valley in all of its complexity. The first movement, the first section, places readers squarely in confrontation with a new environmental threat. To be considered at greatest length here, this section explores how people use language to sort out situations of the unknown and when such an approach is, and is not, successful. The second movement extends across sections two and three. It negotiates a push and pull between the known crisis of pollution, in contrast to the unknown threat just considered, and the still-wild nature of the river itself. In this movement Celati also contrasts inhabitants who ignore the landscape behind closed doors with those who acknowledge it. The third and final movement brings together Celati's observations of the changed and changing landscape and the communicative patterns, his included, of those who inhabit it. It presents no grand epiphanies or overt environmentalist manifesto but is instead simultaneously a love letter to observation and an earnest portrait of the *paesaggio smarrito*, the mislaid – or interstitial – landscape.

In writing about the physical and social terrain of the Po, Celati is careful to describe rather than dictate, for he is intent on faithfully capturing the experience of a witness rather than that of an authority. Patrick Barron connects this desire to the act of translation, a practice dear to Celati.[15] Discussing what he calls "the unmistakable voice of the spirit of place," Barron explains that translation is required "to render this voice intelligible." Like a fully crafted text in possession of its identity, the "spirit of the place" can best be made available to a wider readership not through the work of an interpreter, who imbues meaning, but through that of a translator, who passes it on. Barron defines the process as "depicting while paying close attention to the shifting, subtle appearances of everything other than the self, that despite flowing incessantly before us, are often largely ignored in favor of ready-made or half-remembered impressions (or those simply instilled by society)."[16] This definition describes a move towards objectivity in authorship and, in turn, objectivity in language use. Although such an end is never fully realizable, the journey towards it causes both Celati and his readers to confront the material reality at hand rather than that crafted in the common consciousness.

While Barron does not explicitly address interpretation – speaking for nature – his discussion of translation presupposes a distinction between the two acts that is pivotal to understanding Celati's inclination towards an environmentally minded honesty. The idea of speaking on nature's behalf, at times associated with various sorts of nature writing or environmental criticism, can be discomfiting for the positions it assigns to speaker and natural world. It inevitably runs the risk of ascribing a lack of agency to nature and a full subjective authority to the speaker and the culture that has shaped her or him. Speaking or interpreting for nature implies the sort of universal knowledge and mastery that, Celati suggests, an open-eyed observer, as comfortable in nature as he may be, can never fully gain (wherein, of course, lies the beauty of it all). The act of translation, in contrast, puts the translator at the service of nature. In so doing, it redirects the attention of all involved back to the organic spirit of the place, as nature itself is still the predominant "voice."

The spirit of place that *Verso la foce* describes is, to say the least, in flux – challenged by outside forces but still very much alive. It is conveyed in brief sketches and earnest reflections, such as, "Campagne ondulate con coltivazioni di grano, lattuga, cavoli, erba medica. C'è spazio largo in questo paesaggio, ma non incombente grazie alle ondulazioni," and "Se potessi andrei a guardarli uno a uno quei canali, mi sembrano così favolosi."[17] It is also, however, conveyed in equally earnest portraits like the following: "Un campo tutto pieno di rifiuti, sacchetti di plastica, bottiglie, lattine, pezzi di mobili buttati via; un'estensione grandissima di rifiuti, con sopra centinai di gabbiani che volano come impazziti."[18] Celati describes a site of harmonious balance or a container of epic myth on one page, a confusion of abandoned space and waste on the next. In striving towards an objective report, he translates a landscape that is graceful yet trodden upon, constructively cultivated yet left for dead, nonthreatening and beyond threatened.

He regularly depicts harsh vistas of compromised or degraded land alongside vistas that inspire joy, whether due to the loose loveliness of their shape or the glee they provoke in playing children. In the midst of contemplating polluted riverbanks or cookie-cutter *villette* that are starkly anti-social, and anti-natural, in design, Celati can suddenly rejoice in the unpredictability of the wind or a nearby plant's growth pattern. Such occasional, impromptu celebration conveys an almost

Emersonian experience of transcendence in nature, as Celati once again marvels at the mysteries of the world. Almost Emersonian, but not exactly; the vision of the natural world that transfixes the Italian author is far from the raw, untouched enigma that spoke to the American poet. It is a distinctly second nature, in line with the nature embraced by Celati's British contemporary Derek Jarman, who also wrote of the coexistence of gardens and nuclear reactors – what he calls simply "modern nature."[19]

More often than not, Celati is enchanted by the natural world for its ability to counteract the trappings of society. While this may take the form of a "città vecchia […] ora tutta invasa dalla natura," it is also evident when nature asserts its presence in even the most socially structured, 'cultured' environments.[20] Stumbling one afternoon upon a sea of housing developments and advertising banners, he is saddened until "ad un tratto è arrivata una nube di polline da tutti i pioppeti della zona, gli automobilisti hanno dovuto mettere in opera i tergicristalli, e tutte le insegne publicitarie sono diventate invisibili per dieci secondi."[21] A small pleasure, it provides "dieci secondi di masse opache, dove tutto passava via già da adesso, sparita anche quest'immagine del mondo che ci portiamo negli occhi […] l'effetto di black-out delle immagini pubblicitarie faceva piacere."[22] The copycat houses and brand names that he sees before him are indeed real. By referring to them, however, as the "*image* of the world that we carry in our eyes" (italics mine), Celati suggests that they are not the only reality, simply the one on which we focus out of habit.

As individual landscapes grow increasingly to resemble one another, with structures built according not to their unique environment but to a master plan, it is easy to feel that we've seen it all before. And as Celati muses in a later section of the book, "Se hai la sensazione di capire tutto, passa la voglia di osservare."[23] Why look closely when you sense that you already know what you'll find? A lack of motivated observation has a direct impact for the author on one's relationship with language. As he sees it, a sense that it's all the same leads people to employ a one-size-fits-all lexicon for negotiating the world, which then carries over to a very narrow vision of what that world might be. This is the language the media uses, the same language of consumerism promoted in the scene above by the (momentarily absent) advertisements. The impressively thorough, albeit temporary, ability of nature – a cloud of pollen in this case – to disrupt that image shakes Celati out of his perceptive laziness. It forces him to observe once more with purpose and thus to communicate more carefully with others, with us. As his sharper vision stirs his desire to recount, it also forces him to articulate the scene before him in full detail and, in so doing, reconfigure just a bit the "image of the world that we carry in our eyes." Here lies the core of his environmentalism: observe the landscape in its complexity so as not to dismiss and discount it.

Such an act becomes complicated, however, when what we try to observe is unpleasant or, trickier yet, invisible. For reconfiguring a collective world view grown lazy requires not just sharpening one's gaze but also acknowledging the reality of already occurred denigration and not yet visible obfuscations, such as smog, greenhouse gases, and airborne toxins, all of which are, in 1986, increasingly serious environmental ills Celati can look to the signs of the visible unpleasant in the landscape – contaminated waters, fields made barren by spilled pesticides – to acknowledge what has occurred, but in capturing the immediate effects of the Chernobyl disaster, as he does in the first section of *Verso la foce*, he must turn to social interaction in order to grasp some sense of the not yet known.

In considering as yet invisible environmental damage we enter a discussion of terminology. In the 1980s Ulrich Beck announced the arrival of what he termed the "risk society," which is discussed in his book *Ecological Enlightenment*. He argued that in the post-atomic era, industrial culture had come to abuse the discourse of risk analysis, the science by which the probability of any risk is calculated, in order to move forward with a given action. By casting events such as chemical spills as risks that were calculated, thus understood, and what is of greater importance here, statistically unlikely, the world of industry had permitted regular environmental devestation. Pollution, radiaton, and so forth had simply become "risks" that were worth taking in the name of progress. As Beck established, they were – and still are – much more common than the discourse of risk would suggest. *Verso la foce*'s frequent portraits of semi-rural wastelands left in the wake of industrial production depict the very sort of widespread destruction that results, in his estimation, from a normalization of risk.

Barbara Adam also draws attention in her work to the normalization of environmental damage, but she calls for different terminology. Like Ursula Heise and others, she does build her particular environmental criticism in part on Beck's idea of a risk society. While she seconds much of his basic principle, she finds fault with his use of the term *risk*. What interests me is her explanation for doing so. Adam chooses to reconfigure the risk society as a "hazard society." She explains: "Environmental degradation and hazards [are] [...] *endemic* to the scientific innovations and economic practices characteristic of the contemporary industrial way of life," and notes further, "For hazards arising from the industrial way of life, the past gives no guidance for the future, provides no basis upon which to calculate and quantify risk."[24] In line with Beck's urgency and emphasis on a changed natural environment, Adam's hazard society is particularly caught up with the unpredictable future.

I mention their scholarship and briefly trace this conflict over terminology because both Beck and Adam are key humanist voices in the discussion of industry-induced damage to environment and society. Furthermore, their seemingly discordant approaches to the subject actually complement one another once unpacked and lead to a richer analysis of environmentally engaged texts. Beck underlines the way in which scientific discourse has been manipulated to allow potentially grave dangers to persist as part of standard social life. Adam, for her part, draws our attention to the vast and vastly unknown ramifications of such normalizing actions. Together, they cause us to question what has led to and what will follow from what Frederick Buell calls a "domestication of environmental apocalyptic discourse," the sense that environmental disaster has become a given fact of life and, as such, not exactly cause for alarm.[25] Respecting both of their arguments, I take a middle course and speak of environmental *threat* and its frequent results: environmental damage and, more often than not, environmental crisis, a state that has become so normal these days as to warrant relatively little attention. The notion of threat directs focus back to the (un)predictability of environmental devastation, Beck's original concern, while echoing the endemic and imminent natures of such devastation, as argued by Adam. It is particularly relevant to Celati's approach to environments both natural and social because it emphasizes a not-yet-realized or finalized presence, a rather ominous "something coming."

As *Verso la foce* negotiates a back-and-forth between the threat of environmental damage to come and the crisis that is already here, time imposes a fundamental yet complicated presence. Celati is deeply concerned with the already occurred: the events that have happened, the words that have been pronounced, the physical structures that have been built, and the communities that have been shaped around them. And yet such concern always finds its way to the question of then what to make of these events, words, and structures in the present, and what we will eventually make of them in the future. This attention to the unknown future, and the reevaluations and readjustments that it necessitates, locates Celati's emphasis in the realm of the imminent.

The first section of *Verso la foce* begins on 9 May 1986. This date is less than two weeks after the explosion of a power reactor on 26 April at the Chernobyl nuclear power plant in Ukraine. It is less than one week after 5 May, when the main cloud of radioactive fallout from the explosion passed over Italy.[26] In recent years, losses from the disaster have been estimated at forty thousand human lives and $300 billion, but the effects of Chernobyl continue to unfold.[27] As recently as 2013, Winifred Bird and Jane Braxton Little have written of the dwarf trees, highly contaminated soil, radioactive mushrooms, and genetically mutant birds in what is now referred to as the Chernobyl Exclusion Zone.[28] A report published by the New York Academy of Sciences in 2009 states that Chernobyl's "radioactive contamination has adversely affected all biological as well as nonliving components of the environment: the atmosphere, surface and ground waters, the surface and the bottom soil layers, especially in the heavily contaminated areas of Belarus, Ukraine, and European Russia," and notes that "levels of Chernobyl's radioactive contamination even in North America and eastern Asia are above the maximum levels that were found in the wake of weapons testing in the 1960s."[29] While the nearby town of Pripyat, Ukraine, and the site of the former Chernobyl power plant now stand as uninhabited ghost villages, the results of the nuclear disaster persist in much of the lived world.

In May 1986, however, there was no way yet to gauge Chernobyl's ultimate impact, only its first impression. Celati starts his first entry as a record of the days that have passed since the explosion: "Pensieri di questi giorni, su cui voglio scrivere: notizie sullo scoppio di Černobyl, arrivo della nube atomica, e altri rimuginamenti."[30] In setting the scene he captures the essence of the immediate physical and social ramifications of the disaster, recording its first impressions upon communities from the Tuscan seaside up to the Po Valley:

> Tornati in Maremma, a Capalbio, proprio quando la nube atomica era in arrivo e la televisione diffondeva le prime misure di sicurezza suggerite dagli esperti: vietato vendere verdure in foglia e niente latte fresco per i bambini. Nei negozietti di Capalbio Scalo c'è un'atmosfera che ricorda il tempo di Guerra; si parla delle misure di sicurezza, i clienti restano lì dubbiosi a ripetere le frasi dei giornali, e intanto i prezzi delle verdure in scatola, latte condensato, cibi surgelati, patate e verdure non in foglia, persino il prezzo dell'acqua minerale, ondeggiano secondo le notizie diffuse.[31]

With this snapshot we note initially tangible implications of Chernobyl's aftermath, just as we understand how elusive a grasp on the situation still is. As radiation has presumably fallen into the soil and gathered on leaves, crops are affected and people can neither eat nor sell the produce that they have grown. This has at least two profound ramifications, as both food supply and income are now limited, effects that will inevitably carry over into the future. Regardless of how long the restrictions are in place, consumers will remain cautious about buying particular types of vegetables, and farmers will suffer less-profitable years, thus contributing to larger economic shifts.

In his reflections on Chernobyl just after the explosion, Ulrich Beck notes that "although the dangers remain invisible, they are extremely effective where they are *believed*: markets collapse and new ones emerge (e.g., a shift from fresh vegetables to frozen). Though they look and taste the same, certain products are devalued *tout court*."[32] Note his emphasis on the word *believed*: without concrete evidence, people must make decisions with long-ranging effects based on the information they find most credible. In such a situation the media holds great power, as it is to the word of the media that society responds. Celati and Beck both depict a cycle that is striking for the immediacy of relationship between industry (nuclear power), media ("experts" with early access to information), agriculture (which crops are left to perish, which are grown in the future), consumer culture (where we put our money), and our intimate daily lives (what we put in our bodies).

More perhaps than even this chain of reaction, it is Celati's mention of milk in the paragraph cited above that most directly turns readers' attention to the future while acknowledging the event that has just occurred. As cows must still be fed potentially contaminated grain, their milk is suspect for radiation and there is thus no fresh milk for the children of the community. The result is first felt in the immediate present, as a mundane part of daily life has been altered and patterns must change. It also, however, speaks to both the past and the future. We are sharply aware that no such event has affected past generations of Italians, just as we begin to fathom the implications for a legacy effect bestowed upon the current era's children. It is this next generation, not in any way responsible for the disaster, who will suffer most acutely the long-term consequences.

The newness of it all is apparent in the continually shifting nature of public response reflected by the market economy: "E intanto i prezzi ondeggiano secondo le notizie diffuse."[33] With neither a clear understanding of the actual level of physical danger nor lessons to follow from past experience, people are unsure of how to respond. Their actions shift, and prices fluctuate, as they must repeatedly reassess the situation at hand, made nebulous by the non-concrete nature of radiation. Barbara Adam tells us, "At the level of everyday life, the 'materiality' of radiation falls outside the conventional definition of 'the real', outside conceptions where real means material and where this in turn is defined by its accessibility to the senses."[34] Not only is the situation of radiation new, it is intangible, silent, odourless, and as such, it is resistant to being known. People cannot, for example, see it in the form of a black dusting over that which it has touched, and thus they face yet greater difficulty in understanding its gravity in the present moment.

As an unknown entity, radiation resembles a wartime opponent, a presence that we fear without, perhaps, understanding. Wartime holds a memory that is distinctly communal for older Italian residents and still part of the collective consciousness for the younger members of society. It especially resonates in *Verso la foce* in regards to the rationing of food. Writing from a new town days after his initial entry, Celati reports: "In un negozio di fornaio c'erano molte donne, alcune delle quali arrivate in macchina. Una stava dicendo: 'Ma adesso non ci sarà pericolo anche a mangiare il pane?'"[35] This image of women crowded together at a bakery discussing bread so clearly recalls representations of World War II Italy. In particular, it conjures an early scene from Roberto Rossellini's classic neorealist film *Roma, città aperta* (Rome Open City, 1945), in which the character Pina (portrayed by Anna Magnani) joins a mob of women storming a bakery for their bread. The scenario is decidedly different by 1986. Where once women struggled to get their share from a limited supply, now, in the age of abundance, quantity is not in question so much as is the basic integrity of the product.

Nothing reflects a general uncertainty about the significance of radiation in *Verso la foce* more than the spoken language used to discuss it. Whether quoting statistics from the newspaper or teasing one another in bars, the people Celati encounters display an inability to speak earnestly about the impact of radiation on their land and lives. The teasing and other related modes of communication are particularly intriguing in regards to community. There is the young factory worker who, while watching Celati write in a bar one day, recites in a sing-song voice, "quela vaca che t'a cagà, i Caraibi e Černobyl"[36] Then, in a bar a few towns over, there is the bartender who tells a regular, "Guardi che se non fa il bravo le dò latte contaminato, eh?"[37] Next we might consider the sign hanging by a homeowner's carefully kept flowerbeds, wishing a "radioactive accident" upon local hooligans: "CHE GLI VENGA UN ACCIDENTE RADIOATTIVO A QUELLO CHE MI VIENE A RUBARE I FIORI."[38]

On a basic level, these examples show people communicating with one another about a shared concern, however indirectly. Furthermore, they reveal the first passes towards incorporation into everyday conversation of a semantically flexible, radiation-based lexicon. Such incorporation has mixed implications. On the one hand, bringing the language of radiation exposure into casual speech through jokes, songs, and sarcasm is a way for speakers to touch on a topic that may be troubling them. Moreover, it allows them to harness a bit of ownership over the lexicon of radiation by using it without simply quoting voices of authority. It also, however, allows speakers to shake up assumptions about the gravity of radiation by twisting the context in which it is cited. This is simultaneously a helpful coping mechanism and a means to dismissiveness. It disarms the significance of radiation by daring to bring it, figuratively speaking, into benign situations and thus bypassing the reverence reserved for the truly horrifying. Such action is helpful, empowering even, for a society uncertain of its status. Yet it also runs the risk of allowing people to ignore what might become a devastating state of affairs.

Ultimately, all of this underlines radiation's current identity as a threat rather than a clearly delineated reality. Were it more than just news, more than a danger that has been reported but not physically felt, it would seem beyond distasteful to make jokes about the harm it could cause. This is particularly true in the final two examples cited above, in which people express actual, although we can assume empty, verbal threats of harm to others. In both situations the speakers utilize and simultaneously question the perceived understanding of widespread radiation. They utilize it by holding it above their interlocutors as a potential danger but they also put into question the true level of danger involved.

Repetition of *frasi dei giornali*, mentioned in the long quote above, is a different sort of linguistic response to Chernobyl, and a coping mechanism that quickly proves to be hollow. It bears witness to an overall lack of linguistic authority on an individual level; not possessing a lexicon of their own, people must borrow the language of newspapers and radio. This is a sort of processing that only assuages fears on the surface, as it betrays a lack of individual comprehension and, to follow Celati's logic, communication motivated by dynamic observation. People are simply unable to form an "image of the world" that reflects something still unknown and largely immaterial. Substantial differences exist, of course, between a landscape covered in billboards and housing developments and another shrouded in nuclear radiation. In Celati's framework, such differences are put into perspective through the lens of visual and verbal understanding. Whereas in the pollen whiteout, discussed above, he suggests that people use the language of the media out of complacency, here they do so out of necessity. In both situations it comes down to a matter of seeing: in the first, falling into the habit of not observing closely leads to a struggle to recount and communicate; in the second communication is hampered by the sheer *impossibility* of observation.

People are thus constrained to repeat "notizie giornalistiche e commenti di frasi fatte, in niente diverse dai notiziari sportive," regardless of how lackluster they may ring.[39] Even Celati must at times resort to the language of the media in order to pass through the communities on his path. This is particularly the case when it comes to explaining his mode of travel. Moving by local bus, a hitched ride, or preferably on foot, he does what he can to experience physically the landscape at close proximity. This acutely separates him, already a stranger, from the area's inhabitants who largely ignore the terrain behind their shuttered windows. Walking one day just past Cicognolo in the province of Cremona, the author stops along the side of the road to write. He notes the multitude of trucks that pass by, the still clouds hanging in the air, gothic campanili off in the distance, the stink of industrial pig farms, sloping fields of grain, and at long last, a single bird in the sky.

As he scribbles he is "sorpreso a scrivere" by two policemen, as though caught in a surreptitious act.[40] They want to know if he has a legal address, employment, or purpose for walking and writing in the grass. As readers learn, a car has been stolen in town that morning, and, well, his behaviour (walking, writing) seems suspicious. The relationship that Celati displays with land and language is out of the policemen's normal frame of reference. They quickly reframe the situation in known terms, however, through the clout ascribed to the news media. Celati states, "Ma quando mi hanno chiesto se scrivo per un giornale e ho detto subito di sì, mentendo moltissimo, sono ridiventato normale ai loro occhi. In quanto giornalista, mi hanno offerto un passaggio sulla loro camion."[41] In the role of journalist, someone who writes and observes by profession and not simply natural desire or instinct, Celati fits their image of the world. The officers acknowledge his place in that world by offering to give him a ride. In so doing, of course, they prevent him from continuing in the act of writing, thus impeding his goal and confirming a suspicion that runs rampant in the text, namely that ordered society is averse to the very notions of observance and informed narration. Now satisfied that he is indeed part of the mainstream, the policemen assume that he would prefer to travel, swift and secure, in their automobile, great emblem of culture that it is. For what normal person would rather take his time and walk?

Verso la foce presents many examples of the false authority of language attached to official social roles, often using the humour that West reminds us still colours Celati's later work.[42] Besides Celati's stint as an imposter 'journalist' there is also the noted scholar on the life and land of the valley, who has no real interest in either and would much prefer to stay at home. Then there are the retired teachers-cum-farmers who are sure that anything can be achieved, even the closing of all nuclear reactors in existence, by simply organizing a "forte movimento d'opinione."[43] Both the land scholar and the teachers speak with an assurance that Celati shows to be empty, happy to recount facts as truths based solely on the merit of their roles as experts. In the end, their examples serve to further underline Celati's argument that the only meaningful way to speak about a topic is when we truly believe what we say because what we say reflects what we see.

The discussion thus far betrays an obvious contradiction: for how, then, are people supposed to successfully narrate the tale of recent, largely invisible, radiation if meaningful narration comes from observation? Communication is most effective for Celati in this text when it reflects a first-hand experience of the topic of discourse. When it comes to the state of the Italian environment in the wake of the Chernobyl disaster, however, there is nothing yet to see. Ultimately, he writes,

> Nessuno può dire che effetti avranno le sostanze radioattive venute giù dal cielo, su erbe, alberi, bestie e umani; nessuno può dire che la cosa non potrebbe ripetersi un giorno o l'altro, qui da noi o altrove; nessuno può davvero pensare che le centrali nucleari siano un giorno chiuse, per metterci al riparo da tutte le incertezze e pericoli che verranno. Eppure ognuno di quegli esperti non smetteva mai di mostrare una sicurissima comprensione di quanto è successo e succederà.[44]

While the experts display a sure comprehension of what is to come, Celati himself finds that at journey's end he has "solo incertezza per quello che verrà."[45] His response to that uncertainty is to continue to try to understand and narrate so as not to forget, the default action towards which he suggests we are all inclined.[46] The choice to record with the hopes of one day understanding has two major implications from an environmental perspective. First of all, it confirms that we have entered a new era, at least in the Western world: the radiation of the type caused by Chernobyl is, in 1986, truly an unprecedented situation requiring new modes of thought about the environment. Such a state of affairs is in turn a testament to the fact that we would benefit from engaging what Barbara Adam calls a timescape perspective: awareness of the long-term impact of an event on an area's terrain and community. This includes consideration of a social and environmental landscape's "rhythmicities, [...] timings and tempos, [its] changes and contingencies."[47] That is to say, if we take note of each present moment as it unfolds, recalling the past from which it came and conscientious of the future to which it leads, we have a better chance of acting responsibly towards society and environment.

As Celati concludes the first phase of the work, he leaves us with a suggestive landscape portrait in miniature. Hoping to lead a friend to the banks of the Po in the village of Pomponesco, he instead gets them lost in a wood thick with poplars. Stumbling into a clearing, the men find

> una marea di piante infestanti come non ne ho mai viste; piante a stelo da cui spunta un'unica grande foglia bassa e rigonfia, con superficie molto lustra, brillante, d'un verde che sembra artificiale. E sembravan artificiali quelle piante, per l'eccessiva lucentezza, la sagoma della foglia come quella d'una ninfea, ma rigonfia: come un materiale plastico un po' mostruoso, che ha assunto non si sa come una forma della natura, indistinguibile ormai dalla natura.[48]

This image of a "monstrous" co-mingling of earth and plastic reads as a coda to Celati's musings on the unknown future of a post-Chernobyl landscape. It provides a potential scenario for what may come, a mashup of industrial chemicals and plant life in which colours are too bright and leaves too lustrous. The future it represents is frightening, yet the scenario pertains to a present reality that can only be the result not of the too-recent events at Chernobyl but the past pollution of the everyday. If this disruptive growth results from anything, it is from decades of chemically induced acid rain and industrial runoff from nearby factories. This is the latent environmental crisis explored in the rest of *Verso la foce*.

Adam writes, "Rethinking environmental issues in temporal terms […] gives us considerable theoretical and practical access to their complexity, which in turn provides the potential for alternative socio-environmental praxis."[49] An investigation of socio-environmental praxes is at the forefront of the second movement of *Verso la foce*, made up of sections 2 and 3. Here Celati explores the often-degraded land directly surrounding the Po and the responses of both the area's inhabitants and the river itself to the pollution and neglect that has occurred. Particularly notable in this phase of the book are Celati's stark portraits of polluted land and water and the contrast he unfolds between people who turn their heads away from this reality and those who still communicate with and about it.

While Celati is entranced by the Po's fierce spirit, he does not hold back in portraying its degraded state, in many spots "pieno di bolle e rifiuti."[50] Passing through the town of Pieve di Coriano one day, he overtly connects such degradation to the wealth enjoyed by its residents. We may assume that they have profited from the success of nearby industries, major polluters of the Po. We might also venture, however, that their wealth allows them to contribute even further to waste and pollution of the Po through a lifestyle of steady consuming – constructing ever-larger homes, using chemical fertilizers to produce manicured lawns, adding more and more goods to landfills, and so on. Celati describes a sea of Swiss chalet-style villas with tennis court and pool: "Tutto questo annuncia zone di maggior ricchezza. Infatti, nell'aria c'è un odore grasso che viene da qualche industria e che dura da vari chilometri."[51] The "fat" or "fatty" odour in the air physically comes from factories, yet Celati's use of the conjunction *infatti*, "in fact," relates the *odore di grasso* of the subordinate second sentence to the wealth of the area described in the first, to a state of overabundance.

His description moves immediately from the villas to the vista that they support: "In distanza spuntano tre ciminiere […] contro un cielo quasi nero. Le ciminiere fanno parte della centrale elettrica di Revere, di là dal fiume, una delle tante sul Po […] che scorre pieno di bolle e schiume. Visto di qui, il Po è una vasta corrente nera coperta di rifiuti e macchie oleose e bolle spugnose."[52] Faithful to his mission to *osservare e raccontare*, to observe and recount, Celati provides a portrait of the landscape just as he tells a brief tale of the area's social history. Lives of luxury, robust industry and dirty waters go hand in hand in a state of quotidian environmental crisis.

The term *crisis* may seem gratuitous when discussing contaminated rivers and trash-covered fields but crisis is exactly what these scenarios depict. They mark instability, danger, and a decisive turning point in time. Perhaps the one response often associated with crisis that is missing from the list above is a sense of panic. The turning point has already come, we have altered any semblance of once primary or untouched nature, and yet we are still breathing. In *From Apocalypse to Way of Life* (2003) Frederick Buell highlights the everyday nature of today's environmental crises. He writes that crisis "is not a matter of the imminent future but a feature of the present [...] a process within which individual and society today dwell; it has become part of the repertoire of normalities in reference to which people construct their daily lives."[53] As opposed to the hovering threat represented by the aftermath of nuclear disaster, the crisis state in which we have long placed our natural environment in the name of industrial culture is an accepted part of reality. Like rush-hour traffic on a busy thoroughfare, it is yet another something out of our control that we must simply navigate.

In one of Celati's first entries detailing his experiences at the river's edge, he meets a man who is entrusted with measuring water levels so that he might alert nearby residents to flood danger. This man stands quietly in his rubber boots, taking note of the Po's waxing and waning, as well as its fading aquatic ecosystem. Celati writes: "Parla con tono pacato dell'inquinamento del fiume e dei pesci che si pescano; dice che per lui quel fiume non è lo stesso da quando sono scomparsi gli storioni (per effetto degli scarichi industriali)."[54] The man speaks to Celati of a system permanently changed, reflected by the disappearance of the sturgeon, but his tone is *pacato*, calm or resigned, rather than alarmed. He processes the change by distancing himself, rewriting his conception of relationship to the river. No longer the same entity in his eyes, he must care for and about it less than he once did to avoid feeling that his life has been disrupted. Its degraded state is indeed, as Buell would say, a normality around which he has constructed his life, and his resignation only allows it to persevere.

While Celati's environmentalism is strongly felt in the book's second movement, he goes out of his way to avoid speaking as an expert or preaching his own ideal world view. For as he notes throughout the text, "Parlando in quella lingua di grosse parole che spiegano tutto, diventa difficile accorgersi ogni tanto d'esser qui."[55] And in his sensitivity towards avoiding a stance of pompous authority, Celati is highly aware of his role as outsider in a given community. Denying any ownership of his subject matter, the landscapes and town squares through which he travels, he recognizes his difference from those who, having lived those spaces, hold a greater claim.

Celati's musings on community look forward to Serenella Iovino's discussion of ecological citizenship. Iovino writes that ecology based on citizenship "rilancia l'idea di una condivisione di uno spazio commune e di responsibilità reciproche, secondo i principi della democrazia partecipativa."[56] Furthermore, she notes that "preservando e recuperando l'ambiente commune, è come se la società preservasse e recuperasse se stessa come struttura democratica."[57] Celati, too, in recognizing the bioregional bond that co-inhabitants of an area may have in their shared place knowledge, suggests that strength of community and care for the land lead into one another. By the same token, he fears that a distancing from one's neighbours encourages a lack of investment in the local landscape. He alludes to this at the very beginning of *Verso la foce:*

> Più dell'inquinamento del Po, degli alberi malati, delle puzze industriali, dello stato d'abbandono in cui volge tutto quanto non ha a che fare con il profitto, e infine d'una edilizia fatta per domiciliati intercambiabili, senza patria nè destinazione – più di tutto questo, ciò che sorprende è questo nuovo genere di campagne dove si respira un'aria di solitudine urbana.[58]

In the face of pollution, abandonment, and over-zealous construction, the environmental ill that most shocks Celati is an urban sort of individual solitude. By repeatedly shifting between descriptions of damaged or forgotten lands and individuals lacking community, he draws an overt cause-and-effect relationship between the two.

When he stops to speak with the water measurer referenced above, another local fellow appears. These two men then have a brief dialogue about nearby factories. Standing back to observe, Celati notes: "le cose di cui parlano mi fanno sentire un estraneo, un turista."[59] This is often his reaction in the face of those who speak from experience rather than simply quote the newspaper. It underlines his stance that it takes close observation, perhaps more than that achieved in a single afternoon, to know a place fully. And yet it also supports a different sort of argument.

Knowledge of place built over time, the kind encouraged by Adam's timescape perspective, does promote a deep understanding of a given area. A life-long relationship can also, however, cause one to succumb to a laziness of gaze, a reliance on outdated conceptions or a privileging of certain elements of place over others. At times it takes a fresh view, that of a stranger or outsider, to see the landscape in all its parts and add to a multiaxial understanding of place. In support of that notion, Celati is not the only stranger in *Verso la foce*. As the work unfolds, he slowly pieces together a casual community of strangers, tourists, and outsider figures who, like him, travel on foot and purposefully interact with the landscape. These others are almost always encountered outside, in contrast with resident natives grouped in bars or retreating behind the doors of private homes in a "dichiarazione di guerra con il mondo esterno che sbircia troppo nelle proprietà privata."[60] Outstanding among the bunch are a hunchbacked woman gleaning herbs along the side of the road; an old loner who cleans the crumbling houses, now grown over with vegetation, abandoned along the banks of the Po; a group of ambulant musicians with whom Celati briefly speaks in Arabic; a roadside fishmonger who, to Celati's surprise, is not at all surprised to find the author on foot; and, finally, the young residents of a home for children with Down's syndrome, right along the river's edge.

It is with this last set of "others" in particular that Celati most blatantly questions notions of social normalcy. He contrasts the children, playing and strolling along the riverbank, with speeding drivers on a nearby bridge, eager to get out of town on a Sunday off from work. He reflects: "Le apparenze là fuori vengono avanti sempre diverse e formano i momenti, e i momenti sono ciò in cui gli esseri si raccolgono come quei cosiddetti mongoloidi a passeggio sull'argine." On the other hand, "Il viavai domenicale di machine e motorini verso il ponte è una cosa tanto apatica da farti dimenticare i momenti, andazzo meccanico di dispersi che cercano di salvarsi uscendo con la macchina dall'asfalto sulla costa erbosa."[61] Those who take part in the *viavai domenicale*, the normal coming and going of the mainstream, need to escape from their daily lives in order to find themselves. Conversely, the children with Down's syndrome, a minority group often overlooked in society and thus, in a sense, already considered lost, are able to find peace in daily ritual. Not surprisingly, they do so by embracing the "moments formed by appearances," which is to say, by observing.

Avoiding any implications that people with developmental delay are somehow more "in touch" with nature or natural drives, I focus on how these children, like the old lady gathering herbs, the travelling musicians, and Celati himself are social outsiders. While not exactly *homines sacri*, they are all, in one way or another, outside of the mainstream social group – quite literally, in fact. The children live in a facility assigned just to them, in an "atmosfera non clinica grazie alla vicinanza del fiume," while the others are encountered along roads and in fields, never in social centers.[62] Together, their easy interaction with the landscape underscores the complacency towards it that comes to so many in the mainstream, in need, as they are, of a sudden pollen cloud to wipe their vision "clean."

Ultimately, Celati concludes – as much as he can do so – in the book's brief final section that he, and we, can never completely know a landscape, or any sort of reality, for that matter. We can only keep trying to understand. Finally at the *foce* of the book's title, the mouth of the Po River, he observes, "D'un tratto risuonano richiami di gabbiani, uno chiama e altri rispondono. Anche le parole sono richiami, non definiscono niente, chiamano qualcosa perché resti con noi. E quello che possiamo fare è chiamare le cose, invocarle perché vengano a noi con i loro racconti."[63] His use of calling, or invoking, is right in line with Anna Tsing's work on the act of naming as a way to "order the world."[64] In *Friction: An Ethnography of Global Connection* (2005), Tsing quotes a saying from her mother: "Learning the names of plants is just like learning the names of people you meet; when you know their name, you can get to know them better."[65] As Celati writes about the mixed-use fields, old town centres, and sloping river banks of the Po Valley, naming each area through which he passes, he does get to know them better, just as he reminds his readers, his interlocutors, of their existence in the world. Though he may not be able to comprehend all that he sees before him, in describing, naming, and recounting his observations Celati helps those with whom he communicates to acknowledge material reality.

When that reality involves an oft-degraded second nature, the acts of narrating and naming the landscape inevitably cause us to confront the complicated present and acknowledge a neglectful past. As the book concludes, Celati wryly recalls his earlier considerations of Chernobyl and its still-unknown risk. Near Porto Tolle one afternoon he pauses at a bar to play a pinball game, boldly entitled "VOLTAN ABANDONS THE EARTH." An illustration for he game explains that the protagonists, Wanda and Voltan, must leave an earth grown uninhabitable. Wanda reaches out to her partner, exclaiming in stiff English: "Quick, Voltan, it is going to explode." He responds with, "Too bad, Wanda, it was a nice place where to live."[66] By continuing to observe and recount, even when it is not yet clear what lies before him, Celati works to rewrite this sentence in the present tense. From the unknown environmental legacy of Chernobyl to the disregarded pollution of the Po, he offers a reflective warning: ceasing the struggle to talk about the things around us, to *chiamarle,* call or name them, makes it only too easy to abandon the earth while it still exists.

Chapter Five

Simona Vinci: Provincial Dwellings, Natural Beings

Simona Vinci's work is firmly grounded in contemplation of dwelling and being, the currents of which also run steadily throughout Calvino, Pasolini, and Celati's texts considered herein. *Dwelling* can be nominal as well as verbal, describing a physical space of shelter as well as the physical and psychological act of residing in such a space, what Heidegger defines as a simultaneous state of peace and caretaking.[1] Both forms of the word are appropriate for an environmentally engaged study. Thinking in terms of dwelling(s) allows us to ask several questions: What sorts of shelters and homes do we construct and with what materials, what values? How can these places be in relative harmony with their natural surroundings? Conversely, how might they protect us from or allow us to ignore such surroundings? More generally, just how exactly do we inhabit space as we live our lives? *Being,* too, possesses identities both nominal and verbal, referring either to a living creature or to the very act of existing. In each form the word calls attention to the present moment, the actual space one inhabits and the transitory, constant nature of human life. Anne Whiston Spirn connects the two, noting: "to dwell – to make and care for a place – is self-expression. [...] In German, the roots for building and dwelling and 'I am' are the same. I am because I dwell; I dwell because I build."[2] Through the act of living in a space and constructing some sort of home there, we confirm our very presence on the planet while expressing our subjectivity through the modes of environmental interaction that we choose.

Calvino's texts studied in Chapter 2, *La nuvola di smog* and *La speculazione edilizia,* investigate the ways in which people ignore the natural environment around them for the sake of construction, be it of houses or chemicals. In these works dwelling – and being – are acts that occur behind closed doors and drawn shades. Composed some twenty years later, Celati's *Verso la foce* shifts the discourse to that disregarded environment, the landscape that had served as a stage for the new homes and industries of Calvino's late 1950s. In his efforts to truly see the fields and streams that lie beyond the structures, amid the runoff, Celati emphasizes the need for studied observance of the spaces where we dwell, and of what sorts of beings choose to inhabit these spaces.

Reflecting the important passes made by both authors, Simona Vinci extends the discourse of dwelling and the natural environment, and dwelling *in* the natural environment, one step further. Often writing about the same Emilia-Romagna so loved by Celati, she applies his focus on observance and acceptance of abandoned or interstitial spaces to the very Calvinoesque and equally Pasolinian themes of social alienation and construction. To this mix she adds a healthy dose of psychoanalysis, considering the landscape in symbolic as well as literal iterations as she advocates for an environmental ethics that makes the most of the landscape at hand.

While her predecessors work from positions of lament and uncertainty, Vinci (b. 1970) writes after the fact, that is, after the land has been polluted, the radiation has settled, and people have seemingly gone on with their lives. What results is a study in coping, an ongoing investigation of who acknowledges the change manifested in the landscape and who does not, of how we deal with what has become of our natural and material worlds, and of how those worlds may indeed still help us shoulder the burdens of social existence. Like Celati, Vinci remains steadfast in her message that individual subjects need to maintain connection to the natural world, that they need to know a spirit of place in order to retain their true spirit. A contemporary author at the height of her career, she possesses a gaze and subsequently a notion of just what makes up true spirit of place that is multilayered. In writing about landscape, Vinci incorporates questions of gender and sexuality, ethnic and national identity, and the relationships between language and power. Like all the authorial voices discussed in this book, hers is caught up in an exploration of belonging, of seeking the balance between individual identity and a sense of being part of something larger than the self.

In the end, Vinci's work reads as a rallying cry for finding the organic amid the rubbish, in terms of the individual self as well as the territories this self physically and psychologically inhabits. This cry has two sources. On the one hand, it is prompted by a desire to access the sort of expression motivated by internal drives still unchecked by the grammar of social order, the semiotic realm of significance in Kristevan terms. On the other hand, and yet in fact *resulting* from this desire for the semiotic, it is also prompted by deep concern for the material landscape.

What follows is an analysis in two parts, both grounded in the concept of *dwelling*. The first part traces key environmental motifs throughout Vinci's earlier works, primarily considering their relationship to the semiotic. The second part examines the maturation of these same motifs in Vinci's 2007 novel, *Strada Provinciale Tre*. Whereas in her earlier texts the author is often focused on individual identity and subjecthood – how the individual resides in the world – her attention turns outwards in more recent texts, considering the many people who form communities, and in particular, the physical land upon which we live. The interstitial landscape has an unambiguously positive function for Vinci's protagonists, offering respite from the alienation of contemporary life through access to the natural environment.

Simona Vinci's entrée into literature in 1997 came at a frenzied moment in Italian letters. During the mid-1990s, the publishing industry was transfixed by an exciting new group of young authors who wrote in a graphic, pulp-inspired style.[3] Such authors were eventually given the moniker *i cannibali*, based on an Einaudi anthology, *Gioventù cannibale, La prima antologia dell'orrore estremo* (Cannibal Youth: The First Anthology of Extreme Horror, 1996).[4,5] Though not included in *Gioventù cannibale*, Vinci is featured in a subsequent *cannibale*-centric Einaudi anthology, *Anticorpi: Racconti e forme di esperienza inquieta* (Antibodies: Stories and Forms of Unsettling Experience, 1997). As the title suggests, all the stories gathered in this collection explore the notion of the contemporary and often post-human body, the body modified by science or self.[6] The inclusion of Vinci in this anthology, rather than in the first or in any others associated with the *cannibali*, rightly exposes her willingness to write explicitly about the human body as her most overtly "cannibalistic" feature. Like Aldo Nove or Daniele Luttazzi, Vinci does not hold back in describing the body and its various manipulations, even if this takes her readers into uncomfortable intimacy with sexuality and violence.

The way in which she approaches the body is, however, very far from the realms of consumerism and pulp embraced by her more "cannibalistic" colleagues. While they work with an overt desacralization of the body, parodying today's material culture by way of characters that treat the body as yet another expendable object, Vinci turns to the body as a means of organic defence against that same culture. Roberta Tabanelli has written of the "post-organic" and post-human body in Vinci's work, citing stories in which characters alter their bodies through surgery or self-mutilation and find stimulus in contact with synthetic materials.[7] I agree with much of Tabanelli's work on Vinci, yet I propose that Vinci's fictional manipulation of the body, regardless of the means of manipulation used, is in fact a way to reconnect with the organic elements within the body. In focusing on their physical selves, her characters are brought back to the natural material from which the body is made, even though they may alter it. Furthermore, by engaging their bodies through touch and even mutilation, they are able to experience undiluted feelings of physical pain and pleasure.

Opinion about the true extent of Vinci's "cannibalism" in the 1990s was varied and vague. While she has repeatedly been listed as an author associated with the group, she is inevitably cited as standing somehow apart from it.[8] Since the beginning of her career, her writing style has widely been labelled as more terse, lyrical, and mature than that of her peers. It is this style that set her work apart in the 1990s and that has continued to garner it the greatest amount of attention as the years pass. In the encyclopedic *Letteratura italiana del novecento*, Tommaso Pomilio describes Vinci's language as "una lingua di tersa, inapparente letterarietà (fino al rischio di un certo qual iperlirismo), e sempre starniata dal mimetismo parlato."[9] Similarly, in Stefania Lucamante's English-language introduction to the *cannibali* and co., Filippo La Porta speaks of Vinci's "very personal language, almost obsessed by her desire for precision," calling it "language rich with unusual images, with a sense of estrangement."[10] Compared with, say, the "pulsing techno-rhythm" of Nove's *cannibale*-era writing, or the "needless affectations" of Elena Stancanelli's *cannibale*-esque novel *Benzina*, critics judge Vinci's writing to be particularly refined.[11]

The terse, lyrical language that distinguishes Vinci's early works is linked closely to her engagement with the body, the very element of her work that is, conversely, most in line with the *cannibale* style. Her attention to rhythm, spacing, essential dialogue, and even representations of silence, as La Porta observes, suggests a relationship to language more poetic than pulp.[12] Severino Cesari, for his part, notes that Vinci writes, "Inventando una lingua scarnificata fino all'essenziale eppure misteriosamente piena di vibrazioni, pronta per prove di più distesa narrazione."[13] This final citation truly captures the essence of her style. Although it is *scarnificato*, stripped to the bare minimum, her language is "mysteriously full of vibrations," or, as Fulvio Pezzarossa calls them, "pulsioni."[14] In critical terms, the vibrations or drives notable in Vinci's language are the same drives at work in the creation of the semiotic, as formalized in the work of Julia Kristeva. By reading Vinci's texts in light of Kristeva's work we see that for Vinci, language and an organic connection to the earth, as both a stand-in for the maternal body and a space of free expression in its own right, are deeply entwined. In fact, by acknowledging the semiotic through manipulation of language and narrative content, Vinci demonstrates one solution to Gianni Celati's struggle to *osservare e raccontare*, to observe and recount. As she embraces a fundamental connection between body and earth, observing and expressing the tamed within the body through language is also a means through which to observe and recount the natural world.

Though her work has matured throughout the years, her prose becoming more polished and her narratives more subtle, the themes dear to her heart have remained the same, growing only richer and more assertive over time. Since the publication of her debut novel, *Dei bambini non si sa niente* (What We Don't Know about Children, 1997), Vinci has continued to work with the image of a safe space removed from organized social activity, a primitive hut or organic shelter tucked back in woods or fields, in which characters are at ease to express unchecked instincts and desires. She has also worked extensively with issues of the body, generally female, and the social expectations associated with gender identity. These two thematic categories, the gendered body and spaces of safety, merge in her most forceful common motif – the body literally immersed in earth. Starting with her very first work, Vinci's texts have explored the desire to engage the body physically in the natural world, whether through visions of planting limbs like the roots of a tree or through the completed action of burying a body in dirt as a seed, full of potential.

Such work is undeniably wrapped up in the realms of symbolism and metaphor. Terms like *coping* and *grounding* imply the attribution of values that go beyond the material, just as images of immersing the body in nature cannot but suggest that nature is a symbolic stand-in for the womb and all that the state of pre-subjecthood implies. These sorts of engagement do not in any way negate a real interest in the physical state of nature and the environment, however, and they in fact often lead to and coexist with just such an interest. A feeling of connection, that is, an emotional or psychological attraction to or investment in an entity is a strong incentive indeed for one to yearn for its continued existence. It can also provide a window through which to gaze upon this entity more closely and, subsequently, recognize its practical, material value.

Many of the great environmentally minded writers often grouped in the still solidifying ecocritical canon have such a relationship to nature. From Henry David Thoreau and Ralph Waldo Emerson to V.S. Naipaul and Ananda Devi, we repeatedly find examples of authors who write about the material importance of the landscape from a perspective informed, at least in part, by an assessment of its non-material value. In his work *Modern Nature*, for example, Derek Jarman links a sentimental attachment to his childhood garden with a desire, found later in life, to nurture that same space that had nurtured him. Returning to the garden as an adult he recollects: "These spring flowers are my first memory, startling discoveries […] dividing the enchantment into days and months. […] In that precious time I would stand and watch the garden grow. […] There, in my dreaming, petals would open and close."[15] He then explains, "For two months after moving here [as an adult] I spent hours each day picking up fragments of countless smashed bottles, china plates, pieces of rusty metal. Rubbish had been scattered over the whole landscape."[16] In cleaning the landscape of trash so as to allow flowers to thrive once more, he displays an ecological sensibility of stewardship that stems directly from memories of "enchantment" and "dreaming" inspired by that same space years prior. This process is the same sort we see in the development of Vinci's body of work; responses from the realm of dream or emotion lead to a desire to protect the actual, material landscape.

A clear assessment of Italy's contemporary natural environment does not fully emerge until Vinci's more recent work. Yet a steady focus on landscape does permeate even her earliest titles. As noted at chapter outset, this occurs through a thematic focus on shelters constructed in harmony with or overrun by plant life in woods or fields, and repeated imagery of bodies merging with land. The first motif is present in the novels *Dei bambini non si sa niente* and *Come prima delle madri* (Like It Was Before the Mothers, 2003), along with the theatrical work *Brother and Sister* (2003) and the short story "Fuga con bambina" (Escape with Little Girl) of the collection *In tutti i sensi come l'amore* (In Every Sense Like Love, 1991).[17] This last work tells of a walk to school gone wrong, when the story's fourteen-year-old narrator, Cris, impulsively kidnaps a young girl he has often passed on his morning commute. He takes her because she seems friendly, as opposed to the antagonistic peers that await him at school. Without any set plan, Cris carries the girl to an abandoned villa in a nearby field, the same sort of structure found in *Dei bambini non si sa niente* and *Come prima delle madri*. Secure in his hiding space, he feels free to explore his body as well as that of the young girl, and they are found within the day. It is, to say the least, an uncomfortable read.

Most striking, and what links this text to the others mentioned, is the way in which being tucked among the untamed vines and autonomous trees of the villa, surrounded by the "odore dei campi e il canto dei grilli intorno," allows the narrator to act on unchecked desires, focusing on touch, smell, and sound.[18] Cris says of the villa, "È una vecchia casa in rovina. Ci crescono le piante dentro, non solo cespugli, erba matta e fiori, ma anche alberi veri, ormai grandi e robusti," and describes pulling back branches to enter, crunching over leaves as he walks in, and resting among growing vines.[19] For this reason, he explains, "mi piace" (he likes it). Readers may feel their own skin crawl as Cris acts well beyond the norms of socially appropriate behaviour, but this is Vinci's aim. Her protagonist reaches a level of such comfort nestled within the natural landscape that he is able to explore his physical drives, even those that readers find reprehensible.

The second motif mentioned above, that of physical merger with the landscape, appears in *Dei bambini non si sa niente,* the short story "Agosto nero" (Dark August), also from *In tutti i sensi come l'amore,* and as shall be discussed, the novel *Strada Provinciale Tre* (2007). "Agosto nero" contains the greatest concentration of ready examples: The troubled first-person narrator regularly envisions her young daughter melding with the earth throughout the course of a brief roadtrip. One of the strongest examples is the following, in which the narrator muses, "Vorrei prendere la bambina [...] e piantarla da qualche parte. [...] Tanto sono sicura che non le succederebbe niente, se ne rimarebbe lì ferma come un sasso, parte dell'ambiente naturale: una pietra, un tronco secco, una zolla di terra rossa, fertile e muta. Chissà, poi magari metterebbe radici lì, diventerebbe un albero."[20] Rather than expressing a lack of concern for her daughter's well-being, such visions represent overt acts of salvation from what the narrator experiences as the difficulty of social existence. The narrator imagines that by becoming as still as a stone, as rooted as a tree, her daughter will gain strength and freedom.

The natural setting that presents the greatest potential for release in "Agosto nero" is the sea, itself an active body constantly in flux. Watching the quick movement of waves one day, the narrator notices how forcefully they wash out the crevices of nearby rocks and imagines that the water's potential to effect change might reach her daughter. As she observes the tide creep up the shore she notes, "Ormai è rimasta soltanto una striscia sottilissima di sabbia, il resto se l'è mangiato il mare" and wonders, "E se il mare la prendesse?"[21] This thought reassures the woman, as though her daughter would be safer dissolved in the sea than navigating life with her. She calmly imagines that the girl "flutuerebbe tra i pesci, si dissolverebbe nell'acqua fino a diventare un unico verme pallido, un girino, una cosa simile all'inizio della vita."[22] Rather than images of death, the narrator's visions of her daughter's physical melding with the earth are instead emblems of hope for new life. It is the chance of becoming something 'similar to the beginning of life' that makes physical merger with the earth so attractive to Vinci's characters. They are considered, either by themselves or others, to be safer in physical communion with the land, *fertile* yet *muta*. Like the daughter in "Agosto nero," they are imagined to be unfettered by language and social interaction in this state, yet able to contribute to a communal generation of life in a way perhaps more meaningful than before.

All of the titles listed above feature children on the verge of adolescence, hovering in that treacherous space between the world of play and imagination and the rules and regulations of adult social existence. Natural spaces, such as the untended fields leading out to the sea in *Dei bambini non si sa niente* and "Agosto nero," or the overgrown woods in *Brother and Sister* and *Come prima delle madri*, serve as places of refuge allowing Vinci's young protagonists a moment of respite. Immersed in these landscapes or basic dwellings nestled within them, her protagonists are free from questions of social order and identity. Instead, they are allowed to indulge in curiosity, imagination, fear, and pleasure, all generally stemming from drives within and connected back to their (pre)pubescent bodies. Faced with impending adulthood (sexual maturity of the body, the pressures of social identity, the realization that parents are not faultless, etc.), or, in the case of the adult protagonist of "Agosto nero," struggling with the expectations attached to the roles of woman and mother, they turn to nature as an alternative space of being and expression.

I propose that the drives fuelling their free experiences in nature are the same drives at work in Julia Kristeva's conceptualization of the semiotic. In *Revolution in Poetic Language* (1984), Kristeva describes the act of signification as a process encompassing both symbolic and semiotic modes. The first mode contains set rules of meaning, grammar, and syntax and is dictated by social order. The second mode, stemming from drives within the body, is manifested in expression through rhythm and tone, and not governed by set rules. It is pre-, or even anti-social, and contains multiple and often contradictory instincts. Kristeva conceptualizes these multiple corporeal drives powering the semiotic as a chora: a collective bound in difference, frenetic and yet unified. Possessing drives that may very well be destructive, the semiotic chora is tamed by introduction to the symbolic in linguistic expression. Prior to entering the symbolic realm, however, it is grounded by its relationship to the maternal body, which allows it to exist without erupting in destructive anarchy. From this it must follow that being in a successful state of free expression, a realm unbound by grammar, is akin to the initial stages of life, when the child is still dependent upon the maternal body.

Simona Vinci supports just such a notion, while bringing it specifically into the context of language and writing, in an essay published early in her career. Contemplating her role as writer, she explains that her goal is to "dimenticare l'ossessione di un mondo in forma di parole e tornare all'originale: la forma, quella che è lì, evidente, per tutti."[23] As a writer she consciously manipulates language, and yet she also strives to move away from the world of words in order to return to the original (world), the "form" evident to all. This suggests her interest in a semiotic realm, a celebration of sound and rhythm and a relationship to language that is more free form than that which we generally grow into with social identity. Vinci expresses this desire in the first person in the above citation, relating it to her own formal process, but it is also reflected in her fictional narratives through characters such as the aforementioned Cris, who attempt to access the *originale* through their actions.

Returning to Kristeva's framework, we note that the maternal body is not simply important to the semiotic realm, it is essential for its survival. Kristeva explains:

> Drives involve pre-Oedipal semiotic functions and energy discharges that connect and orient the body to the mother. We must emphasize that drives are always-already ambiguous, simultaneously assimilating and destructive; this dualism [...] makes the semiotized body a place of permanent scission. The oral and anal drives, both of which are oriented and structured around the mother's body, dominate this sensorimotor organization. The mother's body is therefore what mediates the symbolic law

> organizing social relations and becomes the ordering principle of the semiotic *chora*, which is on the path of destruction, aggressivity, and death.[24]

The mother's body manages the frenetic state of the semiotized being. Without it, such a being would simply be overcome by the semiotic chora, which risks being overpowered by the death drive.[25] Thus, although the realm of the semiotic may have great appeal in contrast to the social constraints of the symbolic, lacking the order established by a greater force, it is also anarchical to the point of annihilation. Again, we might think of the character Cris, whose sense of freedom in a safe and semiotized space leads him to an action in the realm of the destructive, inappropriately touching the young girl.

The need for the regulatory maternal body poses a problem for the subject who is already immersed in the social, symbolic order but longs for greater contact with the semiotic. Here we recall the adult narrator of "Agosto nero," who tells readers "certi giorni mi stanco di tutto" and envies her young daughter's ability to distance herself from the social world around.[26] If the narrator wants to act on her desire to reject society and the symbolic without self-destructing, she must, in theory, return to some sort of maternal body for survival. Such a return is of course impossible but this does not keep her from fantasizing about experiences that might *replicate* a return to the maternal body. Encountering an older woman along her journey, she notes: "Aveva un vestito corto arrotolato sulle cosce nude, enormi e abbronzate. Sembravano tenere, ma salde, e io avrei voluto correrle incontro e affondarci la testa, sentire il calore della pelle, farmi tenere da quell'odore sicuramente pulito e sano, appena un po' acido dal caldo."[27] The sight of the unknown woman's solid thighs, evocative to the narrator of maternal strength, inspires in her a desire to literally bury herself in them so as to receive respite from her "vita sempre a metà," full of "cose sporche."[28] Having previously expressed doubt as to her own maternal capabilities and social identity, she identifies physical contact with a sort of ultimate maternal body as a potential source of relief. Her contact with the woman remains only at the level of fantasy, however, in acknowledgment of the fact that one cannot in fact return to the original maternal, especially as a fully acculturated adult.

It is here that the natural landscape enters the equation for Vinci's protagonists, serving as an alternate form of safe grounding between symbolic and semiotic, social structure and unchecked drive. For the narrator of "Agosto nero," envisioning her daughter as "parte dell'ambiente naturale: una pietra, un tronco secco" serves as a wish for the girl's protection. In addition, it allows the woman to imagine her *own* merger with the natural landscape and, thus, break with social order.[29] As she explains, "Mia figlia fa sempre le cose che io desiderei fare"; the girl is in many ways simply an extension of her mother, a freer version of the grown woman.[30] Returning the girl to the land thus serves as an alternative solution to the adult narrator's desired return to a maternal body or other location of grounding in the semiotic.

The realm of physical nature has long seemed the "natural" response to this dilemma of return, a way to experience going back to a different sort of *originale*. The earth provides a zone of new growth and fresh beginnings, a source of nutrition and sustenance, and at least in collective imagination or crafted memory, a potential realm of untouched beauty, found in sprouting buds and newly born creatures. As Richard Mabey comments in the work *Nature Cure*, "The wood and the water, the ancient and the opportunist, are, I suspect, the two poles of natural rhythms. Life begins in the water and reaches its full maturity in the forest – and then it all goes round again."[31] Through entry into the natural landscape we are able to access the potential involved in Mabey's "going round again," tapping into a direct experience of rhythm and instinct not found elsewhere. Melanie Klein suggests, in turn, that "the relation to nature which arouses such strong feelings of love, appreciation, admiration and devotion, has much in common with the relation to one's mother. The manifold gifts of nature are equated with whatever we have received in the early days from our mother."[32] Grateful for the endowment of life, we are often inclined to extend positive feelings from the life-bearing maternal body to the life-bearing natural landscape.

It must be acknowledged, of course, that emphasizing a connection between nature and the maternal comes awfully close to equating the female to nature. Such an equation does then enter dangerously essentialist territory, ill fitting for a study on commingling and crossing over. As Stacy Alaimo explains in her critique of first-wave ecofeminism, "Defining woman as that which is mired in nature thrusts woman outside the domain of human subjectivity, rationality, and agency."[33] By overly stressing the relationship between the female maternal body and nature, we run the risk of reducing that body to one simple function, while simultaneously extracting her from the realms of culture and, in Kristevan or Lacanian terms, the symbolic. Not only that, but we create a woman-as-nature/man-as-culture paradigm in which men are neither allowed to be nurturers nor thought to understand nature fully. I wish to avoid such binaries, for I believe that the female, the male, and other categories of (non)identification run rampant throughout realms natural, cultural, and in-between. Rather, in considering the Kristevan maternal body I wish to redirect focus on the freely expressive semiotic and its need for some zone of mediation. In citing Klein, I move to extend this zone of mediation beyond the maternal body to include also the natural landscape. Recognizing the work of both thinkers, I posit that one of the greatest "gifts of nature" is a safe mode of access to the semiotic.

Vinci herself manages to avoid performing an overt gendering while still asserting her belief in a connection between land and new life. Echoing her statement on writing and the "original" cited above, she writes in the short story "La più piccola cosa" (The Smallest Thing, 2004), "I corpi hanno più risposte di noi, conoscono meglio la terra, perchè è da lì che vengono ed è lì che ritornano."[34] With this she draws a clear correlation between the earth and the initial stages of life yet manages to bypass the question of the maternal body entirely. By going so far as to say that bodies come from *terra*, the land, she surpasses a landscape-maternal body equivalency and privileges the land over the body as a source of life. By then balancing the "coming from" stage of life with the "returning to" stage, she further cements the place of the human life cycle in the ever-cyclical natural world, full of seasonal regeneration.[35] We think once more of Mabey's reminder, cited previously: "Then it all goes round again."

Nowhere is this point more strongly made than in the conclusion of *Dei bambini non si sa niente*, Vinci's first novel. The work tells of five adolescent children who spend their summer days in a sparse shelter tucked into the fields far behind their ex-urban apartment complex. The private realm of their hidden *capanna* allows the children to form a group identity so solid as to become a semiotic chora in their own right, described at one point in the narrative as "questa cosa diversa, questa cosa che erano loro insieme, senza sguardi esterni."[36] Their formation as a collective unfolds through increasingly violent sexual experimentation. Exploring drives of desire, pain, fear, compassion, and destruction, they repeatedly test boundaries and are often afraid, but they are always comforted by their status of being a *loro insieme*, as though their collectivity provides a safe space for any level of expression.

Vinci was both celebrated and lambasted by the press for this work, with critics such as Guido Gugliemi praising her "inquietudine attiva" and others, such as Giulio Ferroni, condemning her "volgarissima banalità pornografica."[37] Both sets of criticism have their place. Scenes of sexual activity, particularly those involving the young female members of the group, as well as descriptions of the pornography that Mirko, the eldest boy, smuggles in, are difficult to read in such sharp detail and bluntness of tone. And yet, as with the similarly themed and previously discussed "Fuga con bambina," difficulty or disgust experienced by the reader is not without purpose. Vinci works not only to express her own "active anxiety," as Guglielmi writes, but also to provoke the same response in readers, causing us to contemplate the life of the adolescent struggling to sort out social existence and young adult identity. The text is of greatest interest to my discussion here for the way in which this struggle plays out in a particularly privileged space, and the way in which this space is established as a realm dominated by free expression in connection to the land.

The fields abutting the children's shared apartment complex are assigned a living character, one that expresses itself in a language of shape and rhythm. In lines such as "I campi erano pieni di vibrazioni, il vento correva in mezzo facendo degli strani disegni e fischiando rapido," readers note how the wind cuts through the fields like drives cutting across the semiotized body.[38] And like a maternal body, a space facilitating free expression, the fields' status as a protective realm attracts the children. Faced at home with domestic chores, blaring television sets, and unfeeling, inattentive parents, the children wish that they could "scappare in mezzo al campo, dentro, e sparire."[39] They do not simply wish to be near this protective realm but to enter fully into it, physically as much as psychologically.

To go to the fields is to go inside a zone that is at once familiar and unpredictable. This is established by the first and last chapters of *Dei bambini non si sa niente*, which begin with a repeated yet ever-changing transitional paragraph. Set in italics on an otherwise blank page, it describes the journey from apartment complex to the children's secret hut, nestled back in untamed fields. Vinci's repetition of the paragraph evolves into a series of interludes that bookend the work. Each new interlude is similar to those that have come before and yet also somehow altered, providing a poetry that is both repetitive and uneven:

> Dritto per cinque minuti dentro il campo, poi ancora dritto,
> seguendo il fosso, tra le ortiche, i fiori gialli e viola, gli insetti. Dentro il fosso con le rane, sempre dritto, fino in fondo. [...]

> Ancora dritto, dentro il fosso, tra le rane e i grilli. In mezzo alle ortiche e ai fiori gialli e viola. Fino alla fine. […]
>
> Camminare dritto dentro i campi per cinque minuti, dritto fino al fosso e poi ancora dentro, tra le ortiche e il fango.[40]

These passages evoke the semiotic in terms of both form and content, tapping into a greater awareness of rhythm, tone, and empty space than other passages in the book, while also defining a natural space to be entered, much like a nest or womb. At the same time, they speak to a celebration of the landscape in its physical form. By slowing down the narrative they create a moment of reverence and establish the space of mud, nettles, insects, and flowers as one to be treated with careful attention. They also recall the landscape-protagonist equivalency so prominent in Pasolini's films of the 1960s, where an edgeland environment welcomes similarly interstitial adolescents on the border between childhood and adulthood. Vinci confirms a deep relationship between human subject and natural environment in her writing: "Non c'è distinzione tra esseri umani e paesaggio, sono convinta che NOI siamo i luoghi che abitiamo, così come noi li modelliamo (spesso li deturpiamo) e li modifichiamo, loro modellano e modificano noi."[41] She sees the relationship between human and land as a simultaneous process of mirroring and reciprocity.

A permanent return to the earth and subsequent rebirth is ultimately achieved in Vinci's first novel through the death of the young character Greta. The actions leading to her death are initially spurred by influence from the outside adult world, as the children recreate pornographic imagery. Their experiments are largely devoid of adult notions of sexuality or conscious violence, however, and can instead be read as an enactment of un-tempered drives. In describing the climax of a scene of violent bondage, Vinci is careful to note the general atmosphere, focusing on the music, the air, all of the elements that tie the children together as a unified entity. About the group, she writes: "Quella corrente violenta e dura li teneva ancora stretti, vibravano tutti quanti, tutta la leggerezza del gioco era esplosa nella furia. Disorganizzati, frenetici."[42] Frenetic and vibrating in unison, they are held tight by the same current. The verb *vibrare* is particularly notable here. Having previously been attributed to the surrounding fields, it draws out a connection between the group's action and the location that has made their expression possible, while also referencing the pulses, drives, and vibrations of instinctive communication unchecked by social order. While the children collectively act as chora, Greta becomes their semiotized body overtaken by the death drive. She is at last able to return to the mediation of something like a maternal body in death, as the group buries her body in the earth of the fields. If we can manage to step back from the brutality of the act, the return to the earth of Greta's body may be considered the narrative's ultimate goal achieved. A representative of the group has finally made her way *dentro*, inside the earth.

The burial scene is narrated for readers by another young girl, meditative in response to Greta's still body. Upon laying her friend in the ground, she recalls images seen in school of a fetus in amniotic fluid. She thinks of the fetus, "così solitario e muto, là dentro. Sospeso in un luogo caldo e silenzioso, lontano dalle voci, lontano dal dolore." Then she reflects, "Forse anche Greta sta così, sospesa in un luogo che non è da nessun parte, con la terra morbida sulla pelle, dentro gli occhi, le orecchie, la bocca. Terra morbida e fresca e il movimento sotterraneo di grilli, cicale, vermi. Una popolazione muta che fa del suo corpo un luogo di passaggio e nutrimento."[43] Readers note key expressions and notions in this passage from other Vinci texts previously cited, as Greta is described as "mute" and facilitating life yet also living as something "before life." In death, she simultaneously becomes womb and fetus, a source of new beginnings and yet herself a brand-new being. Looking down at Greta's body, her friend thinks, "Ecco, proprio un feto. Stava tornando a prima, Greta, a prima della vita."[44] Greta's return to the earth signals the achievement of complete immersion in a space of organic potential, as she is safely grounded in her free-form existence by the mediating force of the natural landscape.

About literary depictions of death, Julia Kristeva writes that "in returning, through the event of death, toward that which produces its break; in exporting semiotic motility across the border on which the symbolic is established, the artist sketches out a kind of second birth. [...] Through themes, ideologies, and social meanings, the artist introduces into the symbolic order an asocial drive, one not yet harnessed by the thetic."[45]

With *Dei bambini non si sa niente* Vinci does just this, drawing readers along on an often painful exploration of drives that insert an element of anarchy into the social order, as she questions a widespread overdependence upon the symbolic. By employing the earth as locus for the death/second birth in which her text culminates, she asserts its value as a realm of creative potential and a space of determinedly nebulous borders.

A link between the semiotic realm and spaces of nature may be brought into sharper focus by returning to the notion of second nature, an underlying theme of this book. As has been well established, we cannot speak of nature at this point without referencing culture, whether consciously or otherwise.[46] The landscape available to the majority of the inhabited world, and certainly Italy, has been modified for centuries upon centuries, in one way or another, by human behaviour. In 1991, for example, Antonio Cederna writes that Italy is the largest producer and consumer of cement in the world, three times that of the United States, a fact he blames on the ruinous construction of houses and roads.[47] The result is that unpaved land is hard to find, while locating land unaffected by the transport and production of material goods is nearly impossible.

As subjects reared within the cultural, we can neither approach the landscape void of ideologies formed by cultural experience, nor pretend that a clear border lies between nature and culture. A similar intermingling exists in Kristeva's discourse on the semiotic. As Terry Eagleton writes of her work: "It is important to see that the semiotic is not an alternative to the symbolic order, a language one could speak instead of normal discourse: it is rather a process within our conventional sign-systems, which questions and transgresses their limits." Citing Lacanian principles from which Kristeva's work stems, Eagleton continues, "Anyone who is unable to enter the symbolic order at all, to symbolize their experience through language, would become psychotic. One might see the semiotic as a kind of internal *limit or borderline* of the symbolic order" (italics mine).[48] Occupying the outer limits of signification, the semiotic is both apart and inseparable from the symbolic. In its role as a threshold or border zone, it allows a subject to step back from the symbolic without denying it, just as the contemporary Italian landscape facilitates an experience with nature despite its overlap with culture. Once again, Vinci's environmental focus is to be located in this same discourse, as it is precisely that interstitial zone of merger in the landscape – the fields that bridge housing development with open sea, the sculpted structures that have begun to let the earth back through – to which she is most drawn.

A physical border zone, that space facilitating the meeting between road and field, is the area of greatest focus in *Strada Provinciale Tre*. In this work the author once again ponders diverse forms of expression and living within the dominant social order. Like *Dei bambini non si sa niente* and the texts that follow it, *Strada Provinciale Tre* examines social (non) conformity, maternity and kinship roles, the relationship to one's body, and the power of the nonhuman world to provide solace in moments of emotional need. At the same time, it surpasses Vinci's previous texts in its insistence on an environment that is explicitly tied to transportation and industry, manifestations of culture in movement. The rambling field or private hut secluded in the woods, so prominent in her earlier work, are no longer primary spaces of interest. That role is assigned instead to the regional highway for which the work is named, the real-world Strada Provinciale Tre, or SP3, which stretches east from Modena to Ravenna. The novel opens and closes in description of this space, and the protagonist turns time and again to it in circular rhythm, stepping momentarily into a town centre or enclosed place of dwelling or labour, only to return once more to the road.

While the particular border space of the highway's edge is fundamental to the protagonist's experience of re-beginning, so too is the geographic and environmental specificity of the SP3. The water-rich land surrounding the highway is an area of the Po Valley long cultivated, dotted with the sorts of flimsy housing developments that industrial growth requires and, in more recent years, somewhat abandoned by industry.[49] This is the same territory explored by Gianni Celati in *Verso la foce* and other texts. Economist Antonio Massarutto describes it as consisting of "small urban centers and isolated fractions [...] discharging into small watercourses; [a] high quantity of small industrial activities, sprawled around in the territory [...]; soil contamination due to landfill and abandoned industrial sites; and finally rainwater contamination."[50] It is a vast expanse of field and stream forever altered by the toxic waste of industry and the ever-increasing cement and asphalt of new extra-urban development. Vinci writes of the area in *Strada Provinciale Tre* as "uno spazio immenso, sconfinato, che un tempo deve essere stato niente che chilometri e chilometri di terra piatta e verde, in certi punti coperta di boschi e faggeti, terra incolta, viva," noting that "adesso le fabbriche abbandonate punteggiano la pianura con le loro ciminiere spente, le recinzioni di filo spinato corrose di ruggine."[51] Similar to the novel's protagonist, who is described as gaunt, weathered, and appearing older than her thirty-eight years, this stretch of the Po Valley bears the mark of wear on its skin.

Like Vinci's earlier characters, the protagonist of *Strada Provinciale Tre* regularly sinks into the physical landscape as a place of respite, yet the land into which she sinks is far from a hearty, uncontaminated nature.

More often than not, it is the earth just past the guardrail of the SP3, a utilitarian space recognized primarily for its access to transport and commerce and generally otherwise ignored. This roadside stretch reveals a life lived frantically on its surface, carrying always the smells and detritus of the workday. One of the novel's first repeated images is of the protagonist face down in the dirt alongside the road, tucked out of view from passing cars and reassured, even reinvigorated, by a mix of smells both fresh and rancid. She sleeps "rannicchiata nell'erba di un fosso, nel fetore della piscia di gatti e cani, tra le ortiche, gli insetti, i rifiuti lanciati dagli automobilisti in corsa."[52] As do so many passages in Vinci's work, this description emphasizes foul odors, harsh surfaces, and, in particular, trash, which can be mentioned numerous times on a single page. All of these elements are tied directly to the SP3, yet they all enter into the woman's perception – and appreciation – of a grass-covered ditch.

The highway's edge is of great importance in *Strada Provinciale Tre* not only for such sensorial reminders of life in process but also for the access it provides to steady physical movement via its ongoing, unobstructed surface. Many days into her journey, the protagonist finds temporary afternoon respite in an empty building. As night falls, she grabs her backpack and slips out the back door. The text reads: "Una folata di vento le ha sbattuto contro la faccia, un odore di concime chimico e gomma sciolta, di erba tagliata e merda di maiale. La notte era lì, un'altra volta, limpida e ferma sopra la sua testa, attorno al suo corpo."[53] Often likened to an animal, in particular a wounded dog, the protagonist feels safer out in the open than inside built structures. And like an animal guided by smell, she is consistently drawn back to her set course. In the passage cited above, "Ha ricominiciato a camminare, senza fermarsi, senza voltarsi indietro a guardare il posto che lasciava. Ha camminato dentro il campo, dritta verso la luce di una casa colonica in lontananza e poi ha sterzato e ha ricominciato a seguire una linea parallela alla strada, orientarsi con la scia di lampioni lontani, alla sua destra."[54] The process of re-beginning ("ha ricominciato") and of returning, is a constant in her experience of the SP3, grounded in a rhythmic physicality directly linked to the sensations of fatigue, strength and hunger. Only after sixty pages dedicated to this protagonist do readers learn that she is named Vera. And only slowly throughout the text do we understand that she has ruptured with a life including partner, home, and career for a bare life experience without money, automated transportation, or set destination. She has made her break unexpectedly, almost unconsciously, so as to find some sort of true experience – one that is *vera*, like her name – something lost long ago. Referring to herself, she muses: "Della tua vera vita, quella che conta, non c'è traccia da nessuna parte," only receipts for items purchased and bank statements from the automated teller.[55] Having blocked out all memories of her past identity, she is as though brand new in the world or, rather, emerging from a deep slumber only to step back slowly into life's basic functions, undergoing her "processo di decomposizione" from a position literally on the interstice.[56]

Although not divulged to readers until the text's end, prior to her rupture Vera worked at an architectural firm called Techniche di Paesaggio (Landscape Technicians). She was a draftswoman who specialized in housing developments, one of the very people responsible for covering the Po Valley in drywall and cement. We read that her architectural passion started early: "Lei ha cominciato da bambina, zitta a disegnare le case, i muri, le porte, le finestre, e ha continuato, tutta la vita spesa e pagata a progettare l'inferno [...] tutta quella immensa necropoli del futuro [...] a invadere la terra."[57] With such a background, images of Vera nestled, skin against dirt, into the same landscape she has helped to mask, function as a refusal of past identity and, what is more important, an awakening to land previously ignored. Vera has experienced what Lee Rozelle terms an awareness of the "ecosublime," that is, "the awe and terror of a heightened awareness of the ecological home."[58] In a distinctly twenty-first-century, post-Romantic sort of awe, she is both frightened by the scarring that the Po Valley has sustained and astonished by the hold that the land still exerts over her. And in her walking practice alongside the SP3, as well as her habit of curling into the land beside it, she refuses her previous role as "technician." No longer seeking to participate authoritatively in the shaping of the landscape, she now seeks to know the form that it already possesses. In this Vera reflects Celati's lesson crafted twenty years prior, observing and acknowledging the land as it is rather than attempting to mold it.

Another active role that she has renounced is that of mother. As readers eventually learn, Vera has aborted a pregnancy in the not-too-distant past. She revisits both the feeling of life within her womb and the feeling of that life leaving her through memories of physical sensation and flashing images of a medical setting. In conversation with a fellow traveller mid-text, Vera shares a memory from an autumn day spent swimming in a thermal pool: "Avevo appena saputo dei bambini e non avevo voglia di dirlo a nessuno, nemmeno al padre. Godermi questa sensazione di essere soli, io e loro. Di essere l'unica al mondo a sapere cosa mi stava sucedendo, almeno per qualche giorno. Volevo stare in un cerchio perfetto, in silenzio, ad ascoltare."[59] Vera's emphasis on the enjoyment of sensation and process, underlined by the past progressive "stava sucedendo," is notable in this passage. As something that is only hers and not yet part of recognized social order, her physical knowledge of pregnancy is an experience truly outside the realm of language. It is a "perfect circle," she explains, yet just as in Kristeva's formulation of the semiotic, Vera finds such perfect balance only in a state pre-determined as fleeting – pregnancy lasts only so long, even when it does reach culmination.

In ecological terms, Vera's renunciation of a potential motherhood and her renunciation of a professional identity as draftswoman are parallel, each an act of remove from direct production. Like Melville's reluctant scrivener Bartleby, an omnipresent figure in Celati's work, and, I would argue, in the works of Calvino and Pasolini considered in this book, Vera "prefers not to." And through this choice not to engage directly, Vinci underlines that not all female bodies are maternal, just as she confirms that one can maintain awareness of and relationship to the natural landscape without actively manipulating it.

Instead, Vera simply walks. Her chosen course, the edge of the SP3, is a space of border crossing on multiple axes in Vinci's novel. It hosts the merger of diverse environmental realities while also facilitating the meeting of human subjects representing different cultural backgrounds and levels of social agency. Such merger is as productive as it is discomfiting; as Vera walks and observes, she re-establishes her set of values regarding both people and space, operating from a newly lowered social position due to her disheveled appearance and lack of money. Finding herself, for example, in a roadside grocery store with scant coins to buy food, she recalls with shame having once judged a man in her same position: "Nessuno si vergogna più di essere ignorante, maleducato, cattivo. [...] Nessuna di queste cose fa vergognare. Solo essere poveri. La povertà, è la cosa peggiore che possa capitarti. Adesso lo capisce. Prima no. Prima, era anche lei come tutti gli altri."[60] Through her 'process of decomposition,' Vera gains direct access to an understanding of diverse social realities through experiences both challenging and illuminating. She re-evaluates her previous approach, for she has a new understanding of what it is to live without all the tools required by the mainstream. In this reevaluation, and in having literally walked the line between highway and field, Vera inhabits the meeting of semiotic and symbolic modes of communication. Her longing for a "true" experience in opposition to the oppressive order of everyday life also reflects a resistance of the symbolic and suggests that ordered social life removes us from instinctual expression.

Strada Provinciale Tre is purely fictional, yet Vinci has been clear about her real-life inspiration to pen the work, in interviews, writings on her personal website, and the final vignette of her eco-noir novella *Rovina* (Ruin), also published in 2007.[61] In the coda to *Rovina,* Vinci mentions her fascination with the endless construction in her native Emilia-Romagna and explains her own daily walking habit: "Cammino sulla Trasversale di Pianura, un giorno dopo l'altro, un mese dopo l'altro, in mezzo a un paesaggio mutante al quale è così difficile dare un nome [...] la terra sventrata, aperta come una ferita."[62] Although the story in *Strada Provinciale Tre* is not Vinci's, the landscape portraits that it contains are directly borrowed from her own roadside journeys, the earth similarly portrayed as a body damaged, disemboweled, and open, like a wound.

Just as the novel adopts the descriptive language of Vinci's personal writing, it also borrows portraits of people from the author's journeys. On a now-defunct personal website, Vinci describes a series of photographs from her explorations of the SP3, along which, we learn, she lived for six years. She first describes in detail the cultivation and construction of the terrain that the images capture: "Centinaia di scatti, alcuni presi da un'auto in corsa, altri dal bordo di una provinciale intasata di camion: cantieri su cantieri, gru, capannoni, villette, campi coltivati." She then notes with admiration "quelle piccole figure, colte per caso o intenzionalmente, che ancora camminano, a dispetto di tutto, e attraversano questi luoghi, e li abitano."[63] These "small figures" that inhabit the spaces in her first-person text also populate her novel; they walk along the border of the SP3, as Vera does, or glean plants in the dirt just past its edge. Their presence contributes to an image of the SP3's margin as host to an alternate sort of social order. By using the adjective *colte* – meaning "gathered," "cultivated," or, best yet, "harvested" – Vinci assigns these walking figures to the hybrid land as though they grew there alongside the nettles and reeds, engulfed in the smell of exhaust. As *Strada Provinciale Tre* progresses, this chorus of socially marginal individuals slowly grows. It is made up of awkward children, ambulant workers, impoverished retirees, and *extracomunitari,* non-Western immigrants. All are depicted as downtrodden but resilient, like the African woman dressed all in white who laughs as she says to Vera: "Evribodi gos auei, diar frend, evribodi ... or do ia zink uirgoin tu stei ir ol ze taim?"[64]

One transitory (non)citizen of the SP3, a young Eastern European truck driver, requires special consideration in terms of realities both social and spatial. Dimà, as he is called, is the first person Vera encounters along the roadside who looks her in the eye with respect, and his silent earnest nature inspires her confidence. As days pass and Dimà joins Vera in her travels for a significant portion of the novel, the two emerge as kindred spirits. Their bond is initially established when he cares for her after an episode of violence at the hands of another trucker: "Non c'è bisogno di dirsi niente, nessuna spiegazione, indicazione, nessun commento. Gesti antichissime e semplici [...] potrebbero sembrare una madre e un figlio, una bizzarra figura mitica rovesciata dato che è lui a compiere i gesti di una madre e lei a riceverli, come un figlio."[65] There is a lack of gender or age identity in their pairing as they alternate roles of caretaker, child, and sexual initiator throughout their time together. Both have turbulent relationships to Italian, the language of the majority culture, and to men and their dominant bodies. Both feel, in their current incarnation as wanderers of the SP3, that they are not treated as full citizens in society. In this interstitial status, they recall Pasolini's Accattone or the many roadside wanderers encountered by Celati in *Verso la foce*. Not surprisingly, Dimà is directly linked to the same environment in which Vera finds comfort. His skin emanates "un odore vegetale, come di erba appena falcita"; he longs simply to live in the countryside one day; and he sleeps in a bare dwelling off of the SP3, an abandoned cottage tucked back among flat, desolate fields described as "un territorio disabitato e alieno, un mondo antichissimo, un mondo prima del mondo."[66] This space in particular, so present throughout Vinci's extant corpus, "a world before the world," cements Dimà's role in the catalogue of interstitial Vinci protagonists. It is also what most posits him, like Pasolini's Accattone, as a *homo sacer* figure, functioning simultaneously within and outside of mainstream Italian society.

As an immigrant, particularly one without papers who has come seeking employment, Dimà represents a contemporary Italy that is far from cultural or ethnic homogeneity. Like (we may assume) the old Eastern European woman dragging her accordion along the side of the road, or the woman who tells Vera that no one stays in one place anymore, cited above, Dimà resides within and upon Italian territory without legal recognition. He is living proof that places and communities change, that borders are fluid, and that the notion of nation does not always mean much to people who live in a space out of necessity. Simultaneously, Dimà also represents a new global environmental reality. He is not just any migrant nomad but one forced from his homeland because of nuclear disaster.

The only member of his family still known to be living, Dimà is a direct survivor of the 1986 Chernobyl explosion. With his original home unsafe for human habitation, he is truly unable to return and must instead remain in movement as he seeks employment as well as spatial and social belonging. This element of his character once again connects Vinci's work to that of Celati. While the latter considers Chernobyl an environmental threat not yet understood, the former is able twenty years later to engage it as a disaster with clear effects on both land and society, still unfolding as they may be.[67] As a survivor, Dimà represents the integration of environmental crisis into the culture of the everyday, and yet his nomadic status is a constant reminder of environmental change that is transnational and long term. As Rob Nixon writes, the Chernobyl disaster is a prime example of slow environmental violence, in which "the different timelines of mutation – international, intranational, intergenerational, bureaucratic, and somatic – are dizzying even to attempt to map."[68] Chernobyl may well have been worked into the collective memory, become a part of shared history, but it has yet to be surpassed.

What Dimà considers his true home, Pripyat, in Ukraine, has been abandoned since 1986. This long-lost home, he tells Vera, is now overrun by a truly wild nature. Vinci writes: "Ha sentito dire che le piante – gli alberi, i cespugli, i fiori selvatici – sono cresciuti dentro le case, dappertutto, e che buttano i rami fuori dalle finestre e dalle porte spalancate delle case. Che gli animali si sono riprodotti in libertà [...] e pensa che dev'essere un posto meraviglioso."[69] Dimà is the ultimate alien, sprung up out of chemical disaster and unable to return home. Yet the land from which he hails has become the closest thing to the very *mondo prima del mondo* so sought after by Vinci's protagonists. That the most lush, untouched natural space in the work is the result of chemical disaster – human error – and, furthermore, a place in which humans cannot dwell, underlines the decidedly post-millenial ecocritical message running throughout Vinci's work. Authenticity is an empty notion and purity of nature beside the point. It is not worth directing our gaze to the unattainable ideal – even this is a contaminated second nature-state, in the above description of an imagined Chernobyl landscape – but rather to the actual.

The actual natural environment that she describes bears deep scars. The real-life SP3 alongside which Vinci situates her novel is often referred to as the Trasversale di Pianura, meaning essentially "road crossing the plains." In describing the relationship between the highway and its surrounding environment, the author emphasizes the notion of crossing as a physical rupture. One of the first landscape portraits in *Strada Provinciale Tre* reads: "La strada è una strada larga che taglia una campagna distrutta. Una distruzione precisa, geometrica."[70] This image of the road "cutting" across the field quickly becomes a common trope. The author writes elsewhere, for example, of "il campo immenso, le spighe a perdita d'occhio e i tralicci dell'alta tensione come suture su un corpo morto," just as she describes how, like a scar across a body, the SP3 "taglia in due un pezzo di pianura," and adds "è una strada mortale, che attraversa piccoli centri – paesi grandi, medi, minuscoli, frazioni – e li deturpa, li soffoca, li ammutolisce."[71]

Deface, suffocate, silence – through such verbs she depicts the plains of the Po Valley as living bodies that have been challenged and wounded, once again drawing a parallel between the maternal body and the natural earth as sites of semiotic mediation. The plains bordering the SP3 are much like the body of Vera's (maternal) travelling companion Dimà, first described in his "pantaloni militari sporchi di terra, la maglietta bianca che aderisce al torace sottile, sporca di terra e umida di sudore, lo zaino buttato su una spalla, le mani callose, piene di tagli e cicatrici."[72] And, just like Dimà, the land serves a care-taking function for Vera, soothing her spirit and her weary body, though distressed they might be. Scars thus become the emblems of life that has been lived, of bodies and spaces that have been put upon and made to work.

The existence of scarring and cutting is largely negative in *Strada Provinciale Tre*, as evidenced by words such as *distrutta* and *soffocare*, above. And yet, scars also contain a certain positive potential when viewed in terms of friction. To return once more to Anna Tsing's definition, we might argue for the productive nature of the scar as that which bares the trace of "heterogeneous and unequal encounters."[73] As permanent reminders of instances of rupture, scars remind viewers that not all "true" experiences are without pain or violence, as Vera knows well. They also serve as a visual affirmation of the possibility for deviation from established patterns of being in the world. They make plain the complicated relationships between order and instinct, between the symbolic and the semiotic, and between the natural landscape and practices of cultivation, communication, and industrial transport. Vinci writes that

Vera "ogni tanto alza lo sguardo per vedere quella campagna morta da una parte e dall'altra della strada. I pali della luce, i tralicci dell'alta tensione che la segnano come suture su un corpo, come cicatrici, certo orribili a vedersi ma necessarie."[74] As disconcerting as scars may be to look at, Vera recognizes their necessity to both bodies and land for the access they provide to multiple modes of experience and expression. In this she surpasses the conflicted attitudes toward overtly modified or interstitial spaces represented by Calvino and Pasolini decades prior. Notable in the above citation is the emphasis on visual acknowledgement: the adjective *necessarie*, necessary, may be applied not only to the high-tension lines, strung like stitches through a body, but also to the very act of seeing them. It is necessary to recognize displeasing effects in the landscape, just as it is necessary to recognize that land's persistent multiple capacities and multiple means of communication.

Vinci's engagement with notions of the semiotic as interstitial space in *Strada Provinciale Tre* is only furthered by Vera's musings on language. Throughout the novel Vera struggles to express herself in words, often simply refusing to speak. She thinks regularly of the small notebook in her backpack but never opens it to write, and she likens her body to an empty sheet of paper, dry and blank. She also questions directly the function of the symbolic, pondering acts of speech and naming as states forced upon us by others rather than chosen. At the novel's outset, for example, upon temporarily entering a structure one day during her walk along the SP3, Vera searches "in un posto ostile che sta dentro la sua testa, i nomi delle cose che vede" but encounters difficulty, unable to come up with the correct words.[75] When she does then find words, they come tumbling out, one after another, as in the following: "Non ricorda niente. Poi torna. All'improviso ricorda tutto. Queste parole che le battono in testa: radice, legame, legaccio, corda che trascina, sasso al collo che affonda, staccarsi, slegarsi, sciogliersi, sgusciare. Le guarda passare, scivolare dentro e fuori dalla testa, le ascolta, e cerca di capire se la marea viene da dentro, da fuori."[76]

In the citations above, Vera interrogates the boundaries of her identity and expressive agency in relationship to language, just as she interrogates the functionality of the systems in place. Notable are the words that do recur: *root, cord, stone, to distance, to loosen, to dissolve, to peel back*. Rather than name the objects before her eyes, in this instance pieces of farm equipment, the words that come to her describe the feeling attached to her relationship to language: it is a weight or physical restraint. They also describe the process that she is undergoing in regards to language, one of separation and liberation. This does not mean, of course, that Vera renounces entirely the use of language. Instead, from her location on the interstices of road and dirt, symbolic and semiotic, Vera is able to be more fully engaged and selective in its manipulation.

This comes as a great relief, for as we read mid-novel, "Le parole pronunciate le sono sempre sembrate faticose." As it turns out, Vera has always had a complicated relationship to language. In fact, as a child, "Pensava a come sarebbe stata la sua vita da bambina sordomuta e la immaginava come una vita di beatitudine perfetta." This perfection is, not surprisingly, related to the natural world for Vera thinks that she would have been "come una vongola adagiata sul fondo del mare, avrebbe percepito soltanto le fluttuazioni del mondo, le spinte, qualche brezza improvvisa."[77] Without language, the younger Vera imagines that she would experience expression through the world's fluctuations, coming and going as an unexpected breeze or the flow of tidal waters.

As an adult, however, reflecting from her position alongside the SP3, she recognizes the impossibility of mute existence: "Forse, pensa adesso, smettere del tutto di parlare è impossibile. Le parole saltano fuori dalla bocca senza che tu neanche te ne accorga, a un certo punto, come le monete magiche di una fiaba, l'unica è sputarle fuori, e condividerle, se non vuoi soffocare."[78] As with a negated fantasy of nestling in to an older woman's skin (strikingly similar to an episode in Vinci's aforementioned short story "Agosto Nero") Vera recognizes the impossibility of total remove from culture and communication.[79] In the passage cited here she continues to depict spoken language as something beyond the speaker's control, yet she attributes value to the act of enunciation as a means by which to at least not be overtaken by the weight of language itself. In this Vera accepts her integration into the very culture that produces the electricity lines and highways cutting across the SP3. She also, however, acknowledges her agency in relationship to the symbolic, choosing when to engage it fully and when to remain along its margins.

Through myriad written explorations of the act of signification, Vinci never fully denies the presence of the symbolic just as she never describes a natural landscape unattached to cultural realities. The question in her work becomes one of tapping back into freeform experience and expression from a position within social grammar, and of benefitting from contact with the natural environment in a hybrid landscape. Depicted as threshold or border zone, the semiotic allows a subject to momentarily step back from the symbolic without renouncing it entirely. It becomes a site of friction, cutting through space like wind in a field as a reminder of natural drives. In this it performs the same sort of function realized by the interstitial space along the highway's edge in *Strada Provinciale Tre,* allowing access to the natural landscape just as it hosts the fumes of trucks plowing by.

In her relationship to language, Vera enacts Michel De Certeau's distinction between the grammar of the architect and the linguistic expression of the walker: "The geometrical space of urbanists and architects," the very space that Vera once worked to shape, "seems to have the status of the 'proper meaning' constructed by grammarians and linguists in order to have a normal and normative level to which they can compare the drifting of 'figurative' language."[80] Having stepped outside of structured urban life, to remain along the highway's edge, connected to both the fields beyond and the detritus of the highway, Vera engages in the figurative language of the drifter. Furthermore, she proves De Certeau's argument that "the long poem of walking manipulates spatial organizations, no matter how panoptic they may be: it is neither foreign to them (it can take place only within them) nor in conformity with them (it does not receive its identity from them)."[81] Vera does not change the structure of the SP3 or, for that matter, of the surrounding landscape. She does, however, use the space in a way that differs from that originally conceived, the transportation of goods and people inside closed vehicles quickly moving from point *A* to point *B*. In walking, she acknowledges those spaces that the road seeks to bypass, thus troubling established "arrangements of culture and power," to return once more to Tsing's description.

Through the figure of Vera in *Strada Provinciale Tre,* Simona Vinci posits questions of value and proposes new expressive modalities. She asks which spaces are prized and which are ignored as she demonstrates the strength of second nature, the smell of auto exhaust and rubber tires motivating her protagonist as much as that of fresh leaves and grass. And by focusing so explicitly on an interstitial space, Vinci argues for the value of border crossing, facilitated by the semiotic, as a means through which to recover one's *vera vita.*

Anne Whiston Spirn has expressed what Vinci has been working towards throughout her career: "The language of landscape reminds us that nothing stays the same, that catastrophic shifts and cumulative changes shape the present. It permits us to perceive pasts we cannot otherwise experience, to anticipate the possible, to envision, choose, and shape the future."[82] She notes further that "to recover and renew the language of landscape is to discover and imagine new metaphors, to tell new stories, and to create new landscapes."[83] From Vinci's initial interest in the language of the semiotic, she has turned to the language of landscape, related so very closely. Her work demonstrates that through active engagement with the land in which we dwell, we gain access to a freedom of expression within the self and a greater understanding of the world around, as complicated as both that self and that landscape may be.

Chapter Six

Daniele Ciprì and Franco Maresco: On Horizons and the Human

In the collaborative films of directors Daniele Ciprì and Franco Maresco, all landscapes successfully embody the interstice without relationship to what lies beyond. Questions of where city meets country and where nature might claim space once lost are not as relevant here as they are for, say, Pasolini. Ciprì and Maresco operate from a place beyond designations like *postindustrial* or *exurban.* The directors present a world in which active industry and a thriving urban culture are so distant as to have vanished from collective memory, and any lingering debate between primary versus second nature is irrelevant, because the latter is the only kind ever imagined. As a result, their interstitial landscapes thrive. In Ciprì and Maresco's films, made primarily in the 1990s but set in an indiscernible time, concern lies less with the health of the environment than with the end-of-days men who inhabit it. Such men – and they are only ever men – comprise a society on its way to extinction, standing in acute contrast to the tenacity and regeneration of the surrounding environment. This is not to say that the directors are not intensely focused on landscape, for they are, simply that the natural landscape is perhaps the least-endangered element in their films.

Neither contemplating what may happen within a given space as time unfolds, nor directly lamenting what has already shaped the history of that space, Ciprì and Maresco focus on the present. That is, they focus on *a* present, suspended in an ambiguous time without a clear past or foreseeable future. In both short and feature-length films of 1995–2004, the directors present a realm so neatly all culture and all nature as to negate the possibility of any lingering memory of spaces once divided, if only ever on the surface. In this way they advance the investigation first launched by Calvino, then carried on by Pasolini, Celati, and Vinci, by proposing a world in which natural space is an integral part of all spatial experience, rather than a quietly languishing other or out-of-bounds locale. The directors' portrayal of a world largely devoid of division between the spaces of city and country, or overt nature and culture, marks the next step in an evolving focus on interstitial Italian landscapes by raising them to a primary plane of consciousness and formal focus. At the same time, the directors question the structural integrity, the health, of a deconstructed humanity.

Rather than the back-to-nature urban wonderland proposed by the character Dimà in Vinci's *Strada Provinciale Tre* – the oddly idyllic yet murderously radioactive modern-day Chernobyl, just one imagined version of a city flush with nonhuman life – Ciprì and Maresco paint a rather hazy portrait of final merger. Theirs is a windswept zone containing only the fossils of buildings, inhabited or otherwise, and dominated by dry, shrub-covered hills on all sides, with mountains in the distance and vast, dramatic skies overhead. The directors' favoured landscape, as both setting and subject, is their natal island Sicily, but this is rarely overt in their films. The realm they craft onscreen is instead often interpreted as a *non-luogo* by viewers and critics, a non-place that is, at least aesthetically, devoid of any indication of geographic specificity.[1]

As an example, we may consider the duo's film *A memoria* (By Memory, 1996). Shortly after its start, viewers are presented with the striking shell of a decrepit, abandoned town. Predominant in this early image are abandoned, crumbling buildings immersed in dry dirt and wild grasses, a mountainous sliver in the distance poking out from behind. A somberly clad man emerges from between the buildings, tiny and ancient. He shuffles steadily towards the left until off-screen, humanity taking its leave from an almost, but not entirely, barren realm. The sky grows increasingly and unevenly dark towards the top of the frame, and no clear horizon is visible where air meets earth. Instead, darkness serves as an imposed limit and finite dimension to the otherwise undelineated space. This wordless introduction establishes the tone for the images and vignettes to follow in the 38-minute *A memoria*. It also reflects the spirit and imagery of Ciprì and Maresco's full-length films *Lo zio di Brooklyn* (The Uncle from Brooklyn, 1995) and *Totò che visse due volte* (Toto Who Lived Twice, 1998). In these films the directors feature landscapes that reveal a complete merger of realms urban and rural, where shrubs grow post-apocalyptically through the walls of apartment buildings and packs of pigs roam abandoned town centres. Against such a backdrop, Ciprì and Maresco explore a fictional society living out its days in a realm full of absence: absence of women, absence of temporal and geographic specificity, and absence of a chance for future generation. As in the scene described above, such elements are foregrounded by the lack of a physical horizon, which only underlines characters' lack of phenomenological horizon, of a temporally informed frame of reference for productively interpreting the world around them.

Both natives of the Sicilian capital, Palermo, Daniele Ciprì (b. 1962) and Franco Maresco (b. 1958) began their careers in film at an early age. Ciprì first worked as a cameraman at the urging of his father, a photographer and movie-camera repairman. Maresco tried his hand working in private radio and television, heading a film cooperative and running a cult-video store. The two men officially joined forces in 1989, when they began collaborating on brief, experimental pieces for a Palermo-based television station, TVM. Their short episodes, grouped under the title *Cinico TV*, quickly moved from TVM to the stations Italia 1 and RaiTre. Thanks to routine play on programs such as the popular news roundups *Blob* and *Avanzi*, as well as Enrico Ghezzi's *Fuori Orario*, the directors and their work gained a relatively wide audience in the early 1990s. *Cinico TV* condemns, among other things, the massification of Italian society and in particular Silvio Berlusconi's liability for it, in shorts such as *La Sucato Family*. Here, a family is interviewed by an off-camera voice about whether TV might provoke *effetti micidiali*, deadly effects, in the family unit. They explain their plan to sue *la televisione* ("La Rai?" "No, Berlusconi") in order to care for a brother who has lost his wits from watching too much of it.

From these beginnings grew a film career, including the feature-length films *Lo zio di Brooklyn*, *Totò che visse due volte*, *Il ritorno di Cagliostro* (The Return of Cagliostro, 2003), and *Come inguaiammo il cinema italiano* (How We Got the Italian Cinema into Trouble, 2004). The first two titles are fictional films, whose protagonists inhabit a hybridized environment of abandoned urban centre and open hillside. The final two titles are both more linear and more urban. The first is a fictional account of the making of a film in 1940s Sicily; the second is a pastiche documentary ode to B-movie legends Franco Franchi and Ciccio Ingrassia. Along the way, Ciprì and Maresco also made various shorter documentary pieces, such as *Enzo, domani a Palermo!* (Enzo, Tomorrow in Palermo! 1999), a semi-satirical investigation of the Sicilian cinema personality Enzo Castagna, and shorter experimental works, like the aforementioned *A memoria* and *Grazie Lia – breve inchiesta su Santa Rosalia* (Thanks Lia – A Short Investigation into Santa Rosalia, 43 min.), both released in 1996. In more recent years, Ciprì and Maresco have returned to working independently from one another.

Since a brief but meaningful series of interventions in the late 1990s to early 2000s, little has been said about the directors, now simply accepted as the "ragazzi terribili" of Italian cinema.[2] Of all their work together, *Lo zio di Brooklyn* and *Totò che visse due volte* received the greatest critical acclaim, produced the most scholarship, and caused the biggest controversy in the public sphere. These films are also, along with the shorter *A memoria*, the works of greatest relevance to this book. Sharing a common setting, cast of characters, and general stylistic approach, the films are further linked by the great attention they pay to physical landscape and natural environment.

Ciprì and Maresco ascribe the landscape such agency in their work that it stands out as an active entity in possession of greater vivacity than the directors' human characters. In this way, they posit the natural environment's resilience as a tool through which to underscore the limited temporality of mankind. While humans wander aimlessly in the directors' films, physically repeating circular paths and backtracking mid-course, the plants surrounding them rhythmically sway in the breeze, rooted firmly into the earth from which they will continue to grow. Rather than inspire regenerative hope, landscape serves as a source of contrast, progressing on into the future in a way that the all-male society in its midst will not. This is not to say that the natural world is exemplary or that a clear human/nonhuman division may be drawn. Instead, we might simply consider that the natural world operates according to a cyclical rhythm not shared by Ciprì and Maresco's characters.

Unlike the abstract *A memoria*, *Lo zio di Brooklyn* and *Totò che visse due volte* both ostensibly have a primary plot. They are overrun, however, by side stories, brief vignettes, and bold images. *Lo zio di Brooklyn* tells the tale of four adult family members assigned to host the mysterious relative of two elderly dwarves in trouble with a mafia don. This absurdist plot is distinctly not the focal point of the film, which is instead the nature of its characters, the realm in which they dwell, and the overwhelming presence of death, signalled by repeated images of coffins and funeral processions.[3] More directly focused on interior spaces than later works, *Lo zio di Brooklyn* nonetheless features a merger of normally discrete environments typical of all three films. It presents an anywhere-Palermo composed of empty housing projects, dark, crumbling apartments, and desolate streets and highways almost entirely devoid of motorized vehicles. Most spaces here, whether an apartment interior or the fields flowing into it, bear the trace of dirt and tumbleweeds.

A certain gradation exists in the spaces that make up the surrounding landscape and those that comprise a town-like structure: the first are light and open; the second are dark and closed. In this sense there is a physical transition between "city" and "country" marked by peripheral zones such as the partly walled, rubble-filled alleys scattered along the edge of town. An ideological division between realms is broken down, however, by a common presence of windswept plant life, dry dirt ground, and roaming animals. In one typical frame from mid-film, viewers encounter a piece of jagged mountain in the upper-right corner, a vaguely 1960s-era housing complex before it, and a bare, sun-bleached, single-storey structure. The dwelling is set centre frame and foregrounded by a dirt path, swaying bushes, a yapping dog, and a man clothed only in undershorts. Nature and culture, ancient and modern.

The omnipresence of physical nature is further enhanced by the crumbling state of all built structures, which allows viewers to see the sky, a near-constant presence, through decomposing roofs. Ciprì and Maresco also establish a uniformity of tone throughout each frame by filming in black and white, as they are wont to do, thus creating a base level of visual continuity between all realms. This relative ideological consistency between spaces of open nature and structured dwelling separates Ciprì and Maresco's peripheral world from that presented, for example, in Pasolini's Roman films of the early 1960s. In films such as *Accattone* and *Mamma Roma*, which often serve as a visual referent for the Sicilian directors, a stark ideological – and thus behavioural – separation exists between open land, the realm of bare life, and city centre, the space of commerce and capital.[4] Conversely, the characters in Ciprì and Maresco's work show no indication of awareness that they are entering a realm where they must conduct themselves in a certain fashion or risk being perceived in a new light. They are equally (ill) at ease wherever they may be; their world is all one fluid, frustrating experience.

Continuing an exploration of the undefined present, *Totò che visse due volte* was officially released to the public in 1998, three years after *Lo zio di Brooklyn*. Ripe with overtones of religious narrative and the imagery of religious idolatry (the first largely mocked, the second oddly revered), this work is divided into three numbered episodes, each dedicated to a different inept character.[5] Abele Longo writes that "più che ne *Lo zio di Brooklyn*, *Totò che visse due volte* si allontana dalla città reale. La Palermo di *Totò che visse due volte* agisce come metafora; metafora della fine dell'Occidente."[6] Inasmuch as the "real city" ever features in the first film, it has even less of a presence in the second. While numerous scenes do occur inside built structures and the city features in the background of certain shots, viewers are never allowed to experience open space when in it; no scenes are shot in common courtyards or along paved roads as in *Lo zio di Brooklyn*. The effect of this is that social life appears to occur only in the wide-open spaces beyond the city, where characters are most explicitly shown to interact. Interior spaces, and particularly those that might be considered more urban, are reserved for private moments or family groupings and are oppressively still, dark, and coloured by death. Such spaces are dominated in the film by a wake, a related scene depicting rats covering the deceased's lover Fefè as he sleeps, and a third-chapter scene featuring a mob hit. Interior spaces thus house no life in this film and are in fact overtly connected to the gradual end of society, as they host or lead to the death of its last living residents.

The film's central vignette sharply contrasts a scene of happier times between Fefè and his lover with scenes of present-day mourning. In flashback, the two men frolic in the countryside, the screen a near whitewash in comparison to the dark tones dominating so much of the film. They dance in an open field richly textured with plants and rocks, and with buildings occasionally visible but always in the background. A musical soundtrack replete with chirping birds accompanies their reverie. In contrast, the interior space surrounding the lover's deathbed is dark, inhibiting clear vision. He is laid out on a bed framed by candles – the only furnishings in the room besides a small table and a random grouping of chairs. The walls of this space are thick and rough, their whitewash so badly chipped as to give the appearance of thick stone. A small gathering of family members in mourners' black surrounds the body, their faces barely emerging from shadow. Shortly after the reluctant Fefè finally comes to visit the body, the camera cuts to an exterior shot of what viewers may infer is the outside of this structure, surrounded by a row of similar buildings along the edge of a canal. It is dusk and all is again obscured, with the exception of one square window, lit from the inside, in the top right corner of the frame. The camera holds on this image for a full six seconds, and all that moves are a scurrying rat and the audible water of the canal – a rare acquatic presence – as it takes on the guise of the river Lethe.

Finally, possessing even less of a narrative, and distributed on a much smaller scale, *A memoria* joins the two titles above for their common landscape and treatment of the men who inhabit it. Released between the two feature-length films, *A memoria* is a series of images and vignettes set to the improvisational work of the saxophonist Steve Lacy. This film is both a testament to the directors' love of jazz and a distillation of the same social and environmental relationships presented in *Lo zio di Brooklyn* and *Totò che visse due volte*. Devoid of language and filmed equally in a ghost-town city space and the open land beyond it, the film is a study in basic visual contrast, not of space but of action. In almost every shot, movement is paired with stillness, as one man performs a repeated action while another stands still, or a lone figure poses against softly undulating plants or the clouds moving behind him, indicative of time moving ever forward. While this film features no scenes or images connected overtly to death, it does communicate an overwhelming presence of death through both its mournful score and the hopeless desire of its characters to remain rooted in a present moment rather than reach an impending end.

In all three films, the space in the landscape that ought to host the meeting of earth and air is consistently blurred or darkened. This obfuscation of horizon lines serves as a productive visual metaphor for the theoretical issues at stake regarding history and temporality. In *Truth and Method* (1960), Hans Georg Gadamer notes, "The horizon is the range of vision that includes everything that can be seen from a particular vantage point."[7] This is a commonly accepted definition, certainly so in physical terms, yet Gadamer's use of the word also includes the following understanding: "A person who has no horizon is a man who does not see far enough and hence overvalues what is nearest to him. Contrariwise, to have an *[sic]* horizon means not to be limited to what is nearest, but to be able to see beyond it. A person who has an horizon knows the relative significance of everything within this horizon, as near or far, great or small."[8] For Gadamer, to have a horizon means to have a broad frame of reference for interpreting the world, to be able to act with foresight and an understanding of long-term consequences. This means that a person in full possession of a horizon acts with awareness of the future, just as it means that "the horizon of the present cannot be formed without the past."[9] To possess a horizon entails recognition of past actions and their results, as well as an awareness of the long-reaching ramifications of present action.[10] It entails an understanding of time as continuous, one moment reaching forward to the next.

This understanding of horizon is exactly what Ciprì and Maresco apply to their craft as filmmakers. Producing films that will be contemplated long into the future, they incorporate the images, sounds, and lessons of past artists. Their sources are varied but always from the world of arts and cinema, serving as homage to the past and a refusal of mainstream contemporary film culture and its norms. The influence of Luis Buñuel, for example, emerges in their predilection for jumping between seemingly unrelated scenes, as well as in the eye-centred sequence at the start of *Lo zio di Brooklyn*, a reference to the Spanish director's surreal groundbreaking short *Un Chien Andalou* (1929).[11]

A studied attention to music and comedy also features heavily in their work. Emiliano Morreale cites the Italian vaudeville star Wanda Osiris, 1920s jazz, and the comic stylings of silent film as particular influences on the Sicilian duo. Franco Maresco also often acknowledges the improvisation and spontaneity of jazz from the 1960s and beyond.[12] All of these influences make for an eclectic formal mix, a visual and auditory memory book possessing a strong nostalgia for past eras of artistic expression paired with an experimental immediacy and adhering to no one period of reference. This filmmaking practice is squarely in possession of the sort of broad horizon noticeably absent in the fictional world that results.

Denied a similar horizon, the characters within Ciprì and Maresco's films lack the tools to act with what Edmund Husserl refers to as intentionality. Husserl asserts that "to every perception there always belongs a horizon of the past, as a potentiality of awakenable recollections; and to every recollection there belongs, as a horizon, the continuous intervening intentionality of possible recollections."[13] As an individual perceives what is before him, he has myriad past images and experiences to serve as reference and thus aid in interpreting the current situation. Each of these past vistas or situations in turn possesses a series of additional pasts to serve as reference and interpretational aid. In this way, every moment of perception functions in Husserl's hermeneutic as an experience informed by a never-ending past and a continual process of selection or intentionality. As Ciprì and Maresco's characters lack this sort of deep horizon and its related intentionalities, their frame of reference and thus their concerns are reduced to the most immediate time and the most immediate material – the body and its needs.

The absence of a clear horizon is just one instance of a lack of distinction between categories in the directors' films. A related lack of distinction is found in the films' total absence of women. In an interview with Massimo Galimberti that accompanies the RaroVideo DVD of *Totò che visse due volte*, Daniele Ciprì attributes the absence of women in his and Maresco's films to the simple fact that the directors are more comfortable working with men. Both directors came of age, he explains, in a Sicilian culture often heavily segregated by gender, and so an all male cast simply feels natural to them. Abele Longo, however, quotes Ciprì and Maresco as explaining elsewhere that women "inspire too much tenderness."[14] Longo suggests that with the term *tenderness* the directors mean to imply that women inspire hope for, as he writes, "continuity." Gendered notions of nurture and caretaking aside, the very capacity of the female body to carry life is able to inspire tenderness in that it may conjure the innocence of the newly born and a hope for the future by way of offspring.

A small number of figures coded through dress as female do appear in all of the directors' fictional films. The characters that portray them are recognized quickly as male, however, because of their rather sloppy drag and overtly male physical traits. The lone female character in *Lo zio di Brooklyn* is played by a scrawny, shrill-voiced man in full modest dress, representing a rather ancient specimen in keeping with the film's focus on aging and death. In the later films, *A memoria* and *Totò che visse due volte*, viewers also find younger, sexualized cross-dressing characters. The initial episode of the first film is devoted to one man's efforts to meet with the town prostitute, a true sight to behold. Displaying herself to customers in her dingy parlor, she stands with muscled legs wide in an authoritative and what can best be described as macho stance, rubbing her large, awkward semblance of breasts. She repeatedly licks her lips as unkempt chest hair spills over the top of her negligee, her messy plastic wig glinting in the moonlight.

A prime focus of desire in the community, she has the ability to break down the distinction between subject and object in her physical representation of both the present male and the absent female. All of her female physical characteristics are mere symbols, however, their status as such underlined by a lack of concern for authenticity. Her breasts, for example, are clearly unattached to her body, lumpy cushions tucked in to an ill-fitting blouse. In the physical masculinity of her actual body – heavy brow, large nose, sharp jaw, hairy chest and legs – this character flaunts her (his) lack of true female form, including female reproductive ability. She is a physical embodiment of Kristeva's treatment of the abject, "where the separation between subject and object is not yet clear but where these two quasi entities are exhausted in fascination and repulsion."[15] *A memoria* features a similar character, silently conjured by a magician for another man's viewing on a ploughed dirt field. This representative of the female also licks her lips and rubs false breasts, shaking her hips and wearing only underwear and socks, her hairy belly hanging over a clearly male groin. Again, she is a source of both fascination and repulsion, the representation of a desired object never to be attained.

Physically, such characters promise a sex devoid of generative potential. On a very basic level, this explains the inability of Ciprì and Maresco's male society to carry forward in new generation. Without women, they simply cannot procreate. Such discourse does, of course, reduce women to mere physical function, but that is precisely the case in Ciprì and Maresco's films. Ciprì and Maresco do reduce women: they reduce them to objects of sexual desire – and, in the instance from *Lo zio di Brooklyn,* noted above, as well as in the set of ancient female mourners in *Totò che visse due volte* – to maternal figures to be ignored or brushed aside, as the "primary ab-ject," in Kristeva's formula.[16] In this reduction, the directors use their cross-dressing characters to lampoon an absence of female agency not only in their cinematic world but also in the world beyond. Their simple "casting choice," while easily misogynistic also reflects and critiques a historical exclusion of women from dominant social power structures in Western society. This abjection of the female thus comes to model abjection of women that is both historical and, in the Berlusconian Italy in which all three films were produced, all too contemporary.

Totò che visse due volte, in particular, is marked by an overarching absence not only of women but of human (pro-)creation, an absence that once more engages in direct dialogue with the natural world. The film's first full scene opens in a communal urinal that seems to double as a porn cinema. A sizable group of middle-aged men are shown to be masturbating over their clothes, all of them staring into the camera, which we take to represent the cinema's screen. Lacking in this image is any indication of direct skin contact or obvious orgasm. The brightness of the stark white room, combined with a lack of physical contact between people, personal skin-to-skin contact, or any physical product of their action by way of semen, again has multiple indications. To begin, the starkness of the room and stoic consistency of the men's actions lend the space an oddly clinical air, further separating their expression of sexuality from the natural world. Second, the absence of any physical product of their sex act suggests a male physical inability to produce the necessary means for procreation, absence of women aside.

From this initial scene the film cuts to an open landscape shot. Bare earth occupies the bottom fifth of the frame, while the rest is dedicated to a textured, moody sky in scales of grey. A small figure moves across the screen, his body in movement signalling and disrupting the hazy space where the horizon ought to be. The right third of the screen is marked by a parallel streak of light that cuts through the clouds and draws the eye towards a distinct transition in the earth. To the right of where the streak (like a lightning bolt in shape) hits the ground, the dirt, seemingly dry and largely devoid of plant life in the majority of the frame, becomes darker, and the formerly bare earth is filled with thick vegetation.

The effect is of a transition to relative fecundity as more and more plants become evident towards the right edge of the screen. The man walks steadily from screen left to right as though drawn to that fertile landscape. His attraction to emblems of fecundity is then underlined by the following shot, which captures his joy and sexual excitement on stumbling across a well-endowed donkey (the animal is shot at mid-body to emphasize the size of its penis). The subsequent shot displays an image of the man as he sits along the shores of a river, a rare glimpse of water in this generally dry territory. As pigs root in the earth behind him, he stares forlorn into the distance. One can infer that his frustration and sadness derive from being surrounded by sexual stimulus and even relative fertility in the plant world, yet lacking his own means of erotic release and creation.

The Galimberti interview noted above cites a loosely translated T.S. Eliot poem as explanation of the directors' work:

> Nascita, e copula, e morte
> Tutto è qui, tutto è qui, tutto è qui
> Nascita, e copula, e morte [17]

Birth, copulation, and death, this citation suggests, are the anchoring elements in the cinematic world of Ciprì and Maresco. Such a reading establishes the directors' films as a model of Freud's opposition of *eros* and *thanatos*, the drive towards life and that towards death.[18] The films outlined above do revolve around physicality and states of being, but the first category listed, *nascita,* is entirely absent in them, even as a notion. The men in Ciprì and Maresco's work cannot create new human life; thus they cannot experience birth. And while copulation is certainly on the minds of many of these men, sex exists for them primarily as a desire, an experience sought, rather than a reality. It is chiefly death, really, that persists without complication in these films, a state that takes the older members of the group and hovers as a spectre for all.

The first third of *Lo zio di Brooklyn,* for example, is visually dominated by death. Shortly after the film begins we see one of its primary characters, a man whose father has just choked to death on his dinner, walking through empty streets littered with mounds of indistinguishable trash. He moves diagonally across the bottom left of a frame filled with bold lines and various shades of grey: the grey of the road in front left, that of the sidewalk after it and the decrepit building beyond that, all stacked up against an increasingly dark sky. As he walks towards the bottom centre of the frame a man passes him in the opposite direction, moving upward on the other side of the division caused by pavement and shadow. This second man carries a coffin hoisted over one shoulder. The first gestures at him in disgust, then moves on, and a third man emerges behind the second, moving in the same direction and also shouldering a coffin. For a full beat, they are the only moving beings on the screen, indicating the direction in which this society heads, towards darkness and death. After a brief interlude featuring corpulent men stuffing their faces with animal parts, bellies jiggling in their boxers and briefs, the film returns once more to images of death, as a full five minutes are given to a wordless series of funeral processions. We see one procession run into another at a traffic intersection, then repeated images of a particular group running first in one direction behind a raised casket, then in another and back again. It is unclear whether the men are running away from death in these images, or towards it.

All of this generative and temporal limitation leads to the element of Ciprì and Maresco's work that has garnered the most notice, their characters' attention to the present state of their bodies. As represented in the three films here in question, such attention is faithful to that demonstrated in Ciprì and Maresco's early television shorts, grouped under the title *Cinico TV,* from which most of their protagonists originally hail. Filmed as always on the streets of a ghost-town Palermo, the shorts feature ragged-looking men who are often naked from the waist up or simply clothed in old white t-shirts and tattered briefs. At certain points they are interviewed by an off-camera voice. At others, they are free to simply and generally wordlessly carry on an action. They frequently and dramatically spit, fart, belch, and mime or truly engage in masturbation or other sexual acts. A prime example is the piece "Fagioli," much posted on the video-sharing site YouTube. Two shirtless men are filmed against a dirty exterior wall of a building, seated at a table. The larger of the two eats a bowl of beans and calmly, loudly, repeatedly passes gas while the other, a favoured actor/character by the name of Pietro Giordano, sits on in silence. It is comic in the basest of ways, absurd and at the same time dark in its suggestion that this is what society has been reduced to in terms, if you will, of communication.

For both their base goals and their brutish appearance, these men are often discussed in the extant criticism as odd others not belonging to mainstream society. Hampson refers to Ciprì and Maresco's characters as "freakish individuals," Fantuzzi sees them as examples of "il deforme, lo sgradevole, il ripugnante," and Scaffidi, summarizing public response, calls them "veri e propri rifiuti della società" in his work on the directors' "universo-immondezzaio."[19] Such descriptions require clarification. The characters in Ciprì and Maresco's work may be considered the garbage of some societies but it is inaccurate to call them the garbage of the society depicted in the film, for they comprise this society in its entirety. The use of the term *garbage* implies a value judgment directly tied to aesthetics. As big-bellied, abnormally large or abnormally small, occasionally disfigured and always unkempt men, these characters are classically "ugly" and thus assumed to be people of little value, garbage to be tossed out.

In presenting an entire populace as a group of people without normative value, however, the directors suggest an alternate scale of normalcy, while simultaneously offering a sharp social critique. If there is no one else to hold greater value, if there are no "beautiful" people like the kind we are used to seeing onscreen, these men are no longer garbage but models for their own sort of normal. Ciprì and Maresco thus reject the narrow beauty aesthetic promoted by mainstream film culture. At the same time, they offer a cannibalized reflection of contemporary Italian society. Their characters' focus on physical consumption reads as a base version of the contemporary Western obsession with another sort of consumption, that of material goods and natural resources. Such criticism is in line with statements the directors themselves make. Ciprì and Maresco are forthright in their negative judgment of Italian society, having declared, for example, "A volte ci dicono siete troppo pessimisti. Beh, guardiamoci attorno. Oggi solo un imbecille può dichiararsi ottimista," and "crediamo che [...] si siano perdute cose come il senso del pudore, della vergogna, della misura."[20] This second judgment is particularly interesting in light of a socially critical reading of their films; Ciprì and Maresco's characterization of actual Italian society is oddly similar to that applied by the media both to the directors' fictional characters, critiqued and banned for their excessive nature (beyond *misura*), and to themselves, chastised for their own lack of shame, *vergogna*. This invitation to a socially critical reading causes viewers to confront our acceptance of aesthetic and behavioural norms. At the same time, it establishes the films in question as a sort of warning, a representation of what may become of contemporary society should it lose a historically informed frame of reference. What results is an extreme and yet extremely basic society: fully homosocial, homogenous, intent only on immediate gratification, and thus without future.

Complementing the corporeal impossibility of future generation in Ciprì and Maresco's films is an environmental refusal of cultural past through means of spatio-historical identification. Such refusal is communicated in the films' absence of geographic markers or landmarks. To return to Husserl, the absence of landmarks negates the "intentionality of possible recollections," for landmarks function not just as spatial identifiers but also as historical indicators, referencing a certain era or marking the passing of time.[21] In this way they serve additionally as "time-marks": indicators of historical identification in both land and cityscape. Landmarks, particularly urban ones such as notable buildings or bridges and works of memorial, commemoration, or public art, carry with them a date of creation or association with a particular moment in a society's history. Whether overtly proclaiming or more subtly signalling this moment, they remind the viewer of where he or she stands in temporal relationship to it.

An example might be the eighteenth-century Villa Malfitana, an English manor in the centre of the real-life Palermo that is distinctly absent from Ciprì and Maresco's films. Through signage and architectural cues at the manor, viewers are made aware of past relationships of cultural exchange and international commerce. They are also made aware of the distance between that time and the present. The experience adds to their understanding of the city as an ever-transitional, multilayered space built on different eras and identities. In phenomenological terms, landmarks are visual cues to help shape viewers' horizons and direct their intentionality, conjuring a vast frame of reference. The men in *Lo zio di Brooklyn*, *Totò che visse due volte*, and *A memoria* lack such cues. Consequently, they are not brought into historical consciousness by the spaces they inhabit.

Their visual remove from any notion of a historically defined city is furthered by a strong presence of the nonhuman in both open and interior spaces. Be it in the guise of plants growing through walls or packs of animals roaming streets and meandering through buildings, the natural is omnipresent in these films. Ciprì and Maresco thus destabilize the very idea of discrete realms like *city* and *country* as they shift their protagonists' scale of visual, phenomenological referents. In establishing a uniform space of being, they surpass traditional depictions of oppositional forces, the city as contrasted with the country and culture with nature. This sort of contrast has historically been the case at least in part owing to different systems of organization and marking; nature marks time through cyclical stages of regrowth while culture or city do so through innovation and progress.

As a result, the natural is often coded as somehow pre-historical, existing outside of record. For this reason Kate Soper, for example, writes about nature as something to "get back to," a non-*time* rather than a non-place.[22] By breaking with these tendencies and bringing nature into their cityscapes, placing it centre-frame in fact, and avoiding temporally coded landmarks, Ciprì and Maresco turn away from cultural means of marking time. This is not to say that time goes unmarked in their filmic world (by means other than aging bodies, of course). Time is demonstrated visually and measured through the shifting of clouds and the growth cycles of plants. But this is a cyclical sort of time rather than a linear one, and Ciprì and Maresco's men seem unable to read its signals.

While mankind progresses towards extinction in the films of Ciprì and Maresco, unilaterally moving forward to a determinate end, the nonhuman world is active and regenerative, healthier than the men in its midst. In particular, the strong visual presence of native grasses, cropping up in organic formation and displaying a diversity of type, negates existing assessments of the directors' landscapes as barren and lifeless. Hampson, for example, writes of "wastelands," while so many others – the directors included – use the term *apocalypse*, indicating the world's end and, oftentimes, natural disaster.[23] An end of days does indeed seem imminent for the men in Ciprì and Maresco's work, yet this does not necessitate an end for the natural world. I cite grasses and shrubs, often minor players in the landscape, as evidence against the land's barrenness not only for their apparent diversity but also for the movement they embody. By directing their lens towards these humble plants the directors attribute dynamism to the land, contrasting movement and stillness in their frames.

This movement is particularly notable in repeated images of men, at times alone but often *en masse*, deposited in front of buildings or scattered along a small mound of earth in relative close-up. On occasion a single individual moves a limb or his torso with the same spirit as the spare but lively soundtrack. Generally speaking, however, the men stand still as trees, a form of plant life largely absent in this dry, southern terrain. The men make a striking portrait against the land, recalling a still-life painting. At the same time, their stance suggests a desire not unlike that felt by Vinci's protagonists: to be a part of this landscape, to root down into it so as not to move forward in their progression towards eventual distinction. The subtle dynamism of the natural environment in Ciprì and Maresco's work serves to underscore the absence of a similar vivacity in the male society inhabiting its space. In the men's yearning to join the land, they expose their desire to root solidly into a source of strength and permanence greater than their own.

A series of images from the midpoint of *A memoria* underscores the elements of contrast and desire in the relationship of man to land in all three films in question. The first image is a landscape shot at far remove, the same stretch of open space from the start of *Totò che visse due volte,* yet all the same tone and evenly dotted by sparse plants. The sky looms heavy overhead, and a man marches across the stillness, backed again by melancholy jazz. The moment is countered by a sense of futility, as he appears to be marching aimlessly, with no goal in sight. The camera then cuts to a much closer image of clouds moving boldly across the sky. It is a transition of sharp contrast, with time passing here in a way that it does not in the previous scene, underlining both temporal progression and the movement of the natural world. Once more, the camera cuts away, now to a still image of seven men spread across a gently sloped hillside. They are older, with hair thinning and paunches protruding beneath their undershirts. Two of the men are propped up by canes while the rest stand unaided and slumped over in one direction or another. They are motionless against the land, human landmarks in the absence of other forms of spatiotemporal commemoration. A figure in a dress enters the frame from bottom right, walking by and in between them all as a twisted image of the unpenetrable female. The sky hangs dark behind, the top two-thirds increasingly blurred out, an unclear meeting point between earth and air.

The men of Ciprì and Maresco's world are far from shameless brutes in this portrait; they do seek greater connection and meaning, but unable to see the horizon before them, they lack the proper tools to attain it. Neither further modifying the world in which they live nor losing themselves in nostalgia for what once was, Ciprì and Maresco's characters experience a natural landscape with a life all its own. This does not negate the directors' clear pessimism regarding contemporary Italian society. It does, however, argue for the agency of the modern Italian landscape, degraded though it may be, as well as the need to acknowledge that landscape's continual transition between the past that it was and the future that it will become.

Afterword

It is a rather somber choice to end this work with the films of Ciprì and Maresco, for the picture they paint is a gloomy one: human culture doomed due to having overlooked the nature in its midst. It is no wonder that the terms *apocalypse* and *post-apocalyptic* have often been applied to the realms of *Lo zio di Brooklyn, Totò che visse due volte,* and *A memoria,* discussed in chapter 6. *Apocalypse* is, after all, commonly interpreted to mean the end of the world. And yet the term possesses another meaning as well: "revelation" or "disclosure," often of something not realized before. This definition also has a place in the directors' films, as they explore and expose the dangers that may (or, indeed, may have already) come with historical and environmental shortsightedness. When read as an ecological model, their emphasis on the present moment engages the same approach cultivated by the other authors and filmmakers discussed here, if only from a different angle. It does so by considering a reality of indirect – but still committed – engagement with environment as both subject and object, by employing an "avuncular" or "intransitive" stewardship.[1] Through nonreproductive protagonists placed in a quietly productive landscape, Ciprì and Maresco – like Calvino, Pasolini, Celati, and Vinci – argue the need to turn our attention to the landscape at hand and recognize the value that it holds.

From the early novellas of Calvino to the more recent films of Ciprì and Maresco, the texts considered in this book map out a particular coming to terms. They confront the difficult acceptance of a modified Italian landscape and the profound, and profoundly messy, relationship it fosters between nature and culture. They contemplate the realities of dwelling in degraded, polluted, and potentially toxic environments, and they explore possibilities for adaptation to a continually evolving natural world. Advocating for nature's primacy of place in creative representations and the world at large, they model the effects of a coping based in acceptance of the *interstitial.*

The gap between two objects of concrete meaning, the space between tissues in the body, the break in content of a printed text, the pause in time. The interstice, that unaccounted-for in-between, is a modest realm. Neither flashy nor loud, it does not call out for attention but rather accepts the hand it is dealt. If we are not careful, we might just look past it entirely. To do so, however, would be to ignore a realm ripe with possibility. When it comes to interstitial landscapes – places like the unmarked earth just beyond a site of construction, the overgrown field behind an apartment complex, or the water's edge near an abandoned factory – that very modesty holds the key. Unassuming landscapes, such spaces provide gentle access to Italy's modern nature, just as they promote a clear-eyed approach. In their overt markings of both nature and culture they cause careful viewers to acknowledge histories of environmental change at the hand of humankind, and to appreciate and care for the land that remains. They encourage a particular sort of caretaking: the stewardship of something that we can neither create nor directly possess ourselves, but to which we may yet be deeply connected.

Notes

1. Introduction: Exploring the Interstice

1 Scarpa, *Batticuore fuorilegge*, 54. Trans.: Evaporating odour of grass / copses of trees on the horizon / two turbines / industrial drainpipes / two towers of silos / the trellises of light / metallic grasshoppers twenty metres high / with soft hooves / small rural Eiffel towers / the electric cables climb across the countryside / they have an itinerary all their own / they have to go on / they have to go on / it makes no sense to think that a giant will arrive and hang his laundry / across them (translation my own, as are all translations without source citations).

2 Jameson, *Postmodernism*, ix.

3 In the past decade anthropological critiques have distanced themselves from binary approaches to nature/culture, guided in large part by Phillipe Descola's 2005 assertion that "the opposition between nature and culture is not as universal as it is claimed to be" (Descola, *Beyond Nature and Culture*, xviii).

4 For Heidegger, "The basic character of dwelling is to spare, to preserve," proposing that humans are preserved, or made to feel safe through the act of dwelling, just as they "save the earth" through that same act (Heidegger, *Poetry, Language, Thought*, 148).

5 Glotfelty, *Ecocriticism Reader*, xix.

6 To date, most work in this vein has been published in the form of single journal articles. Notable exceptions include Barron and Re, *Italian Environmental Literature* (2003); the 2008 edition of *Annali d'Italianistica*, "Humanisms," ed. Lollini and Iovino, *Ecologia Letteraria* (2006). Iovino's work is particularly notable as it, along with Caterina Salabè's *Ecocritica* (2013), provides a much-needed book-length introduction of ecocriticism to Italian-speaking audiences.

7 For an excellent survey of the history of critical landscape studies, see Pagano's "Reclaiming Landscape," *Annali d'Italianistica* 29 (2011).
8 Quaini, *L'ombra del paesaggio*, 12. Trans.: I am in fact convinced that the landscape is not interesting as an analytic category by which to read the environment or territory in scientific terms, so much as it is as a container of myths, dreams, and emotions, an accumulator of metaphors to understand the contradictions and the problems of our time.
9 Schama, *Landscape and Memory*, 6–7, 10.
10 Ibid., 61.
11 Cited in Cohen, "Blues in the Green," p. 16.
12 Antonello, for example, negates the agency of nature entirely in defining landscape as "l'iscrizione dell'umano nel territorio, è la scrittura dell'uomo sull'insignificanza primordiale dell'evento naturale che diventa paesaggio in quanto riconquista semantica della tabula rasa dello stato di natura da parte di chi vi opera" (Antonello, "Paesaggi della mente," 118). Trans.: the inscription of the human in the territory, man's writing on the primordial insignificance of the natural event that becomes landscape as a semantic reconquering of the tabula rasa of the state of nature on the part of he who performs work upon it.
13 Foot, *Modern Italy*, 138.
14 Central Institute of Statistics, *Italian Statistical Abstract 1962*, 227, 228.
15 Ibid., 197.
16 Allum, "Italian Society Transformed," in *Italy since 1945*, 18.
17 A wealth of literature exists on the deeply rooted history of Italy's North/South divide. For an introduction see Gramsci on the "southern question," as well as previously cited works by Duggan, Foot, and Ginsborg.
18 Roberta Piscia et al. note: "Copper started to be recovered from the factory effluent at the end of fifties. The ammonium discharge, however, continued until 1980, when the Italian parliament passed a law regulating the discharge of industrial wastes into freshwaters. The response of the lake was rapid (Bonacina, 2001) and was further accelerated by a liming intervention in 1989–1990 (Calderoni et al., 1991)." "The invasion of Lake Orta (Italy) by the red swamp crayfish *Procambarus clarkii*: A new threat to an unstable environment," *Aquatic Invasions* S46.
19 Conversation with the author, July 2012. Trans.: gave a lot of work to the whole region.
20 Duggan, *Concise History of Italy*, 262.
21 See Forgacs and Lumley, eds., *Italian Cultural Studies*, 273–90.
22 See O. Calabrese, *Carosello o dell'educazione serale*, 1975.
23 Ginsborg, *History of Contemporary Italy*, 240.

24 Ibid., 243.

25 Cederna, *Brandelli d'Italia,* 174. Trans.: In the past thirty years we have witnessed the constant refusal or constant failure of every attempt at urban planning, the exclusive cult of the buildable lot and cadastral map, the indiscriminate deprivation of a good (the landscape, that is) considered, instead of collective patrimony or a resource by definition limited and non-restorable, a no man's land.

26 Tunesi, "Italian Environmental Policies," in McCarthy, *Italy since 1945,* 120. See also Bevilacqua, "The Distinctive Character of Italian Environmental History," in Armiero and Hall, *Nature and History in Modern Italy,* 15–32.

27 Ginsborg, *History of Contemporary Italy,* 234.

28 See Pilat, *Reconstructing Italy.*

29 Cederna, *Brandelli d'Italia,* 77–83. See also Achilli, Cutrera, and Redaelli, eds., "Urbanistica."

30 Tunesi, "Italian Environmental Policies," in McCarthy, *Italy since 1945,* 120.

31 Cederna, *Brandelli d'Italia,* 10.

32 Ginsborg, *History of Contemporary Italy,* 246.

33 Tunesi, "Italian Environmental Policies," in McCarthy, *Italy since 1945,* 119.

34 Ibid.

35 Vittorini, "Industria e letteratura," 99. Trans.: The signifiers of a reality depend on the infinite effects that are produced within it, starting with a certain cause. The peasant reality slowly took its signifiers from the great and mutable world of the effects set in motion by the cultivation of the soil. As for industrial reality, it is from the world of effects set in motion by the factories that it can take its own signifiers.

36 Toni Iermano writes: "Le sollecitazioni proposte sulle pagine del Menabò fin dagli esordi e l'incontro con le diverse posizioni della neoavanguardia ebbero da lì a poco significative conseguenze" (Iermano, "'Non ci sono più personaggi,'" 2). Trans.: The solicitations proposed on the pages of *Menabò* since the beginning, and the meeting of diverse positions of the neo-avant-garde had, from then on, few significant consequences. For more on this argument see Barilli, *La neoavanguardia italiana.*

37 See Benedetti, *Pasolini contro Calvino.* See also *Dialogo con Pasolini,* ed. Cadioli, for an exchange of essays between Calvino and Pasolini in 1965, and Burns, *Fragments of Impegno,* for a full discussion of political commitment in Calvino, Pasolini, and Vittorini.

38 Calvino, *Una pietra sopra,* 11. Trans.: The novel lives in the dimension of history [...] the true theme of a novel will have to be a definition of our time [...] it will have to be an image that explains to us our place in the world.

39 Calvino's fantastic trilogy, published as the volume *I Nostri antenati* (Our Ancestors) in 1960, includes the short novels *Il visconte dimezzato* (The

Cloven Viscount, 1952), *Il barrone rampante* (The Baron in the Trees, 1957), and *Il cavaliere inesistente* (The Non-existent Knight, 1959).

40 Pasolini, *Empirismo Eretico*, 37. Trans.: If the new Italian reality produces a new language, a national Italian, the only way to appropriate it and make it one's own is to know with absolute clarity and courage what the national reality that produces it is, and what this reality is like [...] never as much as today has literature requested such a scientific and rational way of knowing.

41 Legambiente, *Ambiente Italia*, 207.

42 All recent statistics from ibid.

43 Calvino, *La nuvola di smog*, 60. "'This park, this river,' I thought, 'can only be in the margin, a consolation to us for the rest; ancient beauty is powerless against new ugliness'" (Calvino, *Smog*, trans. Weaver, 123).

44 Calvino, *La formica argentina*, 123. "We reached home; the baby was sucking his toy. My wife sat down on a chair. I looked at the ant-infested field and hedges, and beyond them at the cloud of insect powder rising from Signor Reginaudo's garden; and to the right there was the shady silence of the captain's garden, with that continuous dripping of his victims. This was my new home. I took my wife and child and said: 'Let's go for a walk, let's go down to the sea'" (Calvino, *The Watcher and Other Stories*, 179).

45 Celati, *Verso la foce*, 134. Trans.: All at once sound the cries of pigeons, one calls and others respond. Words, too, are calls, they don't define anything, they call something so that it might stay with us. And what we can do is call things, invoke them so that they don't become so estranged as to take off, each on its own, to a different point in the cosmos, leaving us here incapable of recognizing a path by which to orient ourselves.

46 Longo, "Ciprì and Maresco," 189.

47 Buell, *Environmental Criticism*, 45.

2. Economic Expansion, Environmental Awareness in the Early Works of Italo Calvino

1 Calvino, "Natura e storia nel romanzo," cited in the English in Nocentini, *Italo Calvino*, 24. Trans.: An instinctive inclination has always pushed me toward the authors of yesterday and today in which the terms *nature* and *history* (one could also say *society*) appear together.

2 This is not to suggest that Calvino presents city and nature as harmonious but simply as nonexclusive. Martin McLaughlin argues that Calvino does try to reconcile the realms in his earliest work but ultimately fails, and he attributes the scant success of Calvino's early novel *I giovani del Po* largely

to the author's attempts to portray city and nature in harmony (McLaughlin, "Calvino's Visible Cities," 72).

3 Strong critical work has been done in the past decade on Calvino's engagement with the nonhuman, although not regarding the novellas addressed in this book. See Bolongaro, *Italo Calvino;* Iovino, "Wilderness of the Human Other," in Oppermann et al., *The Future of Ecocriticism;* Iovino, "Ecocriticism"; Rohman, "On Singularity"; Ross, "Calvino and Animals."

4 Woodhouse, "Racconti of Italo Calvino," 1970.

5 Along these lines Dana Renga notes, "Calvino's interest in creating male characters that are both narcissistic and controlling is representative of the limited and constricted social/political vision in 1950s Italy. Hence, the over-valuation of work, television, and production in Italy expresses a deficiency of genuine relationships between individuals" (Renga, "Looking Out," 380). The protagonists in the two novellas in question here are quite narcissistic. They constantly ponder their identities and are immersed in the world of work and production. Although unsuccessful in asserting any sort of control, they greatly admire other male characters who manage to do so.

6 Iovino, *Ecologia letteraria,* 21. Trans.: An instrument that may help the reader imagine a universe of more wide-ranging values, a moment of awareness.

7 Berg, *Envisioning Sustainability,* 82.

8 Heise, *Sense of Place,* 61.

9 Cited in Grossi, "50 anni fa," Web. Trans.: I believe that at the present moment a writer or man of opinion not directly involved in political activity can participate in democratic life more effectively outside of the party than in it. For more on the trajectory of Calvino's relationship with the PCI, see again Francese, *Cultura e politica,* 2000.

10 Cited in Nocentini, *Italo Calvino,* vii. Trans.: A sort of history of the Ligurian Riviera and of San Remo in particular.

11 Falcetto, *Romanzi e racconti,* 1318. Trans.: a secure definition of his own style, which makes an ever more decisive choice of the "indirect vision" strategy […] valid also for the problems of today.

12 Cited in Nocentini, *Italo Calvino,* vii. Trans.: useful to the completeness of the portrait.

13 Vera Zamagni writes of the years 1953–63: "This is a period obsessed with enlarging capacity. There was a scramble to produce and to conquer foreign markets and the results are truly amazing: steel production tripled automobiles increased ten times, oil refineries quadrupled their output, electricity doubled its output and many new products like refrigerators,

typewriters, plastic materials, motorbikes (the Vespa) were a great success in the domestic market and abroad" (Zamagni, "Evolution of the Economy," in McCarthy, *Italy since 1945*, 49).

14 Calvino, *La speculazione edilizia*, 85–6. Trans.: "The permanent colony of *** was made up of that so-called bourgeois class, inhabitants of handsome apartments in their own cities that, brick for brick, they reconstruct here (a bit smaller, of course, we are at the sea) in the same enormous residential neighborhoods marked by the same automobile-bound urban life."

15 Joseph Francese, who in 2000 calls *La speculazione edilizia* Calvino's masterpiece, notes that Quinto most resembles the sort of protagonist for whom Calvino fought in the debates surrounding Pratolini's *Metello*, a nuanced protagonist "a tutto tondo," capable of acting on diverse motivations and displaying inconsistencies of character (Francese, "Refashioning," 122).

16 Calvino, *Una pietra sopra*, 16. Trans.: Rebellion against one's nature, characteristic of the intellectual unable to integrate himself, is the sign of condemnation on the part of many who still believe themselves to be, who still wish to be, new men, renovators of history.

17 The term *alienation* is used here in accordance with Marx's writings on alienated labour. In *Economics*, he explains that alienated labour "makes the species-being of man, both nature and the intellectual faculties of his species, into a being that is alien to him, into a means for his individual existence. It alienates man from his own body, nature exterior to him, and his intellectual being, his human essence. [...] An immediate consequence of man's alienation from the product of his work, his vital activity and his species-being, is the alienation of man from man. When man is opposed to himself, it is another man that is opposed to him. What is valid for the relationship of man to his work, of the product of his work and himself, is also valid for the relationship of man to other men and of their labour and the objects of their labour" (Marx, "Alienated Labour," in McLellan, *Selected Writings*, 83). Although Quinto identifies as bourgeois, the above definition of *alienation*, based on a proletariat experience, is still applicable, as he is indeed a worker. Furthermore, as Marx explains, "The propertied class and the class of the proletariat present the same human self-alienation" ("Alienation and the Proletariat," ibid., 134).

18 Calvino, *La speculazione edilizia*, 40. "It depended on privilege in those days, certainly, yet it was still firmly rooted. Nowadays the intellectual belonged to neither the bourgeoisie nor the proletariat" (Calvino, *Real Estate*, 186). Notably, Quinto attributes what he sees as the impending collapse of culture to an upset in the codes of land ownership. For when he thinks that the intellectual bourgeoisie once had *radici solide*, solid roots, he is using

language quite literally, having observed just previously that there was once a time when only landowners could afford to be intellectuals.

19 Ibid., 25. "When he came home, he liked to walk in the countrified outskirts of the town or along the sea front, where he could still recapture the pulsations of the past, the marginal deposits which memory had preserved. But today he felt no nostalgia for a passing order" (Calvino, *Real Estate,* 178). Translator Carne-Ross veers from the original with the final sentence of this passage, as Calvino's text reads "in the city no, everything was ugly," when translated word for word.

20 Calvino, *La speculazione edilizia,* 3. "He raised his eyes from the book (he always read in the train) and rediscovered the landscape piece by piece. The wall, the fig tree, the quarry with its chain of buckets, the reeds, the cliffs – he had seen them all his life but only now, because he was returning, did he really become aware of them. Every time he came home to the Riviera, Quinto renewed contact in this fashion" (Calvino, *Real Estate,* 163). The original text refers explicitly to "his land, the Riviera," emphasizing Quinto's mixed sense of intimacy and ownership toward the land.

21 Calvino, *La speculazione edilizia,* 4–5. "A geometrical arrangement of parallelepipeds and polyhedrons ranked one above the other, corners and sides of house" (Calvino, Real Estate, 164).

22 Calvino, *La speculazione edilizia,* 6–7. "The thing stared him in the face. The district, his district, that amputated part of himself, had taken on a new life, abnormal and graceless perhaps, but for that very reason (such are the contradictions that operate in minds brought up on literature) it was more alive than ever before. And he was excluded" (Calvino, *Real Estate,* 166).

23 Calvino, *La speculazione edilizia,* 6–7. "Bound to the place by no more than a thread of nostalgia and by the devaluation of a semi-urban area with no claim to a view" (Calvino, *Real Estate,* 166).

24 Ibid., 6. "All the same, Quinto was offended by the spectacle of this landscape, his landscape, being overwhelmed by cement before he had ever really possessed it. Basically, though, he was historically minded, anti-nostalgia. He'd seen a bit of the world: hell, what did he care?" (Calvino, *Real Estate,* 165).

25 Calvino, *Saggi,* II, 2722–3; cited in Nocentini, *Italo Calvino and the Landscapes of Childhood,* 62–3.

26 Calvino confirms his negative operation with this work in the essay cited in note 25: "Finora sono riuscito a farlo solo ne La speculazione edilizia, dove un intelletuale costringe se stesso a entusiasmarsi di ciò che sommamente odia, la febbre di nuove costruzioni che sta mutando il volto alla Riviera" (ibid.). Trans.: Thus far I have only succeeded at doing so in *A Plunge into Real Estate,* in which an intellectual restricts himself to

enthusiasm only for that which he fully hates – the fever for construction that is mutating the face of the Riviera.

27 Cronon, *Uncommon Ground*, 20.

28 Calvino, *La speculazione edilizia*, 30. "As a result, Quinto found himself taking the man's side. He was being victimized, the whole city was out for his blood, all the stuffed shirts were against him, and yet the poor bricklaying peasant, armed with only his shy, uncouth nature, was standing up to them" (Calvino, *Real Estate*, 182).

29 Franco Ricci finds Caisotti to be a more powerful agent in the work, arguing that, "the unscrupulous Caisotti, sensing Quinto's ingenuousness, connives to profit from the project by swindling his client," and, "his exploitation of the hopelessly naïve Quinto receives the tacit approval of unscrupulous bureaucrats and lawyers whose own self-interests mirror the depth of society's fraudulent fabric" (Ricci, *Difficult Games*, 96). I largely agree but hold that Caisotti is in many ways as hopeless as Quinto, driven to profit in such a manner by his outsider status.

30 Calvino, *La speculazione edilizia*, 34. "His opponents were now his friends in the big cities in northern Italy, where he had lived all these years, years spent discussing the shape of the new society, the role of the workers and the intelligentsia. Caisotti has won, Quinto told himself" (Calvino, *Real Estate*, 182).

31 Calvino, *La speculazione edilizia*, 19–20. "A shark, or bull perhaps, a bull snorting through its nostrils [with a] fragile innocence" (Calvino, *Real Estate*, 174), literally, "infantile fragility," in the Italian; "as shark, outsize crustacean, crab" (Calvino, *Real Estate*, 174–5).

32 Calvino, *La speculazione edilizia*, 72, 98, 114. "Like a trapped animal who instinctively tries to escape but knows it's no longer any use" (Calvino, *Real Estate*, 207); "quite irresponsible[...] The bastard ..." (Calvino, *Real Estate*, 219); the adjective "savage," cutting in the Italian, has been left out of the English translation; "baffled animal" (Calvino, *Real Estate*, 230).

33 Calvino, *La speculazione edilizia*, 55. "He left home because he'd filled the whole valley with his bastards" (Calvino, *Real Estate*, 196).

34 Agamben, *Homo Sacer*, 105.

35 Ibid.

36 Calvino, *La speculazione edilizia*, 66.

37 Nocentini, *Italo Calvino and the Landscapes of Childhood*, 64.

38 See Plumwood, *Ecofeminism*, 1993; Alaimo, *Undomesticated Ground*, 2000.

39 Calvino, *La speculazione edilizia*, 6. "The Sampieris are adding another floor, there's a new house built by some people from Novara [...] just look at all the digging that's going on there now [...] Now come over to this side, Dear. They couldn't take away any more of our view to the west than

they've done already, but just look at that roof that's popped up over there. I tell you we have to wait half an hour longer every morning for the sun!" (Calvino, *Real Estate,*165).

40 Calvino, *La speculazione edilizia*, 11. "The need for a kitchen garden had gradually lessened [...] So Signora Anfossi had moved in with her flowers and turned it into a kind of clearinghouse, a nursery" (Calvino, *Real Estate,*169).

41 Ibid. "The soil had proved to be moist and exposed to the sun, hence particularly suited to certain rare plants, which, having been granted temporary accommodation there, proceeded to make themselves at home [...] The spot had acquired a mixed air, devoted at once to horticulture, science, and elegance." (Calvino, *Real Estate,* 169).

42 *Random House Webster's Dictionary,* 2005.

43 Pollan, *Second Nature,* 49.

44 Ibid., 194.

45 Ibid.

46 Calvino, *La speculazione edilizia*, 143. "The Signora was in the garden. The scent of honeysuckle was in the air, the nasturtiums were an almost too vivid splash of color. If she didn't raise her eyes to the ranked windows of the apartment buildings all around, the garden was still the garden" (Calvino, *Real Estate,* 249).

47 Calvino, *La speculazione edilizia*, 144. "The shutters were drawn and the room was half dark. They sat with bundles of papers on their knees, calculating once again how long it would be before their capital was amortized. The sun was sinking behind Caisotti's building and the light that filtered through the slats and played over the silver on the sideboard grew weaker and weaker. Now only the upper slats were bright, and slowly the light died, reflected on the polished surfaces of the trays and the teapots" (Calvino, *Real Estate,* 250).

48 Ricci, *Difficult Games*, 335.

49 Calvino, *La nuvola di smog*, v. Trans.: *Smog* is a story continually tempted to become something else: sociological essay or intimate diary, but Italo Calvino is always able to resist these temptations through his defensive tactic based on comic gags and shrugging of shoulders.

50 Calvino, *La nuvola di smog*, 5. "A new job, an unfamiliar city – had I been younger or had I expected more of life, these would have pleased and stimulated me; but not now, now I could only see the grayness" (Calvino, *Smog*, 79).

51 Calvino, *La nuvola di smog*, 21. "As far as I was concerned, I had no ideals, nor did I want to have any; I only wanted to write an article he would like, to keep my job, which was no better or worse than another, and to

continue my life, no better or worse than any other possible life" (Calvino, *Smog*, 92).

52 Calvino, *La nuvola di smog*, 54. "Cordà himself was the smog's master; it was he who blew it out constantly over the city, and the IPUAIC was a creature of the smog, born of the need to give those working to produce the smog some hope of a life that was not all smog, and yet, at the same time, to celebrate its power" (Calvino, *Smog*, 117).

53 Calvino, *La nuvola di smog*, 26. "Will we solve it? We are solving it" (Calvino, *Smog*, 96).

54 Calvino, *La nuvola di smog*, 25. "We are one of the cities where the problem of air pollution is most serious, but at the same time we are the city where most is being done to counteract the situation!" (Calvino, *Smog*, 95).

55 Laskin, "The Great London Smog," 2006.

56 Calvino, *La nuvola di smog*, 25; "rival cities here in our own country" (Calvino, *Smog*, 126).

57 Calvino, *La nuvola di smog*, 23. "The situation is serious, yes, more serious than your article would lead the reader to believe. Let's speak frankly: the danger of air pollution in the big cities is huge, we have the analyses, the situation is grave" (Calvino, *Smog*, 93).

58 Calvino, *La nuvola di smog*, 23. "And precisely because it is grave, we are here to solve it" (Calvino, *Smog*, 93).

59 Calvino, *La nuvola di smog*, 45. But she wasn't listening to me, she was attracted by something she had seen flying, a flight of birds; and I stayed there, looking for the first time, from outside, at the cloud that I inhabited and that inhabited me, and I knew that, in all the variegated world around me, this was the only thing that mattered to me" (Calvino, *Smog*, 139).

60 Calvino, *La nuvola di smog*, 44. "A sense of vastness had seized me [...] looking at the countless aspects of the landscape. [...] At this point I saw the thing" (Calvino, *Smog*, 138–9).

61 Bertone, *Lo sguardo escluso*, 25. Trans.: *Landscape* is only a modern, bourgeois, refined word, sprung up like a fountain long restrained in the dark organs of the earth.

62 Calvino, *La nuvola di smog*, 60. "Beauty has to be constantly invented" (Calvino, *Smog*,149).

63 Quaini, *L'ombra del paesaggio*, 12. Trans.: The landscape is not interesting as an analytic category by which to read the environment or territory in scientific terms; but it is as a container of myths, dreams, and emotions, as an accumulator of metaphors for understanding the contradictions and problems of our age.

64 Calvino, *La nuvola di smog*, 70. "But listen, dear sir, do you truly believe in this danger of radioactivity?" (Calvino, *Smog*, 156).
65 Calvino, *Una pietra sopra*, 41–2. Trans.: Revolutionary is the man who does not accept what is given as natural and historical and wants to change it. The surrender to objectivity, a historical phenomenon of this post-war era, is born in a period in which man's faith in directing the course of things is lessened, not because he is reduced by a burning defeat but, on the contrary, because he sees that things (the great politics of the two opposing systems of strength, the development of technology and the domination of natural forces) go forward on their own; they make up a structure so complex that the most heroic effort can be applied only to trying to understand how it's made, to comprehend it, to accept it.
66 Calvino, *La nuvola di smog*, 74. "You see so many things without paying attention to them; maybe these things you see have an effect on you but you aren't aware of it; and then you begin to connect one thing with the other and suddenly it all takes on meaning" (Calvino, *Smog*, 158).

3. Pier Paolo Pasolini: Boundaries and Mergers in (Ex)Urban Film

1 Steimatsky, Rhodes, Jewell, Naldini, Biondillo, and Gandy, all to be discussed here, beautifully address landscape and cityscape in Pasolini's films. There is still more work to do, however, on the relationship between the two.
2 Soper writes, "For if nature is conceptualized and valued, as it sometimes is in environmentalist philosophy, as that which is independent of human culture, then rather little of the environment corresponds to the concept: hardly anything we refer to as natural landscape is natural in this sense, and its supposed value might therefore be seen to be put into question" (*What Is Nature?* 152).
3 Lefebvre, *Landscape and Film*, xiii.
4 Soper, *What Is Nature?* 155–6.
5 Commenting on the director's tendency to overlap cultural references, Peter Bondanella cites the word *contaminated* as Pasolini's "favorite term" (Bondanella, *Italian Cinema*, 182). Noa Steimatsky notes that "contamination in Pasolini's film practice finds its primary moment in his first use of Bach's *Matthäus-Passion* over the scene of a pimp's fight in the dust in *Accattone*" (Steimatsky, *Italian Locations*, 125–6).
6 Antonioni's attention to landscape is certainly *a*, if not in fact, *the*, key element of his work and one deserving of study in its own right. In *Red Desert* we note perhaps the strongest presence of a landscape-protagonist correspondence, as Monica Vitti's troubled Giuliana is repeatedly drawn to the

foggiest scapes that Ravenna has to offer. And yet her relationship to the land is not exactly one of parallel identity, most noted in the fear that she expresses once fully surrounded by fog out in the marshes. Her character corresponds more to that of the mother in Pasolini's *Teorema* than that of an Ettore or Accattone, in that she is dominated by her neuroses. Furthermore, while he does visually expose the great pollution already undergone by the Po, Antonioni is not particularly concerned with environmental health. Instead, he explores the beauty to be found in the industrial, the beauty of the cityscape. Seymour Chatman cites the director as stating: "It's too simplistic to say – as many people have done – that I am condemning the inhuman industrial world which oppresses the individuals and leads them to neurosis. My intention [...] was to translate the poetry of the world, in which even factories can be beautiful. The line and curves of factories and their chimneys can be more beautiful than the outline of trees, which we are already too accustomed to seeing" (Chatman, *Michelangelo Antonioni,* 91).

7 Agamben, *Homo Sacer*, 9.

8 Anzaldúa, *Borderlands*, 1.

9 On the notion of *friction*, Anna Tsing notes: "A wheel turns because of its encounter with the surface of the road; spinning in the air it goes nowhere. As a metaphorical image, friction reminds us that heterogeneous and unequal encounters can lead to new arrangements of culture and power" (Tsing, *Friction*, 5).

10 David Ward deftly unravels Pasolini's conceptions of *cinema* and *film* in Rumble and Testa's anthology. He explains, "Whereas 'film' is the conventional artefact we see at movie theatres, 'cinema' for P means the reproduction of the entirety of the language of reality in 'written' but unedited form. [...] 'cinema' is an entirely hypothetical idea whose key element is an uninterrupted, infinite long take" (Ward, *A Poetics of Resistance*, 129).

11 Regarding juxtaposition, Pasolini frequently pairs contrasting cultural references in his films. Examples include the aforementioned scene of lounging pimps and hustlers set to a Bach score in *Accattone*, or in *Uccellacci e uccellini* the image of country boys doing synchronized dance moves to British-style pop music in front of a sign reading "Bar Las Vegas," amid open fields. Bondanella notes that such contrast "forces the viewer into an awareness of the loss sustained from industrial development and the acquisition of self-consciousness – for Pasolini, a bourgeois vice – and it underlines the mythical qualities of life abandoned by modern culture" (Bondanella, *Italian Cinema*, 181).

12 Trans.: "those proper to memories and dreams, which prefigure and offer themselves as the 'instrumental' premise of cinematographic

communication." Pasolini, "The Cinema of Poetry," trans. Luise Barnett and Ben Lawton, 171–2.

13 Giuliana Bruno briefly notes Pasolini's "potential contribution, complex and controversial as it may be, to feminist research" (Bruno, "Heresies," 36). His explorations of film semiotics make just such a contribution.

14 "The visual communication which is the basis of film language is, on the contrary, extremely crude, almost animal-like," and so, "concrete, never abstract." Pasolini, "The Cinema of Poetry," trans. Luise Barnett and Ben Lawton, 171–2.

15 Bruno, Atlas of Emotion, 31.

16 Though the city holds wealth, those that live beyond it struggle financially to keep up with changing ways of life.

17 Pilat, *Reconstructing Italy*, 5.

18 Ibid., 27.

19 Lefebvre, *Landscape and Film*, 29.

20 Pasolini, *Scritti corsari*, 129. Trans.: "In the early 1960s, due to the pollution of air and, particularly in the countryside, due to the pollution of water (the blue lakes and clear canals) the fireflies began to disappear. The phenomenon was instant and striking."

21 Kazama et al., "Characterization of Firefly Habitat," 2009.

22 Jusoh et al., "Firefly Distribution," 2010.

23 Pasolini, *Scritti corsari*, 130. Trans.: Something similar is happening in Italy, and with even greater violence as the industrialization of the 1970s constitutes a decisive "mutation" in regards to the German industrialization of fifty years ago.

24 Ibid. Trans.: a new epoch of human history, that human history with millenarian deadlines.

25 Ibid. Trans.: anyhow, as far as I am concerned (if that matters any to the reader) let's be clear: I would give all of Montedison, multinational corporation that it is, for one firefly.

26 Mariniello, "Toward a Materialist Linguistics," 160. Trans.: The guest, beautiful and silent, reader of Rimbaud, inserts himself with extreme naturalness in the life of the family and his relationship with the various characters it comprises is based not so much on words but on gestures, glances, on a complicity and an almost silent understanding.

27 Bart Testa notes: "Clearly, Emilia lives within a different law, a different selfhood, and without benefit of Pasolini's theory, before and after the encounter. When she loses herself, she alone finds herself, to be recognized by the villagers both as Emilia and as a saint. Pasolini leaves her enigma open, but it is also classical as an imitation, while he systematically nails

down the 'meaning' of the other characters, whose case histories form a predictable theoretical arc. He makes a point of this by cutting from key moments in Emilia's transformation to each of theirs – Emilia's tale hovers over almost all of the third segment – and suggests that, for her, the 'violence of Jesus actually has come in the form of the theoretical stranger. For Emilia, he is not the theoretical stranger, but God, although a sexual, and so a heretical (more precisely, a Gnostic) God" (Rumble and Testa, *Pier Paolo Pasolini,* 203).

28 Pasolini, *Pier Paolo Pasolini,* 51–3. Trans.: But amid the stubborn explosion of the/rock-crusher, which blindly dismembers, blindly/crumbles, blindly grabs,//as though, without direction,/a sudden human scream is born/ and periodically returns,//so crazed with pain it seems suddenly/human no longer and becomes once more/a dead screech. Then slowly it's/reborn in the violent light/among the blinded buildings, a new/steady scream that only someone dying,/in his last moment, could hurl/into this sun, which still cruelly shines,/though softened by touches of sea air....//The scream is the old excavator's,/tortured by months and years/of morning sweat – accompanied/by silent swarms of stone-/cutters; but it's also the freshly/convulsed earth's, or, within the narrower/limits of the modern horizon,/the whole neighborhood's.... It is the city's/plunged into the festive brilliance//– it is the world's. The crying is for/what ends and begins again – what was/grass and open space and has become//waxy white courtyards/enclosed within a resentful decorum;/what was almost an old fairground//. (Pasolini, *Pier Paolo Pasolini: Poems*, 26–7).

29 Pasolini, *Teorema*. Trans.: I did not come here to die but to cry. And mine are not tears of pain. No, they will be a spring, but not a spring of pain.

30 Colleen Ryan-Scheutz reads the bulldozer as the referent of "ciò" in this poem, rather than the earth: "The digger cries out against herself, or despite herself, for she is the agent of development or change whose actions 'silence' the unspoiled roots of humanity that lay beneath the surface of life" (Ryan-Scheutz, *Sex, the Self, and the Sacred*, 159).

31 Described by Zanoli as "l'interpretazione di un'opera d'arte scelta per ragione affettiva da personaggi famosi," (the interpretation of a work of art chose for sentimental reasons by famous people) "Io e ..." came after "Capolavori nascosti" (Hidden Masterpieces, 1968–9) and before "In difesa di ..." (In Defence of ..., 1974) (from Zanoli's notes housed at the Cineteca di Bologna).

32 Brunatto, *Io e ... Pasolini e la forma della città*. Trans.: They belong to another world, and so they have stylistic features that differ completely from those

of the ancient city of Orte, and the mixture of the two things is troubling, it's a discord, a disturbance of the form, the style.

33 Ibid. Trans.: Having chosen the form of the city as my argument, I'd like to clarify that the form of the city manifests itself, reveals itself, appears through its confrontation with a natural backdrop.

34 Ibid. Trans.: But there is always the problem of respecting the confrontation of the natural border between the form of the city and the surrounding countryside.

35 Ibid. Trans.: They disturb in particular the relationship between city and nature.

36 Ibid. Trans.: The form of the city of Orte appears as such because it is on the edge of this brown hill, devoured by autumn, with this fog in front and a grey sky behind.

37 Soper, *What Is Nature?* 15.

38 Gandy, "Heretical Landscape," 299.

39 From producer Dino De Laurentiis's collection, *Le streghe*. One of the director's less-studied films, it is, in its brevity, an extreme and bitterly comic example of the messages (the false idol of capitalist values), characters (the bourgeois father-son duo, angelic martyrs, and savvy whores), and, finally, landscapes (industrial, city centre, and most prominent, peripheral lumpen proletariat no man's land) found in Pasolini's earlier works. It is a short film, absurd in plot and even more so in visual effect. At times it feels like the story unfolds on a stage set, yet the domestic setting it features, a Dust Bowl–style shantytown, could well be the Testaccio housing complex where *Accattone* was filmed. Residences there are as basic as can be and seem to sprout willy-nilly from the dry earth, composing a visual hybrid of open space and future city structure. A tumbleweed would not be out of place. For more, see the introduction to Steimatsky's *Italian Locations*.

40 Farley and Roberts, *Edgelands*, 5.

41 Much has been made of Pasolini's passion for the mythical, the spiritual, the rites of eras past, and the ways of less technologically advanced cultures. These poles of attraction may be grouped as elements representing bare life, that which, according to Aristotle, is the "simple natural life [that] is excluded by the *polis* in the strict sense." In Aristotle's definition of "simple natural life," we are to imagine a life that is connected to the natural environment and based on relationships of survival and pleasure. Pasolini's attraction to bare life is expressed in his general fascination with the lower classes, as well as his emerging interest in developing nations, evident in projects such as *Appunti per un'Orestiade africana* (Notes towards an African Orestes, 1975).

42 While not subproletariat figures, the mythical Oedipus and Medea of *Edipo Re* (1967) and *Medea* (1969) are both embodiments of *omines sacri* in their connection to an older way of life, and their difficulty in adjusting to new social structures and doomed fate. We need only recall Medea's concern upon seeing her young groom tossing about hoops with a group of boys one day, a representation of both technological progress and the male peer structure of modern politics. Furthermore, in resembling the protagonists of *Accattone* and *Mamma Roma*, Epido and Medea posthumously lend a mythic, timeless quality to these modern subjects.

43 Agamben argues that *homo sacer* is an intrinsic part of the political structure, as his existence is required to affirm the identity of he who is sovereign in a relationship of reciprocity and opposition. The Latin *sacer* means both sacred and damned, and this paradoxical position is firmly supported by Agamben's reading of the sacred man, a figure outside of both divine and human law. Following the tradition of Rodolphe Jhering, the Italian philosopher also places the figure of the bandit, as understood by Germanic and Scandinavian tradition, alongside the Roman *homo sacer*. The bandit, as he explains, is the wrongdoer who may legally be killed or considered already dead. Agamben's blending of the bandit figure with that of *homo sacer* is particularly suited to the outsider status of Pasolini's characters, such as Accattone and Ettore of *Mamma Roma*. These men are never able to enter into the legally recognized market economy and, again like the bandit, face predestined death.

44 Pasolini confirms Accattone's sacredness in this scene, as well as his vulnerability, by filming him from below, bare-chested and open-faced with nothing behind but clear blue sky and a striking statue of angels bearing the cross. A sense that he has one foot already in the grave only persists in the scenes to follow. This is seen when Accattone suddenly slumps into another man's lap at a bar one afternoon; then again when, held in a room at the local prison as a suspect in Maddalena's beating, he cannot endure the experience of confinement and the processes of the legal system, acting out in animalistic frenzy and crying both "*Io voglio morire*" and "*ma io son pure malato*"; and, finally, in the repeated suggestions that Accattone is literally starving.

45 The struggling hustler Accattone must embrace legal work as a day labourer within Rome's urban limits if he is to move forward and survive in Italy's still emerging post-war economy. Yet he appears nearly dead after unsuccessfully attempting to do so one day toward the end of the film, physically and ideologically unable to exist within the modern urban structure.

4. Observation and Acknowledgment in Gianni Celati's *Verso la foce*

1 All of these identities, in their own way, have aided in his being recognized as one of Italy's most important contemporary scribes, yet notice of Celati was relatively slow to reach the shores of American academia. A significant contribution came in the form of Rebecca West's *Gianni Celati: The Craft of Everyday Storytelling* (2000), the first full-length study on the author in English. Celati's work has, furthermore, been translated fairly extensively, particularly in German and English.

2 *Narratori delle pianure* holds a place of importance as Celati's first published text after *Lunario del paradiso;* its tone does reflect that of Celati's texts from the 1980s on. It does not actually represent his first written work after *Lunario del paradiso*, however, as much of *Verso la foce* was written in 1984.

3 On Celati as storyteller see West, cited above, as well as Cannon, "On the Path of Gianni Celati"; Lausten, "L'abbandono del soggetto"; Lumley, "Gianni Celati"; and more.

4 Moroni, "Il paradigma dell'osservazione," 308.

5 Lorenzini, "Tecniche di 'divagazione,'" 119. For more on Celati's work on photography and his long-standing collaboration with Luigi Ghirri, see Marco Sirroni's *Geografie del narrare.*

6 Walter Pedullà also reads a strong overtone of death in *Verso la foce*: "Il libro ha un così intenso odore e sapore di morte" (trans.: the book has such a strong smell and taste of death). Paradoxically, Pedullà calls the work the mark of Celati's "second birth" as a writer. Borsellino and Pedullà, *Letteratura Italiana del Novecento*, 365).

7 Spunta, "Lo spazio delle pianure," 11. Trans.: A renewed feeling of marvel for simple things.

8 Celati, *Verso la foce*, 97. Trans.: We are never estranged from any part of what happens around us, and when we are alone, even less so. The body is an organ to immerse in the outside world, like stone, lichen, leaf.

9 West, *Everyday Storytelling*, 24–5. The quote comes from her discussion of Baratto, a character in Celati's 1987 work *Quattro novelle sulle apparenze.* Taking a cue from Melville's "Bartleby, the Scrivener," Baratto decides one day to stop participating in "the ceremony of linguistic exchange," as it seems to get in the way of thinking. Notably, one of the first clear thoughts he has on the day that he stops speaking is "*C'è del fumo in questo paesaggio,*" there's smoke in this landscape (Celati, *Quattro novelle sulle apparenze*, 11). Like Celati himself in *Verso la foce*, Baratto is grounded through observation.

10 Celati, *Verso la foce*, 115. Trans.: We are eager to observe when we have a desire to show others what we see. It's the connection with others that colors the things we see, which otherwise seem dull.
11 Ibid., 54. Trans.: Against the sky on a riverbank poppies moved by the wind, and a sky so dark, so heavy. Empty fields. All this makes me want to write, as though the words followed something outside of myself.
12 Spunta, "Lo spazio delle pianure," 18. Trans.: bears witness to the most acute attempt to liberate oneself from a narrative structure conceptualized at the writing desk and to make the moments of perception, observation, and reflection coincide with that of writing.
13 As defined in the *Zingarelli minore*.
14 The text reads in the Italian: "un viaggio pieno di incertezze," Celati, *Verso la foce*, 10. Trans.: A voyage full of uncertainties.
15 Since 1966, Celati has translated works by Swift, Céline, London, Melville, Stendahl, and others.
16 Barron, "Gianni Celati's Poetic Prose," 326.
17 Celati, *Verso la foce*, 63, 100. Trans.: Undulating hills with plots of grain, lettuce, cabbage, medicinal herbs. There's big, open space in this terrain, big but not overwhelming thanks to the undulations; [...] if I could, I would go and look at them one by one, those canals, so fabulous do they seem.
18 Ibid., 110. Trans.: A field totally full of garbage, plastic bags, bottles, cans, pieces of thrown out furniture; a huge expanse of trash, with hundreds of pigeons overhead, flying like they're crazed.
19 See Jarman, *Modern Nature*.
20 Ibid., 76. Trans.: An old city now completely invaded by nature.
21 Ibid., 37. Trans.: All of a sudden a cloud of pollen arrived from all of the little poplar trees, drivers had to turn on their windshield wipers and all of the advertising banners became invisible for ten seconds.
22 Ibid. Trans.: Ten seconds of opaque masses, where everything had already gone away, even this image of the word that we carry in our eyes had disappeared. [...] The blackout effect on the images of advertisement was pleasing.
23 Ibid., 95. Trans.: If you have the sensation of understanding everything, the desire to observe passes.
24 Adam, *Timescapes of Modernity*, 82.
25 As cited by L. Buell, "Environmental Memory."
26 Yablokov, Nesterenko, and Nesterenko note: "There were several radioactive plumes, but the main Chernobyl fallout cloud passed over northern Italy on May 5, 1986. [Ninety-seven per cent] of the total deposition in Italy occurred between April 30 and May 7" ("Chernobyl,"12).
27 F. Buell, *From Apocalypse to Way of Life*, 91.

28 Bird and Little, "Contaminated Forests," 2013.

29 Yablokov, Nesterenko, and Nesterenko, "Chernobyl," 232.

30 Celati, *Verso la foce*, 14. Trans.: Thoughts from these days, about which I want to write: news about the Chernobyl explosion, arrival of the atomic cloud, and other rumblings.

31 Ibid., 15. Trans.: Back in the Maremma, in Capalbio, just as the atomic cloud was arriving and the TV transmitted the first security measures recommended by the experts: It was forbidden to sell leafy greens and no fresh milk for children. In the shops of Capalbio Scalo there's an atmosphere reminiscent of wartime; people speak of security measures, clients stay there nervously repeating lines from the newspapers, and in the meantime the price of canned vegetables, condensed milk, frozen food, potatoes and non-leafy vegetables, even the price of bottled water, waver according to the news on the street.

32 Beck, *Ecological Enlightenment*, 64.

33 Celati, *Verso la foce*, 15. Trans.: and in the meantime prices fluctuate according to the news broadcast.

34 Adam, *Timescapes of Modernity*, 10.

35 Celati, *Verso la foce*, 34. Trans.: But won't it be dangerous now even to eat bread?

36 Ibid., 29. Trans.: That cow that shit on you [i.e., what bad luck], the Caribbean and Chernobyl ….

37 Ibid., 38. Trans.: Look, if you're not good I'll give you contaminated milk, eh?

38 Ibid., 45. Trans.: Trans.: MAY A RADIOACTIVE ACCIDENT BEFALL WHOEVER STEALS MY FLOWERS!

39 Ibid., 16. Trans.: Journalistic news and comments in pre-formed sentences, no different from the sports pages.

40 Ibid., 28. Trans.: surprised (while) writing.

41 Ibid. Trans.: […] but when they asked me if I write for a newspaper and I right away said yes, lying heavily, I became normal again in their eyes. As I was a journalist, they offered me a ride in their truck.

42 West argues that "there is more continuity over time among Celati's superficially diverse writing projects than might first seem to be the case" (West, *Everyday Storytelling*, 24). She links, in particular, the comic element of the "absurd" search for meaning in Celati's later work to his more overtly comic texts, such as *Le avventure di Guizzardi.*

43 Celati, *Verso la foce*, 32. Trans.: strong opinion-movement.

44 Ibid., 48–9. Trans.: No one can say what the effect will be of these radioactive substances fallen down from the sky, on the grass, the trees, the animals and people; no one can say that it couldn't happen again someday,

here on our land or elsewhere; no one can really think that the nuclear reactors will one day be closed, to shelter us from all the uncertainties and dangers that will come. And yet each one of those experts would never stop showing a sure understanding of what had happened, and of what is still to come.

45 Ibid., 49. Trans.: only uncertainty for what will come.

46 Celati calls this "la dimenticanza che dovunque ci avvolge e ci porta," the forgetfulness that everywhere envelops and takes us (ibid.).

47 Adam, *Timescapes of Modernity,* 11.

48 Celati, *Verso la foce,* 46–7. Trans.: A sea of invasive plants like I had never seen; stemmed plants with one fat leaf, low and swollen, jutting out of them, with a very glossy, shining surface so green it seemed fake. And those plants seemed fake, for their excessive sheen, the leaf's profile like that of an inflated waterlily: like a rather monstrous plastic substance that has assumed, who knows how, a form of nature, indistinguishable from nature.

49 Adam, *Timescapes of Modernity,* 19.

50 Celati, *Verso la foce,* 72. Trans.: full of bubbles and trash.

51 Ibid., 68. Trans.: All of this announces areas of major wealth. There's even a fatty odor in the air that comes from some industry and lasts for a number of kilometres.

52 Ibid. Trans.: In the distance three chimneys sprout up […] against an almost black sky. The chimneys are part of the Revere power plant on the other side of the river, one of many along the Po […] that teem with bubbles and froth. Seen from here, the Po is a vast black current covered in garbage and oily stains and sponge-like bubbles.

53 F. Buell, *From Apocalypse to Way of Life,* 76.

54 Celati, *Verso la foce,* 71. Trans.: He speaks with a calm tone about the pollution of the river and the fish caught there; he says that for him that river hasn't been the same since the sturgeon disappeared (an effect of industrial dumping).

55 Ibid., 116. Trans.: Speaking in that language of big words that explain everything, it becomes difficult every now and then to remember we're here.

56 Iovino, *Ecologia letteraria,* 55. Trans.: […] reintroduces the idea of sharing common space and that of reciprocal responsibilities, according to the principles of participatory democracy.

57 Ibid., 55–6. Trans.: Preserving and recovering the shared environment, it's as though society preserves and recovers itself as a democratic structure.

58 Celati, *Verso la foce,* 9. Trans.: More than the pollution of the Po, the sick trees, the industrial stink, the state of abandon of everything that doesn't have to do with profit or the construction of cookie-cutter domiciles without

homeland or destination – more than all of this, what is surprising is this new generation of countryside in which one breathes an air of urban solitude.

59 Ibid., 71. Trans.: The things they speak about make me feel like a stranger, a tourist.

60 Ibid., 36. Trans.: A declaration of war against the outside world that sneaks too close a look at private property.

61 Ibid., 74. Trans.: Out in the world appearances always come forth differently to form moments, and moments are what beings gather themselves up in, like those so-called "mongoloids" out strolling along the bank. [...] The Sunday back and forth of cars and scooters toward the bridge is a thing so apathetic as to make you forget the moments, a mechanical trend of lost souls looking to save themselves, heading out in their cars on the asphalt along the grassy coast.

62 Ibid. Trans.: nonclinical atmosphere, thanks to the proximity of the river.

63 Ibid., 134. Trans.: All of a sudden pigeon calls ring out; one calls, and others respond. Words, too, are calls, they don't define anything, they call out to something so that it might stay with us. And all that we can do is call things, invoke them so that they might come to us with their stories. *Chiamare* is an interesting choice of verb here, as it means both to call to someone or something, and to call someone or something by a name.

64 Tsing, *Friction*, 168.

65 Ibid., 158.

66 Celati, *Verso la foce*, 138.

5. Simona Vinci's Provincial Dwellings, Natural Beings

1 Heidegger, *Poetry, Language, Thought*, 143–59.

2 Spirn, *The Language of Landscape*, 16.

3 See Lucamante, ed., *Italian Pulp Fiction*; Pezzarossa, *C'era una volta il pulp*; or entries in encyclopedic works such as those by Borsellino and Pedullà, eds., *Letteratura italiana del Novecento*.

4 Pierpaolo Antonello would have us note, however, that the term is also connected to the magazine *Cannibale*, founded in 1977. Antonello, in fact, suggests that we "assume cannibalism as a sort of name brand of the historical avant-garde" (Antonello, *Italian Pulp Fiction*, 39).

5 This text marked the first publication for many of the eleven voices included and served as the first in a line of books featuring splatter-style narratives. As occurs with so many movements labelled as such by others, most of the authors associated shied away from group identification at the

time. With the passing years, the majority have moved on to new styles and genres. Already in 2004 Aldo Nove discussed the *cannibali* as part of a long-lost era: "Quanto ai Cannibali, dico che furono una cosa bellissima" (Polese, "Aldo Nove." Trans.: As far as the *cannibali*, I say that they were a beautiful thing). Riddled with the imprint of a consumer-obsessed and mass media-filtered contemporary culture, the texts that *cannibale* authors produced were often graphically violent, sexually explicit, and intentionally exploitative of a twentieth-century obsession with consumerism and a television-driven cult of fame and celebrity. Their formal structures displayed either an apparent lack of concern for established literary and social codes or an intentional destabilizing or dismantling of canonical texts and their forms. Authors such as Niccolò Ammaniti, Aldo Nove, Andrea Pinketts, Tiziano Scarpa, and, to a lesser extent, Vinci, Isabella Santacroce, and Silvia Ballestra, among others, were linked to the group.

6 Hayles asserts, "The posthuman view thinks of the body as the original prosthesis we all learn to manipulate, so that extending or replacing the body with other prostheses becomes a continuation of a process that began when we were born" (Hayles, *How We Became Posthuman,* 3). Donna Haraway, in turn, has written extensively on the cyborg as a variation of the post-human: "By the late twentieth century, our time, a mythic time, we are all chimeras, therorized and fabricated hybrids of machine and organism; in short, we are cyborgs" (Haraway, *Simians, Cyborgs, and Women*, 150). My suggestion that Vinci's ecological sensibility is rooted in a Kristevan reading of the semiotic goes against Haraway's assertion that the cyborg "slips the step of original unity, of identification with nature in the Western sense" (ibid.,151). I do, however, hold that the world of which Vinci writes reflects Haraway's cyborg-world, in which "nature and culture are reworked; the one can no longer be the resource for appropriation or incorporation by the other" (ibid.).

7 Tabanelli, "Il post-umano (femmineo) di Simona Vinci," 379.

8 See again *Encyclopedia of Italian Studies*, Lucamante's texts previously cited, and the articles from the *Corriere della Sera* in the bibliography in this book.

9 Pomilio, "Le Narrative Generazionali," 674. Trans.: A language of terse, unapparent literary quality (to the point of risking a certain hyper-lyricism) and always substantiated by the mimicry of spoken language.

10 La Porta, "Simona Vinci," 66.

11 At the time of this writing Vinci has penned four novels, one collection of short stories, two children's books, two novellas, a travel memoir, and numerous short stories for anthologies.

12 La Porta, "Simona Vinci," 65.

13 Cesari, "Dopo i cannibali." Trans.: inventing a language skinned down to the essential and yet mysteriously full of vibrations, ready for trials of more extended narration.

14 Pezzarossa, *C'era una volta il pulp,* 11. This is a term often used in describing Vinci's work. Grazia Menechella, for example, writes "I corpi descritti da Vinci sono motivati e ossessionati da pulsioni fisiologiche" (Menechella, "I corpi 'a pezzi' di Simona Vinci," 135). Trans.: The bodies described by Vinci are motivated by and obsessed with physiological drives.

15 Jarman, *Modern Nature,* 7.

16 Ibid., 8.

17 *Dei bambini non si sa niente* and the story "Agosto nero" are discussed at greater length here than the other works mentioned for multiple reasons, not least of which is the question of space. These texts provide a representative portrait of Vinci's earlier works in terms of format, for she easily alternates between short and long works, as well as narrative voice, which is even, steady, and often, but not always, in the first person; they are the two pieces in which a shared knowledge of body and land is most explicit; and, ultimately, they lead most directly into Vinci's most environmentally focused work. Her other works are strung through with considerations of landscape and spaces of free expression: *Brother and Sister* features a group of siblings spending their last night together in a dark wood before facing a morning reality, while *Come prima delle madri* is rife with mysterious characters likened to animals or possessing "una bellezza che aveva a che fare con la terra, con la solidità degli alberi" and features many a safe forest hiding place. (Vinci, *Come prima delle madri,* 198). Trans.: a beauty that had to do with the earth, with the solidity of the trees.

18 Vinci, *Dei bambini,* 174. "The perfume of the fields and the song of the crickets around us" (Vinci, *In Every Sense Like Love,* 134).

19 Ibid. "There are plants growing inside, not just moss, but grass and flowers, even full-size trees, tall and strong after all these years" (ibid.).

20 Vinci, "Agosto nero," 12. "I would like to take my little girl […] and plant her somewhere in the middle of the Maremma […] I'm sure nothing would happen to her. She'd stay there as still as a rock, become a part of the nature. A stone, a dead tree trunk, a clump of red earth, fertile and mute. Maybe she'd put down roots. She'd turn into a tree, a thick bush" (Vinci, *In Every Sense,* 4–5).

21 Ibid., 15. "And what if the sea took her?" (Vinci, *In Every Sense,* 7).

22 Ibid., 16. "Her body would float among the fish, dissolve in the pure water, become a single pale worm, a tadpole, something like the beginning of life" (ibid.).

23 Vinci, *Incubatoio* 16:1. Trans.: Forget the obsession with a world in the form of words and return to the original: the form, that which is there, evident, to everyone.
24 Kristeva, *Revolution in Poetic Language*, 28.
25 Kristeva's and, I believe, Vinci's, use of the death drive corresponds to the work of Melanie Klein. In her work titled simply *Melanie Klein*, Kristeva suggests: "Under the effects of the death drive, the psyche expresses a fear for life. For the sake of life, it affords itself a way to respond to the fear of annihilation of life, and its most fundamental mechanisms are nothing more than defenses against any such annihilation" (Kristeva, *Melanie Klein*, 83). The death drive in Kristeva's formulation and *in Dei bambini* is a pre-emptive defense mechanism, reacting against the perceived threat of harm due to social existence.
26 Vinci, "Agosto nero," 11–12. "Some days I get tired of it all" (Vinci, *In Every Sense*, 4).
27 Ibid., 9. "She was wearing a short dress, rolled up over her massive tanned thighs. Her lap seemed soft and strong. I would have liked to run to her and bury my head in it, feel the warmth of her skin, let her smell wash over me – a clean and healthy smell, but a little sour and salty from the heat" (Vinci, *In Every Sense*, 2).
28 "My half-hearted life" (ibid, 3); "dirty, unkempt, run-down [things]" (ibid, 2).
29 Ibid., 12; "part of the nature. A stone, a dead tree trunk" (Vinci, *In Every Sense*, 5).
30 Ibid., 9. "My daughter always does the things I want to do" (Vinci, *In Every Sense*, 3).
31 Mabey, *Nature Cure*, 12.
32 Klein, *Love, Hate and Reparation*, 108.
33 Alaimo, *Undomesticated Ground*, 2.
34 Vinci "La più piccola cosa," 6; Trans.: bodies have more answers than we do, they know the land better, because it is from there that they come to to there that they return.
35 An emphasis on the body's memory potential surfaces in many Vinci texts. Menechella comments: "Il concetto che il corpo ha più memoria della mente e dell'anima viena affermato più di una volta in diversi racconti in *In tutti i sensi come l'amore*" ("I corpi 'a pezzi,'"135). Trans.: The concept that the body has more memory than the mind or spirit is confirmed more than once in various stories in *In tutti i sensi come l'amore*.
36 Vinci, *Dei bambini*, 47. "This thing between them, this thing that was about them – together. No outsiders looking in" (Vinci, *In Every Sense*, 46). Left

out of Proctor's translation of the passage above is the adjective *diversa*, different, found in the original. A literal translation reads "this different thing between them."

37 Cited in Fiori, "I critici alla battaglia dei cannibali," *Corriere della Sera*; Ferroni, "Perversioni infantili in salsa pulp," *Corriere della Sera.*Trans.: active inquietude; very vulgar pornographic banality.

38 Vinci, *Dei bambini*, 15. "The fields were full of vibrations. The wind whistled right through the middle, leaving exotic patterns" (Vinci, *In Every Sense*, 15).

39 Ibid., 29. "Escape into the middle of the fields, go inside, and disappear."

40 Ibid., 11, 30, 154. "Straight ahead for five minutes through the fields, then keep going straight ahead, along the ditch, through the nettles, the purple and yellow flowers, the insects, down into the ditch with the frogs. Keep going straight, to the end" (Proctor, 11); "Keep going straight, into the ditch with the frogs and crickets. Through the middle of the nettles, the yellow and purple flowers. All the way to the end" (31); "Keep going straight on for five minutes, into the fields and then continue on. Follow the ditch for another five minutes, through the mud and nettles" (149).

41 Trans.: There is no distinction between human beings and landscape, I am convinced that WE are the places we inhabit, just as we shape (often we disfigure) and modify them, they shape and modify us (personal email correspondence with the author, 13 August 2012).

42 Vinci, *Dei bambini*, 144. "The violent, hard current held them tightly, vibrating through them. All the lightness of the game had exploded into a messy, frenetic rage" (Vinci, *In Every Sense*, 130).

43 Ibid., 164. "Curled up, all alone there inside its mother's body. Suspended in a hot and silent place, far from voices, far from pain. Maybe Greta was like that now too, suspended in a nowhere place, the soft earth on her skin, in her eyes, her ears, her mouth. Soft, cool dirt and the underground movement of crickets, cicadas, worms. A silent population making a passage and nourishment of her body" (Vinci, *In Every Sense Like Love*, 152).

44 Ibid. "She was just like a fetus. She was going back to before, before Greta, before life."

45 Kristeva, *Revolution in Poetic Language*, 71.

46 Seminal texts previously cited include the works of Bill Cronon, Bill McKibben, Serenella Iovino, Michael Pollan, Ursula Heise, Lawrence and Frederick Buell.

47 Cederna, *Brandelli d'Italia*, 10.

48 Eagleton, *Literary Theory*, 164–5.

49 In the summer of 2012 it was also devastated by a series of earthquakes. For more from Vinci on housing practices in Emilia-Romagna, see *Rovina* (2007).

50 Massarutto, "Agriculture," 6.

51 Vinci, *Strada Provinciale Tre*, 6. Trans.: an immense, unconfined space, that at one time must have been nothing but kilometres and kilometres of flat, green land, at certain points covered with woods and glens – uncultivated, vibrant land. […] Now the abandoned factories dot the plains with their stilled chimneys, their barbed wire covered in rust.

52 Ibid., 10. Trans.: curled up in the weeds of a ditch, among the nettles, the insects, the garbage tossed by passing drivers.

53 Ibid., 90. Trans.: A gust of wind hit her in the face, an odor of chemical fertilizer and disintegrating rubber.

54 Ibid. Trans.: She began again to walk, without stopping, without turning back to look at the place she was leaving. She walked into the field, straight toward the light of a farmhouse in the distance, and then swerved and began once more to follow a line parallel to the road.

55 Ibid.,153. Trans.: There is no trace anywhere of your true life, the one that counts.

56 Ibid.,107. Trans.: process of decomposition.

57 Ibid., 222. Trans.: She began as a child, quietly drawing houses, walls, doors, windows, and continued on, her whole life spent and paid designing Hell […] that whole immense necropolis of the future […] invading the land.

58 Rozelle, *Ecosublime*, 1.

59 Ibid., 167. Trans.: I had just learned about the babies and I didn't want to tell anyone, not even the father. Just to enjoy this feeling of being alone, them and me. Of being the only one in the world who knew what was happening to me, at least for a few days. I wanted to be in a perfect circle, in silence, listening.

60 Vinci, *Strada Provinciale Tre*, 45. Trans.: No one is embarrassed anymore to be ignorant, rude, mean. […] None of these things cause embarrassment. Just being poor. Poverty is the worst thing that could happen to you. Now she understood. Not before. Before, she was just like all the others.

61 Vinci's narrative focus continues to hone in on the landscape of Emilia-Romagna, particularly in terms of architectural development. *Rovina*, mentioned above, is a novella commissioned by the VerdeNero campaign of Legambiente and detailing the failure of housing development crafted without respect for the law, land, or area residents. A similar theme is

treated in the short story "Suino pesante padano," included in the collection *Il gusto del delitto* (2008).

62 Vinci, *Rovina*, 117. Trans.: I walk along the county highway, one day after the other, one month after the other, in the middle of a mutating countryside so hard to name [...] the land eviscerated, open like a wound.

63 Vinci, "Anima e luoghi e storie." Trans.: hundreds of snapshots, some taken from a moving car, others from the edge of a highway blocked by trucks, construction site upon construction site, cranes, hangars, houses, cultivated fields [...] those small figures, seized by chance or intentionally, that still walk, in spite of everything, that cross through these places and live them.

64 Vinci, *Strada Provinciale Tre*, 61.

65 Ibid., 104. Trans.: There's no need to say anything, no explanation, direction, or comment. Ancient and simple acts. [...] They could seem like a mother/son, a bizzare mystic figure in reverse since it is he who enacts the gestures of a mother and she who receives them, like a son.

66 Ibid.,131, 101. Trans.: A vegetable odour, like freshly cut grass; an uninhabited, alien landscape, an ancient world, a world before the world.

67 Twenty years after the event Keith Braverstock and Dillwyn Williams report in *Environmental Health Perspectives* (2006): "There is no previous experience of an accident such as this, and the long-term risks cannot be predicted with any certainty either in the heavily exposed areas or in the much wider areas with low-level exposures. Certainly there is a clear indication that there is a risk for low dose and low dose rate exposure [...] but there are also large uncertainties regarding its magnitude. [...] Without these studies, society will not be able to assess the future risks associated with nuclear accidents, judge what precautions need to be taken, or plan the proper provision for health care" (Braverstock and Williams, "The Chernobyl Accident," 1315).

68 Nixon, *Environmentalism of the Poor*, 49.

69 Vinci, *Strada Provinciale Tre*, 131. Trans.: He'd heard that the plants – the trees, the shrubs, the wild flowers – had grown into the houses, everywhere, and that branches jut out of the windows and open doors of the houses. That the animals had reproduced freely [...] and he thinks that it must be a marvelous place.

70 Ibid., 6. Trans.: The road is a large road that cuts through a destroyed countryside. A precise, geometrical destruction.

71 Ibid., 219; 8. Trans.: the immense field, the spikes as far as the eye can see and the web of power lines like sutures on a dead body; [...] cuts in two a piece of the plain [...] it is a deadly road that cuts through little

centres – big, medium, minuscule, towns, fractions of town – and devastates them, suffocates them, mutes them.

72 Ibid., 39. Trans.: military pants dirty with mud, a white t-shirt, muddy and damp with sweat clinging to his slender chest, his backpack tossed over one shoulder, calloused hands covered in cuts and scars.

73 Tsing, *Friction*, 5.

74 Ibid., 30. Trans.: Every now and then she lifts her gaze to see that dead land on both sides of the road. The streetlights, the net of high tension wires that marks it like sutures on a body, like scars, horrible to see, of course, but necesarry.

75 Ibid., 18. Trans.: in a hostile place inside her head the names of things she sees.

76 Ibid., 23. Trans.: She doesn't remember anything. Then it comes back. All of the sudden she remembers everything. These words that hit her in the head: root, link, rope, cord that tugs, stone around the neck that is sinking; to break away, to come undone, to melt, to escape. She watches them pass by, sliding in and out of her head. She listens to them and tries to understand if the tide comes from inside, or from outside.

77 Ibid., 122. Trans.: Uttered words always seemed exhausting to her, even when she was a child […] sometimes, in her bed, before falling asleep, she thought about what her life would have been like if she were a deaf-mute, and she pictured it as a life of perfect beatitude. She would have been like a clam laid gently on the shore; she would have perceived only the fluctuations of the world.

78 Ibid. Trans.: Maybe, she thinks now, it is impossible to stop talking entirely. At a certain point, words jump out of your mouth before you even realize it, like magic coins in a fairytale. The only thing to do is spit them out and share them, if you don't want to suffocate.

79 A few days into her walking journey Vera spies a solidly built older woman sitting outside of a building along the SP3 and longs for the comfort that might come from proximity to this woman's physicality. We read: "Vorrebbe sedersi su quel gradino insieme a lei e posarle la testa contro una spalla, percepire il fresco asciutto della sua pelle grinzosa e maculata, aspirarne l'aroma – che sarebbe certamente di lavanda e limone – e restare anche lei lì immobile, gli occhi socchiusi nella luce del tramonto, a osservare i frutti viola, rossi e verdi, lucidi, globosi che pendono verso terra come seni gonfi di latte." Through the contact of skin and the inhalation of its odor, Vera imagines she would feel calm, grounded, and nurtured. The older woman's physically maternal function and, notably, her connection in this role to the natural world, are rendered explicit. Vera's imagined

physical connection to the woman's body thus reads as a desire for return to the first stages of life, in which an infant depends on the mother's breast for sustenance. In emphasizing immobility in this brief fantasy, Vera momentarily seeks to negate the inevitable passing of time. She also negates her primary mission – endless forward movement along the SP3. It is a self-aware negation, however, and a brief one, for just as she engages in her fantasy she also recognizes its limitations. We read how "questo pensiero arriva, si construisce. È un'immagine, una storia, una possibilità. Poi perde forza, si sfibra. La realtà tornano ad essere i suoi piedi massacrati nelle Superga disfatte. Il sudore colloso che la avvolge come una membrana." Vera is able in this instance to draw a clear line between image and reality, between what may be desired and what is, in fact, real. She could go lay her head on the older woman's shoulder, but the chances of that woman welcoming such an action are slim and the moment would be fleeting regardless. What Vera knows instead to be certain is the current state of her body conditioned by her daily walking regimen, her tired feet, and sweat-soaked skin. She thus simultaneously desires the grounding of a maternal body and recognizes its impossibility, turning instead to the physical environment.

80 De Certeau, *Everyday Life*, 100.

81 Ibid., 101.

82 Spirn, *The Language of Landscape*, 26.

83 Ibid., 25.

6. Daniele Ciprì and Franco Maresco: On Horizons and the Human

1 Nino Scaffidi, for example, describes the landscape in Ciprì and Maresco's films as "un paesaggio disastrato, composto da ruderi, rifiuti, scheletri industriali, da una natura scarna e almeno altretanto mostruosa e selvaggia dei personaggi che la abitano," stating further, "la città di Palermo, la sua infinita periferia degradata è il non-luogo arcaico nel quale si svolge il drama eterno dell'aiezione" (web). Trans.: a ravaged landscape made up of ruins, refuse, industrial skeletons, and of a nature that is bare and at least as monstrous and savage as the people who inhabit it. The city of Palermo, its infinite degraded periphery is the archaic non-place in which the eternal drama of alienation unfolds. Scaffaldi's use of 'non-place' is representative of the majority of Ciprì and Maresco criticism, while his reading of monstrosity and alienation in this landscape is an attitude I seek to challenge here.

2 Manin, "Ciprì e Maresco," 33. The criticism I refer to is largely cited in this analysis. See, among others, Hampson, "Daniele Ciprì and Franco

Mareso"; Longo, "Films of Ciprì and Maresco"; and Morreale, *Ciprì e Maresco*.

3 The mafia subplot does, more than any other narrative element, serve to tie the film together. It also suggests a particularly southern Italian, and in fact Sicilian, culture not to be overlooked in Ciprì and Maresco's dreamscapes, one involving myth, rite, and a don-centred patriarchy. Thus, while the landscape betrays no visual identifiers, the film's narrative is directly tied to Sicilian culture. For more on mafia in Ciprì and Maresco, see Hampson, "Mocking the Mafia."

4 Longo cites Pasolini's *Uccellacci e uccellini*, instead, as "the principal model for Ciprì and Maresco's city-text" (Longo, "Films of Ciprì and Maresco," 189).

5 Religious narratives surface through enactments of crucifixion, a last supper, and the resurrection of a messiah figure, while devotional artwork is evident in the visual staging of these events. Fantuzzi observes that, just as in Pasolini's self-conscious film *La ricotta* (1962), the images of a Christ figure in *Lo zio di Brooklyn*, both in the film's initial plucking of the eyeball and later images of crucifixion, reference the work of fifteenth-century painter Antonella da Messina. It is important to note here that da Messina was, like Ciprì and Maresco, a Sicilian artist. For as much as the directors criticize Sicilian culture they are also deeply faithful to it.

6 Longo, "Il commiato funebre," 21. Trans.: More than in *Lo zio di Brooklyn*, *Totò che visse due volte* distances itself from the actual city. The Palermo of *Totò che visse due volte* serves as a metaphor; a metaphor for the end of the Western world.

7 Gadamer, *Truth and Method*, 269.

8 Ibid.

9 Ibid., 273.

10 Author and playwright Dacia Maraini summarizes this sentiment well, explaining: "When you compare today's life, the current way of living or the current culture, with what existed in the past, you learn a lot of things. If you don't have something to compare with today, you can't understand. You can't understand today if you don't have yesterday, no? And you can't project the future, tomorrow, if you don't know today and yesterday" (Seger, "Interview with Dacia Maraini," 30).

11 Exemplifying the depth of the directors' referential abilities, Ernest Hampson notes that the eye sequence in *Lo zio di Brooklyn* actually recalls not only Buñuel's work but also Pier Paolo Pasolini's *The Gospel According to Matthew*, as well as the notion of the film camera's "eye," and the "'cine-eye' movement of Dziga Vertov," the Soviet documentarian (Hampson, "Daniele Ciprì and Franco Mareso," 139). It is also in dialogue with

Bakhtin's discussion of the grotesque, which states: "The eyes have no part in these comic images; they express an individual, so to speak, self-sufficient human life, which is not essential to the grotesque" (Bakhtin, *Rabelais and His World*, 316). Following this line of thought, images of eye removal (*A memoria* and *Lo zio di Brooklyn*) and what looks like the eating of cow's eyes (*Totò che visse due volte*) become active negations of self-sufficient life.

12 Morreale, *L'invensione della nostalgia*, 237; Michelone, "Noi e il Jazz ovvero," 19.

13 Husserl, *Cartesian Meditations*, 44.

14 Longo, "Films of Ciprì and Maresco," 190.

15 Kristeva, *Intimate Revolt*, 260.

16 Ibid.

17 Cited in Galimberti, "Caso Censura: Lo sguardo eccessivo" (DVD booklet).

18 Defined by Freud as "the urge of living matter to return to a lifeless state" (Freud, *Beyond the Pleasure Principle*, 137).

19 Hampson, "Mocking the Mafia," 90; Fantuzzi, "Ciprì e Maresco," 10; Scaffidi, "Brutti, sporchi e cattivi."

20 Ciprì and Maresco, "Ciprì & Maresco contro tutti," 19.

21 Husserl, *Cartesian Meditations*, 44.

22 Soper, *What Is Nature?* 181–7.

23 Hampson, "Daniele Ciprì and Franco Maresco," 138.

Afterword

1 Sarah Ensor defines this as a "slanted or oblique relationship to the linear" (Ensor, "Spinster Ecology," 416).

Bibliography

Accattone. Dir. Pier Paolo Pasolini. Arco Films. 1961.

Achilli, M., A. Cutrera, and G. Redaelli, eds. "Urbanistica: Vertenza aperta. I soggetti, i tempi, i modi della riforma." In *Quaderni Socialisti*. Vol. 1. Florence: Arti grafiche So. Po. Al., 1970.

Adam, Barbara. *Timescapes of Modernity: The Environment and Invisible Hazards*. New York: Routledge, 1998.

Agamben, Giorgio. *Homo Sacer: Sovereign Power and Bare Life*. Daniel Heller-Roazen, trans. Stanford: Stanford University Press, 1998.

Alaimo, Stacy. *Undomesticated Ground: Recasting Nature as Feminist Space*. Ithaca: Cornell University Press, 2000.

Allum, Percy. "Italian Society Transformed." In Patrick McCarthy, ed., *Italy since 1945*, 10–41. New York: Oxford University Press, 2000.

A memoria. Dir. Daniele Ciprì and Franco Maresco. Cinico Video and Tea Nova. 1996.

Antonello, Pierpaolo. "Paesaggi della mente: Su Italo Calvino." *Forum Italicum* 32:1 (Spring 1998): 108–31.

Anzaldua, Gloria. *Borderlands/La Frontera: The New Mestiza*. San Francisco: Aunt Lute Press, 1987.

Armiero, Marco, and Marcus Hall, eds. *Nature and History in Modern Italy*. Athens: Ohio University Press, 2010.

Augé, Marc. *Non-places: Introduction to an Anthropology of Supermodernity*. London: Verso, 1995.

Bakhtin, Mikhail. *Rabelais and His World*. Helene Iswolsky, trans. Bloomington, IN: Indiana University Press, 1984.

Baracchi, Claudio. "Looking at the Sky: On Nature and Contemplation." *Annali d'italianistica* 26 (2008): 319–32.

Barbalato, Beatrice. *Sul palco c'è l'autore*. Leuven, Belgium: Presses Universitaires de Louvain, 2006.

Barilli, Renato. *La neoavanguardia italiana: Dalla nascita del "Verri" alla fine di Quindici*. Bologna: Il Mulino, 1995.

–. "I racconti di Calvino." *Mulino* 8:4 (1959): 160–6.

Barilli, Renato, Nanni Balestrini et al., eds. *Narrative Invaders: Narratori di Ricercare 1993–1999*. Turin: Testo & Imagine, 2000.

Barron, Patrick. "Gianni Celati's Poetic Prose: Physical, Marginal, Spatial." *Italica* 84:2–3 (Summer–Autumn 2007): 323–44.

–, and Anna Re, eds. *Italian Environmental Literature: An Anthology*. New York: Italica, 2003.

–. "Gianni Celati's *Verso la foce*: 'An Intense Observation of the World.'" *Forum Italicum* 39:2 (Fall 2005): 481–97.

Battaglia, Salvatore. "I racconti di Italo Calvino tra realtà e favola." *Filologia e Letteratura* 17 (1971): 514–25.

Beck, Ulrich. *Ecological Enlightenment: Essays on the Politics of the Risk Society*. Mark Ritter, trans. Atlantic Highlands, NJ: Humanities Press International, 1995.

Belpoliti, Marco. *Storie del visibile: Lettura di Italo Calvino*. Rimini: Luisè Editore, 1990.

Benedetti, Carla. *Pasolini contro Calvino: Per una lettura impura*. Turin: Bollati Boringhieri, 1998.

Bennet, Michael, and David Teague. *The Nature of Cities: Ecocriticism and Urban Environments*. Tucson: University of Arizona Press, 1999.

Berg, Peter. *Envisioning Sustainability*. San Francisco: Subculture Books, 2009.

Bertone, Giorgio. *Lo sguardo escluso: L'idea di paesaggio nella letteratura occidentale*. Novara: Interlinea, 1999.

Biondillo, Gianni. *Pasolini: Il corpo della città*. Milan: Edizioni Unicopli, 2001.

Bird, Winifred, and Jane Braxton Little. "Contaminated Forests: Management after Chernobyl and Fukushima." *Bulletin of the Atomic Scientists*, 1 August 2013. Web: 12 November 2013.

Bolongaro, Eugenio. *Italo Calvino and the Compass of Literature*. Toronto: University of Toronto Press, 2003.

Bondanella, Peter. *Italian Cinema: From Neorealism to the Present*. 3rd ed. London: Continuum, 2001.

Borsellino, Nino, and Walter Pedullà, eds. *Letteratura italiana del Novecento*. Milan: Rizzoli, 2000.

Boselli, Mario. "Apparenze e caducità." *Nuova Corrente: Rivista di Letteratura* 41:114 (July–December 1994): 253–65.

–. "Pensare-immaginare." *Nuova Corrente: Rivista di Letteratura* 42:115 (January–June 1995): 19–26.

Bottiglieri, Nicola. *I luoghi di Calvino: Guida alla lettura di Italo Calvino*. Cassino: Università degli Studi di Cassino, 2001.

Brandolini, Alessio. "Intervista a Simona Vinci." Gialloweb. Rome, 23 February 2001. Web: 7 December 2009. http://www.gialloweb.net/interviste/vinci.asp

Braverstock, Keith, and Dillwyn Williams. "The Chernobyl Accident 20 Years On: An Assessment of the Health Consequences and the International Response." *Environmental Health Perspectives* 114:9 (September 2006): 1312–17.

Bruno, Giuliana. *Atlas of Emotion: Journeys in Art, Architecture, and Film*. New York: Verso, 2002.

–. "Heresies: The Body of Pasolini's Semiotics." *Cinema Journal* 30:3 (Spring 1991): 29–42.

Buell, Frederick. *From Apocalypse to Way of Life: Environmental Crisis in the American Century*. New York: Routledge, 2003.

Buell, Lawrence. *The Future of Environmental Criticism*. Hoboken, NJ: Blackwell Manifestos, 2005.

–. "Uses and Abuses of Environmental Memory." Madison: University of Wisconsin. Presentation. 15 April 2009.

Burns, Jennifer. *Fragments of Impegno: Interpretations of Commitment in Contemporary Italian Narraitive, 1980–2000*. Leeds: Northern Universities Press, 2001.

Cadioli, Alberto, ed. *Dialogo con Pasolini: Scritti, 1957–1984*. Rome: L'Unità, 1985.

Calabrese, Giuseppe Conti. *Pasolini e il Sacro*. Milan: Jaca Book, 1994.

Calabrese, O. *Carosello o dell'educazione serale*. Florence: Cooperativa Libraria Universitaria, 1975.

Calvino, Italo. *Difficult Loves; Smog; A Plunge into Real Estate*. William Weaver and D.S. Carne-Ross, trans. 1970. Reprint. London: Vintage Classics, 1999.

–. *Gli amori difficili*. Turin: Einaudi, 1970.

–. *Il barone rampante*. Turin: Einaudi, 1957.

–. *Il cavaliere inesistente*. Turin: Einaudi, 1959.

–. *Il visconte dimezzato*. Turin: Einaudi, 1952.

–. *I nostri antenati*. Turin: Einaudi, 1960.

–. *I racconti*. Turin: Einaudi, 1958.

–. *La nuvola di smog & La formica argentina*. 1965. Reprint. Milan: Mondadori, 1996.

–. *La speculazione edilizia*. 1957. Reprint. Milan: Mondadori, 2002.

–. *Marcovaldo*. Turin: Einaudi, 1963.

–. *Romanzi e racconti*. Claudio Milanini, Mario Barenghi, and Bruno Falcetto, eds. Vol. 3: *Meridiani*. Milan: Mondadori, 1994.

–. *The Watcher and Other Stories*. William Weaver and Archibald Colquhoun, trans. Orlando, FL: Harcourt Brace, 1971.

–. *Una pietra sopra: Discorsi di letteratura e società*. Turin: Einaudi, 1980.

Canclini, Nestor Garcia, ed. *Hybrid Cultures: Strategies for Entering and Leaving Modernity*. Minneapolis: University of Minnesota Press, 2005.

Cannon, JoAnn. "On the Path of Gianni Celati: A Reading of *Narratori delle pianure*." *Rivista di Studi Italiani* 19:2 (December 2001): 62–72.

Canova, Gianni. "Conversazioni in Sicilia: I 'documentary.' " In Stefano Curti and Enrico Ghezzi, eds., *Kind of Cinico: Daniele Ciprì e Franco Maresco*, 9–14. RaroVideo, no. 55. Rome: Minerva Pictures Group Srl., April 2005.

Casarino, Cesare. "Oedipus Exploded: Pasolini and the Myth of Modernization." *October* 59 (Winter 1992): 27–47.

Cederna, Antonio. *Brandelli d'Italia: Come distruggere il bel paese*. Rome: Newton Compton, 1991.

–. *I vandali in casa*. 2nd ed. Bari: Laterza, 2007.

Celati, Gianni. *Cinema naturale*. Milan: Feltrinelli, 2001.

–. *Comiche*. Turin: Einaudi, 1971.

–. *Finzioni occidental*: Fabulazione, comicità e scrittura. Turin: Einaudi, 1975.

–. *Le avventure di Guizzardi*. Turin: Einaudi, 1973.

–. *Lunario del paradiso*. Turin: Einaudi, 1978.

–. *Narratori delle pianure*. Milan: Feltrinelli, 1985.

–. *Quattro novelle sulle apparenze*. Milan: Feltrinelli, 1987.

–. *Verso la foce*. 1989. Reprint. Milan: Feltrinelli, 2002.

Central Institute of Statistics. *Italian Statistical Abstract 1962*. Rome: Istituto Poligrafico dello Stato, 1963.

Cesari, Severino. "Dopo i cannibali." *Carmilla on line*. 4 June 2003. Web. 8 December 2009. http://www.carmillaonline.com/2003/06/04/dopo-i-cannibali/

Chatman, Seymour. *Michelangelo Antonioni: The Investigation*. London: Taschen, 2004.

Chierici, Anna Maria. "Spazio emozionale: Celati e Hillman." *Rivista di Studi Italiani* 22:2 (December 2007): 164–72.

Ciora, Pippo. "Adriati-città: Notes on a Post-industrial Landscape." In Robert Lumley and John Foot, eds., *Italian Cityscapes: Culture and Urban Change in Contemporary Italy*, 199–203. Chicago: University of Chicago Press, 2004.

Ciprì, Daniele, and Franco Maresco. "Ciprì & Maresco contro tutti." *Il Porto ritrovato*. Web: 6 September 2010. http://www.ilportoritrovato.net/html/cipr%C3%AC.html

Clifford, James. *Routes: Travel and Translation in the Late Twentieth Century*. Cambridge: Harvard University Press, 1997.

Cohen, Michael P. "Blues in the Green: Ecocriticism under Critique." *Environmental History* 9:1 (January 2004): 9–36.

Come inguaiammo il cinema italiano. Dir. Daniele Ciprì and Franco Maresco. Cinico Cinema, Istituto Luce, and Lucky Red. 2004.

Confalonieri, Luca Badini. "Calvino e il racconto." In Giorgio Bàrberi Squarotti, ed., *Metamorfosi della novella*, 413–27. Foggia: Bastogi, 1985.

Cronon, William, ed. *Uncommon Ground: Rethinking the Human Place in Nature*. New York: W.W. Norton, 1995.

Curti, Stefano, and Enrico Ghezzi, eds. *Kind of Cinico: Daniele Ciprì e Franco Maresco*. RaroVideo, no. 55. Rome: Minerva Pictures Group Srl., April 2005.

–. *Totò che visse due volte: Daniele Ciprì e Franco Maresco*. 1998. RaroVideo. Rome: Minerva Pictures Group Srl., 2005.

De Certeau, Michel. *The Practice of Everyday Life*. Steven Rendall, trans. 1984. Reprint. Berkeley: University of California Press, 2011.

De Lauretis, Teresa. "Language, Representation, Practice: Re-reading Pasolini's Essays on Cinema." *Italian Quarterly* 82/83 (Fall 1980–Winter 1981): 159–66.

Descola, Philippe. *Beyond Nature and Culture*. Janet Lloyd and Marshall Sahlins, trans. Chicago: University of Chicago Press, 2013.

De Vivo, Alberto. *Il tempo: Ordine e durata nei Racconti di Italo Calvino*. Abano Terme: Piovan, 1990.

Duggan, Christopher. *A Concise History of Italy*. New York: Cambridge University Press, 1994.

Eagleton, Terry. *Literary Theory*. 2nd ed. Minneapolis: University of Minnesota Press, 1996.

Ensor, Sarah. "Spinster Ecology: Rachel Carson, Sarah Orne Jewett, and Nonreproductive Futurity." *American Literature*, 84:2 (2012): 409–35.

Fabbro, Elena, ed. *Il Mito Greco Nell'Opera di Pasolini*. Udine: Forum Editrice, 2002.

Fantuzzi, Virgilio. "Il De Profundis di Ciprì e Maresco." In Stefano Curti and Enrico Ghezzi, eds., *Kind of Cinico: Daniele Ciprì e Franco Maresco*. RaroVideo, no. 55. Rome: Minerva Pictures Group, Srl., 2005.

Farley, Paul, and Michael Symmons Roberts. *Edgelands: Journeys into England's True Wilderness*. London: Random House, 2011.

Ferroni, Giulio. "Perversioni infantili in salsa pulp." *Corriere della Sera*. 6 October 1997. Page 27. Web: 9 December 2009. http://archiviostorico.corriere.it/1997/ottobre/06/Perversioni_infantili_salsa_pulp_co_0_9710062578.shtml

Fiori, Cinzia. "I critici alla battaglia dei cannibali." *Corriere della Sera*. 14 October 1997. Page 33. Web: 9 December 2009. http://archiviostorico.corriere.it/1997/ottobre/14/critici_alla_battaglia_dei_cannibali_co_0_971014615.shtml

–. "'Scandalosa' Vinci accolta negli Usa." *Corriere della Sera*. 28 December 1997. Page 30. Web: 9 December 2009. http://archiviostorico.corriere.it/1997/dicembre/28/Scandalosa_Vinci_accolta_negli_Usa_co_0_971228 13788.shtml

Foot, John. *Modern Italy*. New York: Palgrave Macmillan, 2003.

Forgacs, David. "Film Culture in Rome." *Film Quarterly* 61:3 (Spring 2008): 40–7.

Forgacs, David, and Robert Lumley, eds. *Italian Cultural Studies: An Introduction*. New York: Oxford University Press, 1996.

Fornara, Bruno. "Uomini e zii tra terra e cielo." *Cineforum* 372:2 (March 1998): 3–6.

Francese, Joseph. *Cultura e politica negli anni cinquanta: Salinari, Pasolini, Calvino*. Rome: Lithos Editrice, 2000.

–. "The Refashioning of Calvino's Public Self-Image in the 1950s and Early 1960s." *The Italianist* 27:1 (2007): 125–50.

Francioso, Monica. "Impegno and Alì Babà: Celati, Calvino, and the Debate on Literature in the 1970s." *Italian Studies* 64:1 (Spring 2009): 105–19.

Freud, Sigmund. *Beyond the Pleasure Principle*. Todd Dufresne, ed. Gregory C. Richter, trans. Peterborough, ON: Broadview Press, 2011.

Gadamer, Hans-Georg. *Truth and Method*. Sheed and Ward Ltd., trans. 2nd ed. New York: Seaberry Press, 1975.

Galimberti, Massimo. "Caso Censura: Lo sguardo eccessivo." In Curti, Stefano, and Enrico Ghezzi, eds. *Totò che visse due volte: Daniele Ciprì e Franco Maresco*. 1998. RaroVideo. Rome: Minerva Pictures Group Srl., 2005.

Gandy, Mathhew. "The Heretical Landscape of the Body: Pier Paolo Pasolini and the Scopic Regime of European Cinema." *Environment and Planning D: Society and Space* 14:3 (1996): 293–310.

Gérard, Fabien. "Una passione per le immagini." In Peter Kuon, ed., *Corpi/Körper*, 35–62. Frankfurt: Peter Lang GmbH, 2001.

Ghezzi, Enrico. "Illuminati a futura Memoria dell'oscurità." In Stefano Curti and Enrico Ghezzi, eds., *Kind of Cinico: Daniele Ciprì e Franco Maresco*, 3–4. RaroVideo, no. 55. Rome: Minerva Pictures Group Srl., April 2005.

Ginsborg, Paul. *A History of Contemporary Italy: Society and Politics, 1943–1988*. New York: Palgrave Macmillan, 2003.

Girardello, M. et al. "Identifying Important Areas for Butterfly Conservation in Italy." *Animal Conservation* 12 (2009): 20–28.

Glotfelty, Cheryll, and Harold Fromm, eds. *The Ecocriticism Reader: Landmarks in Literary Ecology*. Athens: University of Georgia Press, 1996.

Goldmann, Silvana Tamiozzo. "Palinsesti contemporanei (storie senza fine o fine delle storie?): Le narrazioni di Celati, Vassalli e Scabia." *Testo: Studi di Teoria e Storia della Letteratura e della Critica* 25:48 (July–December 2004): 93–107.

Goodall, Mark. "Mondo Roma: Images of Italy in the Shockumentary Tradition?" In Richard Wrigley, ed., *Cinematic Rome*, 97–107. Leicester: Troubadour, 2008.

Gordon, Robert S.C. *Pasolini: Forms of Subjectivity*. Oxford: Clarendon Press, 1996.

Greene, Naomi. *Pier Paolo Pasolini: Cinema as Heresy*. Princeton: Princeton University Press, 1990.

Grazzini, Giovanni. "Lettura dei Racconti di Calvino." *Letterature Moderne* 9 (1959): 621–37.

Grossi, Alessia. "50 anni fa: Su *l'Unità* l'addio di Calvino al PCI." *Sito Comunista*. Web: 6 January 2009. http://www.sitocomunista.it/pci/documenti/calvino_1957.html

Hampson, Ernest. "Mocking the Mafia: Ciprì and Maresco's Sicilian Apocalypse." In Wendy Everett, ed., *The Seeing Century: Film, Vision, Identity*, 88–97. Atlanta: Editions Rodopi, B.V., 2000.

–. "Daniele Ciprì and Franco Maresco: Uncompromising Visions – Aesthetics of the Apocalypse." In William Hope, ed., *Italian Cinema: New Directions*, 131–50. Bern: Peter Lang, 2005.

Haraway, Donna. *Simians, Cyborgs, and Women: The Reinvention of Nature*. New York: Routledge, 1991.

Hayles, N. Katherine. *How We Became Posthuman: Virtual Bodies in Cybernetics, Literature and Informatics*. Chicago: University of Chicago Press, 1999.

Heidegger, Martin. *Poetry, Language, Thought*. Albert Hofstadter, trans. New York: Harper Colophon Books, 1971.

Heise, Ursula. *Sense of Place and Sense of Planet: The Environmental Imagination of the Global*. Oxford: Oxford University Press, 2008.

Herrington, Susan. *On Landscapes*. New York: Routledge, 2009.

Husserl, Edmund. *Cartesian Meditations: An Introduction to Phenomenology*. Dorion Cairns, trans. The Hague: M. Nijhoff, 1960.

Iermano, Toni. "'Non ci sono più personaggi': Ritratto di Paolo Volponi." *Testo e Senso* 9 (2008). Web: 27 January 2013.

Il ritorno di Cagliostro. Dir. Daniele Ciprì and Franco Maresco. Cinico Cinema, Istituto Luce, and Rai Cinema. 2003.

Io e … Pasolini e la forma della città. Dir. Paolo Brunatto. Rome: RAI, 1974.

Iovino, Serenella. "Ecocriticism, Cultural Evolutionism, and Ecologies of Mind: Notes on Calvino's Cosmicomics." *CoSMo: Comparative Studies in Modernism*, 2 (2013): 113 –26.

–. *Ecologia letteraria*. Milan: Edizioni Ambiente, 2006.

–. *Filosofie dell'ambiente: Etica, natura, società*. Rome: Carocci, 2004.

–. "Restoring the Imagination of Place: Narrative Reinhabitation and the Po Valley." In Tom Lynch, Cheryll Glotfelty, and Karla Armbruster, eds., *The Bioregional Imagination: Literature, Ecology and Place*, 100–17. Athens: University of Georgia Press, 2012.

–. "The Wilderness of the Human Other: Italo Calvino's *The Watcher* and a Reflection on the Future of Ecocriticism." In S. Oppermann, U. Ozdag,

N. Ozkan, and S. Slovic, eds., *The Future of Ecocriticism: New Horizons*, 1–18. Cambridge: Cambridge Scholars Publishing 2011.

Jackson, John Brinkerhoff. *Discovering the Vernacular Landscape*. New Haven: Yale University Press, 1984.

Jameson, Fredric. "The End of Temporality." *Critical Inquiry* 29 (2003): 695–718.

–. *Postmodernism, or, The Cultural Logic of Late Capitalism*. Durham: Duke University Press, 1991.

Jansen, Monica. "Il mondo salvato dai ragazzini: Un'ottica infantile sulla guerra e sulla violenza in *Come prima delle madri di Simona Vinci*." In Alain Sarrabayrouse, ed., *Images littéraires de la société contemporaine*, 9–21. Grenoble: Université Stendahl, 2005.

Jarman, Derek. *Modern Nature*. London: Random Century, 1991.

Jewell, Keala Jane. "Pasolini: Deconstructing the Roman Palimpsest." *SubStance* 16:2 (1987): 55–66.

Jusoh, Wan, Faridah Akmal Wan, Nor Rasidah Hashim, and Zelina Z. Ibrahim. "Firefly Distribution and Abundance on Mangrove Vegetation Assemblages in Sepetang Estuary, Peninsular Malaysia." *Wetlands Ecology and Management* 18 (2010): 367–73.

Kazama, So, Satoru Matsumoto, S. Pryantha Ranjan, Hiroshi Hamamoto, and Masaki Sawamoto, et al. "Characterization of Firefly Habitat Using a Geographical Information System with Hydrological Simulation." *Ecological Modeling* 209 (2007): 392–400.

Klein, Melanie. *The Psycho-analysis of Children*. 1932. Reprinted as *The Writings of Melanie Klein*, Vol. 2. London: Hogarth Press, 1975.

–, and Joan Riviere. *Love, Hate and Reparation*. New York: Norton, 1964.

Kristeva, Julia. *Desire in Language*. Thomas Gora, Alice Jardine, and Leon Roudiez, trans. New York: Columbia University Press, 1980.

–. *Intimate Revolt*. Jeanine Herman, trans. New York: Columbia University Press, 2002.

–. *Melanie Klein*. Ross Guberman, trans. New York: Columbia University Press, 2011.

–. *Revolution in Poetic Language*. Margaret Waller, trans. New York: Columbia University Press, 1984.

Klopp, Charles. "The Return of the Spiritual, with a Note on the Fiction of Bufalino, Tabucchi, and Celati." *Annali d'Italianistica* 19 (2001): 93–102.

La Porta, Filippo. *Pasolini, uno gnostico inamorato della realtà*. Florence: Le Lettere, 2002.

–. "Simona Vinci." In Gaetana Marrone, Paolo Puppa, and Luca Somigli, eds., *Encyclopedia of Italian Literary Studies*, 64–6. Vol. 1. New York: Routledge, 2007.

Laskin, David. "The Great London Smog." *Weatherwise* 59:6 (2006): 42–5. Web: 12 November 2013.

Lausten, Pia Schwarz. "L'abbandono del soggetto: Un'analisi del soggetto narrato e quello narrante nell'opera di Gianni Celati." *Revue Romane* 37:1 (2002): 105–32.

–. "Verso la foce del pensiero." *Revue Romane* 37:2 (2002): 249–70.

Lawton, Ben, and Maura Bergonzoni, eds. *Pier Paolo Pasolini: In Living Memory*. Washington, D.C.: New Academia Publishing, 2009.

Lefebvre, Martin. *Landscape and Film*. New York: Routledge, 2006.

Legambiente. *Ambiente Italia 2012*. Duccio Bianchi and Giulio Conte, eds. Milan: Edizioni Ambiente, 2012.

Le streghe. Dir. Luchino Visconti, Franco Rossi, Pier Paolo Pasolini, Mauro Bolognini, and Vittorio De Sica. Prod. Dino De Laurentiis. Productions Artistes Associés. 1967.

Lollini, Massimo, ed. "Humanisms, Posthumanisms, and Neohumanisms." *Annali d'Italianistica* 28 (2008).

Longo, Abele. "Il commiato funebre di *Totò che visse due volte*." In Stefano Curti and Enrico Ghezzi, eds., *Kind of Cinico: Daniele Ciprì e Franco Maresco*, 19–23. RaroVideo, no. 2. Rome: Minerva Pictures Group Srl., April 2005.

–. "Palermo e il commiato funebre del cinema di Ciprì e Maresco." In *La forma del passato: Questioni di identità in opere letterarie e cinematografiche italiane a partire dagli ultimi anni Settanta*, 237–48. Sabina Gola and Laura Rorato, eds. Bern: Peter Lang, 2007.

–. "Palermo in the Films of Ciprì and Maresco." In Robert Lumley and John Foot, eds. *Italian Cityscapes: Culture and Urban Change in Contemporary Italy*, 185–95. Chicago: University of Chicago Press, 2004.

Lorenzini, Niva. "Tecniche di 'divagazione' e di 'erranza' nella narrativa contemporanea." *Studi Novecenteschi: Rivista Semestrale di Storia della Letteratura Italiana Contemporanea* 32:70 (July–December 2005): 115–23.

Lo zio di Brooklyn. Dir. Franco Maresco and Daniele Ciprì. Filmauro Distribuzione and RaroDVD. 1995.

Lucamante, Stefania. "Cannibali." In Gaetana Marrone, Poalo Puppa, and Luca Somigli, eds., *Encyclopedia of Italian Literary Studies*, 373–4. Vol. 1. New York: Routledge, 2007.

–. "Come prima delle madri: Un thriller edipico dei toni noir?" *Narrativa* 26 (2004): 81–96.

–, ed. *Italian Pulp Fiction: The New Narrative of the Giovanni Cannibali Writers*. Madison, NJ: Fairleigh Dickinson University Press, 2001.

Lumley, Robert. "Gianni Celati: 'Fictions to Believe in.'" In Zygmunt G. Baranski and Lino Pertile, eds., *The New Italian Novel*, 43–58. Edinburgh: Edinburgh University Press, 1993.

–, and John Foot, eds. *Italian Cityscapes: Culture and Urban Change in Contemporary Italy*. Chicago: University of Chicago Press, 2004.

Lynch, Tom, Cheryll Glotfelty, and Karla Armbruster, eds. *The Bioregional Imagination: Literature, Ecology and Place*. Athens: University of Georgia Press, 2012.

Mabey, Richard. *Nature Cure*. Charlottesville: University of Virginia Press, 2005.

Mamma Roma. Dir. Pier Paolo Pasolini. Arco Film. 1962.

Manin, Giuseppina, Ulivi Stefania, and Cavallaro Felice. "La Censura: Ciprì e Maresco perversi e bestiali." *Corriere della Sera*. 5 March 1998. Web: 24 October 2010. http://archiviostorico.corriere.it/1998/marzo/05/censura_Cipri_Maresco_perversi_bestiali_co_0_98030511321.shtml

Mariniello, Silvestra. "Toward a Materialist Linguistics: Pasolini's Theory of Language." In Patrick Rumble and Bart Testa, eds., *Pier Paolo Pasolini: Contemporary Perspectives*, 106–26. Toronto: University of Toronto Press, 1994.

Marrone, Gaetana, Paolo Puppa, and Luca Somigli, eds. *Encyclopedia of Italian Literary Studies*. Vol. 1. New York: Routledge, 2007.

Marx, Karl. *Selected Writings*. David McLellan, ed. Oxford: Oxford University Press, 1977.

Massarutto, Antonio. "Agriculture, Water Resources and Water Policies in Italy." *FEEM Working Paper* No. 33 (1999). Web: 26 January 2013. http://papers.ssrn.com/sol3/papers.cfm?abstract_id=200151

McCarthy, Patrick, ed. *Italy since 1945*. New York: Oxford University Press, 2000.

McLaughlin, Martin L. "Calvino's Visible Cities." *Romance Studies* 22 (Autumn 1993): 67–82.

Menechella, Grazia. "I corpi 'a pezzi' di Simona Vinci, Rocco Fortunato e Sandra Petrignani." *Italian Culture* 20:1–2 (2002): 135–48.

Meynardi, Riccardo. "Ciprì e Maresco: Luttazzi and Co. non sono martiri." <*Ragionpolitica.it*> 13 January 2006. Web: 6 September 2010. Inactive site.

Michelone, Guido. "Noi e il Jazz ovvero <<il nostro cinema è un jam-session>>: Intervista di Guido Michelone a Franco Maresco sul jazz e sulla colonna sonora." In Stefano Curti and Enrico Ghezzi, eds., *Kind of Cinico: Daniele Ciprì e Franco Maresco*, 18–23. RaroVideo, no. 55. Rome: Minerva Pictures Group Srl., April 2005.

Milanini, Claudio. *L'utopia discontinua*. Milan: Garzanti, 1990.

Minghelli, Giuliana. "Haunted Frames: History and Landscape in Luchino Visconti's Ossessione." *Italica* 85:2–3 (Summer–Autumn 2008): 173–96.

Moroni, Mario. "Il paradigma dell'osservazione in *Verso la foce* di Gianni Celati." *RLA: Romance Languages Annual* 4 (1992): 307–13.

Morreale, Emiliano. *Ciprì e Maresco*. Alessandria: Falsopiano, 2003.

–. "L'invensione della nostalgia: Il vintage nel cinema italiano e dintorni." Rome: Donzelli, 2009.

–. "Maceria e memoria." In Stefano Curti and Enrico Ghezzi, eds., *Kind of Cinico: Daniele Ciprì e Franco Maresco*, 15–17. RaroVideo no. 55. Rome: Minerva Pictures Group Srl, April 2005.

Naldini, Nico. *Pasolini, una vita*. Turin: Einaudi, 1989.

Nixon, Rob. *Slow Violence and the Environmentalism of the Poor*. Cambridge: Harvard University Press, 2011.

Nocentini, Claudia. "Calvino in Turin: The Industrial City as a Desk." *Italian Quarterly* 40:157–8 (Summer–Autumn 2003): 55–9.

–. "Il paessaggio ricorrente nella narrativa di Italo Calvino." *Bulletin of the Society for Italian Studies* 20 (1987): 13–22.

–. *Italo Calvino and the Landscapes of Childhood*. Leeds: Northern Universities Press, 2000.

"Nursery." In *Random House Webster's Unabridged Dictionary*. 2nd ed. New York: Random House, 2005.

O'Beirne, Emer. "Mapping the *Non-Lieu* in Marc Augé's Writings." *Forum for Modern Language Studies* 42:1 (2006): 38–50.

Pagano, Tullio. "La Liguria ubaga di Italo Calvino." *Narrativa* 27 (January 2005): 125–34.

–. "Liguria: Un precaria identità conflittuale." *Annali d'Italianistica* 24 (2006): 65–85.

–. "Reclaiming Landscape." *Annali d'Italianistica* 29 (2011): 401–16.

Pagliarani, Elio. *I romanzi in versi: La ragazza Carla; La ballata di Rudi*. Milan: Mondadori, 1997.

Palladini, Irene. "Simona Vinci: Corpo io sono." *Griseldaonline* VIII (2008–2009), 5 October 2009. Web: 7 December 2009. http://www.griseldaonline.it/temi/metamorfosi/simona-vinci-corpo-sono-io.html

Pasolini, Pier Paolo. *Empirismo Eretico*. Milan: Garzanti, 1972.

–. *Heretical Empricism*. Ben Lawton and Louise K. Barnett, trans. Washington, D.C.: New Academia Publishing, 2005.

–. *Le ceneri di Gramsci*. Milan: Garzanti, 1957.

–. *Passione e ideologia, 1948–1958*. Milan: Garzanti, 1960.

–. *Pier Paolo Pasolini: Poems*. Norman MacAfee, ed. and trans. New York: Vintage, 1982.

–. "10 febbraio 1975. L'articolo delle lucciole." In *Scritti corsari*, 160–8. Milan: Garzanti, 1975.

–. *Scritti corsari*. Milan: Garzanti, 1975.

–. *The Ashes of Gramsci*. David Wallace, trans. Peterborough, Cambridgeshire, UK: Spectacular Diseases, 1982.

– et al. "Pier Paolo Pasolini: An Epical-Religious View of the World." *Film Quarterly* 18:4 (Summer 1965): 31–45.

Peterson, Thomas E. "The Allegory of Repression from *Teorema* to Salò." *Italica* 73:2 (Summer 1996): 215–32.

Pezzarossa, Fulvio. *C'era una volta il pulp: Corpo e letteratura nella tradizione italiana*. Bologna: CLUEB, 1999.

Pilat, Stephanie Zeier. *Reconstructing Italy: The INA-Casa Neighborhoods of the Postwar Era*. Burlington, VT: Ashgate, 2014.

Piccolo, Pina. "Gianni Celati's Silence, Space, Motion and Relief." *Gradiva: International Journal of Italian Literature* 4:2 (1988): 61–5.

"Pier Paolo Pasolini." *Pasolini.net*. Web: 23 August 2010. http://www.pasolini.net/

Piscia, Roberta, Pietro Volta, Angela Boggero and Marina Manca. "The invasion of Lake Orta (Italy) by the red swamp crayfish *Procambarus clarkii* (Girard, 1852): A new threat to an unstable environment." *Aquatic Invasions* 6:1 (2011): S45–8.

Plumwood, Val. *Ecofeminism and the Mastery of Nature*. New York: Routledge, 1993.

Pollan, Michael. *Second Nature: A Gardener's Education*. New York: Grove Press, 1991.

Pomilio, Tommaso. "Le Narrative Generazionali Dagli Anni Ottanta Agli Anni Novanta." In Nino Borsellino and Walter Pedullà, eds., *Letteratura italiana del Novecento*, 671–80. Milan: Rizzoli, 2000.

Quaini, Massimo. *L'ombra del paesaggio*. Reggio Emilia: Edizioni Diabasis, 2006.

Ranieri, Polese. "Aldo Nove, il ritorno del giovin cannibale." *Corriere della Sera*, archivio. 14 April 2004. Web: 28 November 2009. http://archiviostorico.corriere.it/2004/aprile/14/Aldo_Nove_ritorno_del_giovin_co_9_040414101.shtml

–. "Vite perdute lungo la strada." *Corriere della Sera*. 25 November 2007. 35. Web: 9 December 2009. http://archiviostorico.corriere.it/2007/novembre/25/Vite_perdute_lungo_strada_co_9_071125062.shtml

Renga, Dana. "Looking Out: Calvino's Vision of the 'Economic Miracle.'" *Italica* 80:3 (Autumn 2003): 371–88.

Rhodes, John David. *Stupendous Miserable City: Pasolini's Rome*. Minneapolis: University of Minnesota Press, 2007.

Ricci, Franco. *Difficult Games: A Reading of "I racconti" by Italo Calvino*. Waterloo, ON: Wilfrid Laurier University Press, 1990.

Rizzanti, Massimo. "Per Gianni Celati." *Nazione Indiana*. 7 October 2008. Web: 10 March 2010. http://www.nazioneindiana.com/2008/10/07/per-gianni-celati/

Rohman, Carrie. "On Singularity and the Symbolic: The Threshold of the Human in Calvino's *Mr. Palomar*." *Criticism: A Quarterly for Literature and the Arts* 51:1 (2009): 63–78.

"New Immigration Statistics Released." *Wanted in Rome* (2 November 2009). Web: 9 June 2010. http://www.wantedinrome.com/news/6406/new-immigration-statistics-released.html

Rorato, Laura. "Alla ricerca del diverso: Il mare come estrema soglia ne *Il filo dell'orizzonte* di Antonio Tabucchi e *Verso la foce* di Gianni Celati." In Bart Van den Bossche, Michel Bastiaensen, and Corinna Lonergan, eds.,*"E c'è di mezzo il mare": Lingua, letteratura e civiltà marina*, 421–35. Vol. 2. Florence: Cesati, 2002.

Ross, Silvia. "Calvino and Animals: The Multiple Functions of Marcovaldo's Poisonous Rabbit." *Spunti e Ricerche*, 18 (2003): 29–40.

–. *Tuscan Spaces: Literary Constructions of Place*. Toronto: University of Toronto Press, 2010.

Rozelle, Lee. *Ecosublime: Environmental Terror and Awe from New World to Oddworld*. Tuscaloosa: University of Alabama Press, 2006.

Rumble, Patrick. "Accattone." In Giorgio Bertellini, ed. *The Cinema of Italy*, 103–11. New York: Columbia University Press, 2005.

–. *Allegories of Contamination: Pier Paolo Pasolini's Trilogy of Life*. Toronto: University of Toronto Press, 1996.

–, and Bart Testa, eds. *Pier Paolo Pasolini: Contemporary Perspectives*. Toronto: University of Toronto Press, 1994.

Rusconi, M. "In questo mondo di maniaci: Intervista a Simona Vinci." *L'Espresso* (11 February 1999): 90–91.

Ryan-Scheutz, Colleen. *Sex, the Self, and the Sacred: Women in the Cinema of Pier Paolo Pasolini*. Toronto: University of Toronto Press, 2007.

Salabè, Caterina, ed. *Ecocritica: La letteratura e la crisi del pianeta*. Rome: Donzelli, 2013.

Sanguinetti Katz, Giuliana. "Le 'adolescenze difficili' di Italo Calvino." *Quaderni d'Italianistica* 5:2 (Autumn 1984), 247–61.

Sanguinetti, Tatti. "Totò, Ciprì, Maresco e la Censura." In Stefano Curti and Enrico Ghezzi, eds., *Kind of Cinico: Daniele Ciprì e Franco Maresco*, 4–9. RaroVideo no. 2. Rome: Minerva Pictures Group Srl., April 2005.

Scaffidi, Nino. "Brutti, sporchi e cattivi: Un cinema diverso, il caso di Ciprì & Maresco." *Immagini latenti: Cinema e disabilità* 2003/3. 1 January 2003. Web: 8 September 2010. http://www.accaparlante.it/articolo/brutti-sporchi-e-cattivi

Scarpa, Tiziano. *Batticuore fuorilegge*. Rome: Fanucci Editore, 2006.

Schama, Simon. *Landscape and Memory*. New York: Vintage Books, 1996.

Schilirò, Massimo. "I paesi introvabili: Il pellegrinaggio ai luoghi parentali in Gianni Celati." *Compar(a)ison: An International Journal of Comparative Literature* 1–2 (2005): 107–14.

Seger, Monica. "A Conversation with Dacia Maraini." *World Literature Today* 85:4 (2011): 30.

Sironi, Marco. *Geografie del narrare: Insistenze sui luoghi di Luigi Ghirri e Gianni Celati*. Reggio Emilia: Diabasis, 2004.

Soper, Kate. *What Is Nature?* Oxford: Blackwell, 2005.

Sorice, Michele. *La città ideale: Italo Calvino dal "pessimismo dell'intelligenza" all'intelligenza dell'utopia*. Rome: Merlo Editore, 1990.

Spunta, Marina. "Ghirri, Celati e lo 'spazio di affezione'." *Il lettore di Provincia* 36:123–4 (May–December 2005): 27–39.

–. "Conversazione con Gianni Celati." In Franca Pellegrini and Elisabetta Tarantino, eds., *Il romanzo contemporaneo: Voci italiane*, 117–31. Leicester, Eng.: Troubadour, 2006.

–. "The New Italian Landscape: Between Ghirri's Photography and Celati's Fiction." In Ashley Chantler and Carla Dente, eds., *Translation Practices: Through Language to Culture*, 223–37. Amsterdam, Netherlands: Rodopi, 2009.

–. "Lo spazio delle pianure come 'territorio di racconti': Verso la foce con Gianni Celati." *Spunti e Ricerche: Rivista d'Italianistica* 18 (2003): 5–28.

Spirn, Anne Whiston. *The Language of Landscape*. New Haven: Yale University Press, 1998.

Steimatsky, Noa. *Italian Locations: Reinhabiting the Past in Postwar Locations*. Minneapolis: University of Minnesota Press, 2008.

Tabanelli, Roberta. "Il post-umano (femmineo) di Simona Vinci." *Annali d'Italianistica* 26 (2008): 379–88.

Teorema. Aetos Produzioni Cinematografiche. 1968.

"Tentativo." In *Lo Zingarelli minore*. Edizione Terzo Millenio, 2001.

Totò che visse due volte. Dir. Franco Maresco and Daniele Ciprì. Istituto Luce, Tea Nova, and RaroDVD. 1998.

Trimble, Stephen. "The Scripture of Maps, the Names of Trees: A Child's Landscape." In Gary Paul Nabhan and Stephen Trimble, eds., *The Geography of Childhood: Why Children Need Wild Places*, 15–32. Boston: Beacon Press, 1994.

Tsing, Anna Lowenhaupt. *Friction: An Ethnography of Global Connection*. Princeton: Princeton University Press, 2005.

Tunesi, Simonetta. "Italian Environmental Policies in the Post-war Period." In Patrick McCarthy, ed., *Italy since 1945*, 118–32. New York: Oxford University Press, 2000.

Uccellacci e uccellini. Dir. Pier Paolo Pasolini. Arco Film. 1966.

Vinci, Simona. *Brother and Sister*. Turin: Einaudi, 2003.

–. "Anima e luoghi e storie." *Intuttisensi* 4 (August 2009). Web: 8 December 2009. http://intuttisensi.wordpress.com/2009/08/04/anima-e-luoghi-e-storie/

–. *Come prima delle madri*. Turin: Einaudi, 2003.
–. *Dei bambini non si sa niente*. Turin: Einaudi, 1997.
–. *In Every Sense Like Love*. Minna Proctor, trans. London: Random House, 2001.
–. *In tutti i sensi come l'amore*. Turin: Einaudi, 1999.
–. "La materia dell'idea." *Incubatoio* 16:1 (February 1996). Web: 8 December 2009. http://www.arcobaleno.com/incubatoio16/1/simona.htm
–. "La più piccola cosa." *Ragazze che dovresti conoscere: The Sex Anthology*. Turin: Einaudi, 2004.
–. *Rovina*. Milan: Edizioni Ambiente, 2007.
–. *Strada Provinciale Tre*. Turin: Einaudi, 2007.
–. *What We Don't Know about Children*. Minna Proctor, trans. New York: Alfred A. Knopf, 2000.
Vitti, Antonio, ed. *Incontri con il cinema italiano*. Rome: Salvatore Sciascia Editore, 2003.
Vittorini, Elio. "Industria e letteratura." *Il Menabò* 4 (1961): 13–20.
Ward, David. *A Poetics of Resistance: Narrative and the Writings of Pier Paolo Pasolini*. Cranbury, NJ: Associated University Presses, 1995.
West, Rebecca. "Gianni Celati and Literary Minimalism." *L'Anello Che Non Tiene: Journal of Modern Italian Literature* 1:2 (Spring 1989): 11–29.
–. *Gianni Celati: The Craft of Everyday Storytelling*. Toronto: University of Toronto Press, 2000.
–. "Gianni Celati's *La strada provinciale delle anime*: A 'Silent' Film about 'Nothing.'" *RLA: Romance Languages Annual* 4 (1992): 367–74.
–. "Pasolini's Intoxication and Celati's Detoxification." *RLA: Romance Languages Annual* 9 (1997): 390–6.
–. "Lo spazio nei Narratori delle pianure." Giuseppe Sertoli, trans. *Nuova Corrente: Rivista di Letteratura*. 33:97 (January-June 1986): 65–74.
Williams, Raymond. *The Country and the City*. New York: Oxford University Press, 1973.
Winicott, D.W. *The Child and the Outside World*. New York: Basic Books, 1957.
Woodhouse, J.R. "Fantasy, Alienation and the *Racconti* of Italo Calvino." *Forum for Modern Language Studies* 6 (1970): 399–412.
Yablokov, Alexey, Vassily Nesterenko, and Alexey Nesterenko, eds. "Chernobyl: Consequences of the Catastrophe for People and the Environment." In *Annals of the New York Academy of Sciences*. Vol. 1181. Hoboken, NJ: Wiley, 2010.
Zamagni, Vera. "Evolution of the Economy." In Patrick McCarthy, ed., *Italy since 1945*, 42–68. New York: Oxford University Press, 2000.

Index

www.ingramcontent.com/pod-product-compliance
Lightning Source LLC
LaVergne TN
LVHW090159080826
844660LV00013B/875/J
9781442649194